From Nazi Inferno
To Soviet Hell

From Nazi Inferno
To Soviet Hell

By
Larry Wenig

KTAV Publishing House, Inc.
Hoboken, New Jersey

Copyright©2000
Larry Wenig

Library of Congress Cataloging-in-Publication-Data

Wenig, Larry
From Nazi inferno to Soviet hell/ by Larry Wenig.
p. cm.
ISBN 0-88125-683-8
1. Wenig, Larry. 2. Jews--Poland—Biography. 3. Holocaust,
Jewish (1939-1945)—Poland—Personal narratives. 4. Political
prisoners—Soviet Union—Biography. 5. Immigrants—New York
(State)—Biography. 6. New York (N.Y.)—Biography. I. Title.

DS135.P63 W4 2000
940.53'18'09438--dc21
                                                        00-031485
                                                              CIP

Distributed by
Ktav Publishing House, Inc.
900 Jefferson Street
Hoboken, NJ 07030

Contents

Preface..vii

Childhood in Dynów 1

The Threat of Hitler..25

The War Is Upon Us 43

Escape to the East 69

The Expulsion..113

Arrival in Gulag 149 125

On the Road to Freedom 191

Reversal of the War..239

The War Is Coming to an End................................261

Freedom But Not Liberty 291

Epilogue 321

Preface

Friends, relatives, fellow lawyers, and several judges in the New York City courts have urged me to write a book about my experiences during World War II, especially about my five years as a political prisoner in the Soviet Union during the Stalin era.

When I arrived in America in June 1946, my only material possessions were the clothes on my body, and I had no knowledge of the English language.

My uncle Irving and his family were kind to us, and he provided my parents, sister, and me with a completely furnished apartment in a building he owned at 50 East 191st Street in the Bronx.

Several days later I was introduced to some Yiddish-speaking neighbors, who took me for a walk. As we strolled along Fordham Road, I saw two policemen and took off like a shot. My companions ran after me and asked why I was running. I explained that in the Soviet Union one avoided the police, because they could haul you off to prison for any reason or for no reason at all. My companions assured me that I had nothing to fear from American policemen. That in the United States the function of the police is to protect the people, not to persecute them.

Despite these assurances, I continued, for the next several months, to cross the street whenever I saw a policeman. It was a conditioned reflex.

During these first weeks in America, I simply could not digest food. My stomach could not accustom itself to the good American food after five years of starvation. Many a time, during those five years, my family and I, in our prayers, had promised God that if He would only give us bread, we would never ask for anything else.

My relatives gave me all kinds of advice on how to get a job and earn a living, especially since I did not understand English. My mind, however, was set on continuing my education, as I had always had a scholarly bent.

Lacking the financial means to attend school as a full-time student, I was forced to compromise. I worked during the day and attended school in the evenings. I landed a job as a jewelry apprentice at L&D Jewelry Company on Maiden Lane in Manhattan, earning forty cents an hour, or sixteen dollars for a forty-hour week, and attended evening classes at Theodore Roosevelt High School.

After graduating high school, I enrolled in the evening session at City College, majoring in social and political science, subjects of great interest to me. From City College I went on to the evening session of Brooklyn Law School. Even in law school I still had to make use of a Polish-English dictionary. I attended five nights a week, and took courses in the summertime as well in order to speed up my graduation. I took no vacation at all.

Around that time I came across a photograph of a beautiful girl. The people in the apartment where I saw the photo only mentioned her first name, Selma. They refused to give me her last name, address, or phone number. I finally persuaded them to spill her last name and the borough in which she lived. Upon obtaining this information, I ran to the nearest candy store that had a telephone booth, leafed through the Queens directory, and found the name Werber in Long Island City. I dialed the number, and indeed Selma Werber answered. I introduced myself, told her who had given me her name and number, and said they had suggested I should ask her for a date. She obviously believed me, and agreed to go out with me the following Saturday. On that first date I fell in love with Selma and decided to marry her. We were married 10 months later, on June 13, 1954.

Meanwhile, I graduated from Brooklyn Law School and worked for several law offices, eventually entering into my own law practice.

At the same time, I became the father of two wonderful children, a daughter, Phyllis, and a son, Alan. In due course they both married, and now Selma and I are grandparents. My Phyllis gave us three grandchildren: Matthew, Michelle, and Elena. My son Alan gave us two grandchildren, Alex and Arielle.

My law practice has been very successful. My son Alan is now a lawyer too, and is my partner in the firm of Wenig & Wenig.

Despite my wonderful marriage, beautiful children and grandchildren, and very successful law practice, I have not forgotten my past. I am very grateful to my adopted country, America, for in no other country could I have found such happiness and been so successful.

Childhood in Dynów

The roses in the garden were shimmering in the fleeting summer sun. Storm clouds were gathering in the July sky, but I was heedless of their rumbling. The pages of my book were thundering in my mind. *Pan Tadeusz*, by the Polish writer Adam Mickiewicz, was all-absorbing. A glorious Poland had existed in the eighteenth century, and I was deeply involved in every one of the famous exploits I was learning about. Exultant over my country's military glory. Totally engrossed in the book on my lap, I was only vaguely aware of the rising wind and brooding sky.

Suddenly I heard Hania's shrill voice calling, but I paid little attention. Accustomed to our maid Hania's shaking with fear whenever lightning spiked the sky, I remained engrossed in *Pan Tadeusz*. Her calls, more ominous and insistent, eventually tore me away from my book.

"What is it, Hania?" I asked impatiently.

"Go! Go at once to your grandfather's house," She insisted.

How strange. Grandfather was usually displeased by any interruption of his busy daily routine. Reluctantly I walked back to my grandfather's house, which was next door to our own.

I was startled by the scene that greeted me.

Grandfather's usually pleasant, untroubled face was exceedingly pale; his tranquil blue eyes, sad and misted. My mother was there, a handkerchief in her trembling hand, wiping her tears. Noticing the fear in my questioning eyes, my grandfather extended his arms, whispering softly.

"Come sit on my lap, Eliezer."

His arms enfolded me, and I felt the warmth and kindness in his short, stocky body.

"Starting tonight, you will have to say Kaddish, the prayer for the dead," my grandfather said in a trembling voice.

"For whom?" I almost screamed, my voice full of disbelief.

"Your father," he replied softly.

"It can't be, I just saw him a few hours ago," I said with conviction. I tried to explain that he was making a mistake, that it couldn't be true. My eyes raced from his face to my mother's for clarification.

"Your real father," I heard my grandfather say. His body pressing against mine in a comforting embrace did not diminish the fear engendered by these strange words.

This was the zeidah (grandfather) who was always so attentive to me, the grandfather who took pride in my good grades, and often confided his hopes that I would become a rabbi. Now he was trying to share another confidence.

"You are too young to understand, Eliezer," he said with sadness in his voice, "but you had a different father. Your mother was married to another person when you were born. A man named Aaron Sarna; and when you were one year old, your mother divorced him. Your mother suffered a great deal. The father you know is not your real father."

He was relating events I could not connect with the parents I knew, it was all so shocking and confusing.

"Explain it to me," I pleaded, turning first to him, then to my mother.

"I can't," she sobbed.

The two people who were the stalwarts of my life, in whom I had faith, whom I loved and respected, were stumbling, unable to explain the troubling mixup I was facing. Behind their tearful eyes I could see the pain and anguish.

I ran from them. Across the garden, to my home, to my room, to a cave I made under the blankets of my bed, hiding from the revelation that was shaking the very foundation of my life, my home, my family. I beat the pillows, tormented by thoughts of disbelief. I hid my muffled cries from my brothers, who were not my brothers now.

That evening, searching the faces of everyone I knew for the answers my mother and grandfather had been unable to give me, I walked with my grandfather to the synagogue. Distressed, I followed the gabbai (sexton) in pronouncing the Kaddish for my father. From that day on, like one of the faithful, I continued to recite the prayer for the dead, morning and evening, for the eleven prescribed months. Haunting me all that time were questions about the man for whom I was saying Kaddish, a prayer to honor the memory of a man who had turned my life upside down.

Why had I never been told about my real father? Why had my father and mother divorced? I had never heard of people divorcing each other. I questioned aunts, uncles, friends of the family, beginning to understand from their discomfort that there was something to hide, something shameful they didn't want to disclose. I began to sort through my mother's actions, through the actions of the man I had known as my father and of the boys I had thought were my older brothers. I saw reasons for my mother's special tenderness. The extra hug or kiss that was a measure of compensation for the hurt and the separation from true ties. Now I understood why she paid more attention to me than to my brothers. I understood why I was my grandfather's favored grandson, getting perhaps excessive attention beyond what my good grades would have warranted. I did not waver in my respect or affection for my grandfather, but felt there was a degree of deception in his conduct. I now attributed my stepfather's detachment, which had seemed so natural in the past, to the lack of blood ties, and began to feel my own kind of detachment. I could see why my stepbrothers Shmulek and Mundek ignored me, something I had attributed to differences in age and my better grades at school.

From the bits and pieces offered by relatives, I pieced the tale together. In Jewish circles, when my mother came of marriageable age, it was taken for granted that the daughter of a wealthy man would wed a talmudic scholar. No one was more revered than the scholar. Nobody had higher status in communal life.

A shadchan (marriage broker) introduced young Miriam Kasser to Aaron Sarna. He may have been an ardent student of the Talmud, but he was no observer of the strict tenets of Jewish law. Soon rumors reached my grandfather that his son-in-law had been seen walking the street without a yarmulka (skullcap) or any other head-covering, in violation of the conduct of an observant Jew, and worse, was smoking on the Sabbath. Desecrating the Sabbath was a grave sin. Other rumors stated that he ate bacon and ham, absolutely forbidden foods for an observant Jew.

"How can your daughter be married to such a sacrilegious man?" people would ask my grandfather, causing him enormous embarrassment. Grandfather was devastated by the gossip. He saw no choice but to rid his household of the culprit. He arranged for a divorce.

Now, the man who had fathered me was dead, and such was the respect for fatherhood that I, his son, was obligated to say Kaddish for him. The sorrow and grief in my mother's eyes made me believe there had been love between them at the time of their marriage.

I wanted to know more about Aaron Sarna. Questioning my grandfather, I found out that the local rabbi had received a message with news of his death from a rabbi in Zurich. After the divorce, he had remarried and had moved to Switzerland, where he died on July 30, 1932.

Somewhere in the vicinity of Warsaw, where my father had been born, were three uncles whom I had never met and a half-sister of mine, Susi, from his second marriage. Separated as we were, they still seemed part of me, a part shorn from my self.

In the aching hours of the night, I thought of myself as set apart from the family I lived with. All the silences and unfriendly gestures of my brothers, which I had never understood, were now potent with new meanings. I imagined nocturnal conversations I would conduct with my uncles in Warsaw, men revered for learning with whom I suddenly had blood ties.

This was 1932, I was eight years old and drawn to reading and studying. I was entering a higher level of cheder (religious school) to learn with Moishe Elazar, a respected teacher of the Talmud. The world would spin on its axis as it had been doing in my little world centered in the Polish town of Dynów.

My little world had already suffered an upset the year before when I came home to see my mother in bed. Next to her, in swaddling clothes, was a baby. Where had it come from? My aunt told me the stork had brought her.

My mind raced to the Feigenbaum store on our street, above which hung a sign, picturing a stork with a baby hanging in a sling from its beak.

There was not much more I could draw out from the adults, so I sought out my friend Dufciu Feigenbaum. He would know more about the woman called a midwife who made the arrangements with the stork. She occupied an apartment in their house.

"Where does the midwife keep the babies when the stork brings them?" I asked with curiosity.

"In the attic," Dufciu told me. "When the women get sick and go to bed, then she brings them the baby."

My curiosity aroused, I asked, "Can I go up to the attic to see where she keeps the babies?"

"She keeps them in a commode, up in the attic," he offered.

His answer made me more inquisitive.

"Dufciu, take me up there."

He led the way up a high ladder, sharing curiosity, sharing a secret. The steps creaked under our weight. "What if they catch us doing this?" I whispered.

"She's not home now. She must be delivering babies."

Dufciu opened the attic latch and there was the commode. Inside was a batch of clothing.

"She must have delivered all the babies. She must be waiting for a new supply."

But the forbidden door to life's secrets had been opened. Questions needed answers. I knew some older boys, three or four years older than I. They had accepted me into their circle because I was a good student, an avid reader in Polish and Yiddish, and a source of information on Poland's history and its great romantic poets. I was only too eager to share this information with them, and could also explain lessons on military history or drill them on the poems we had to memorize. Actually we bartered information. From them I learned where babies come from. Girls began to have a new meaning for me.

My new friends had more adult pleasures to share with me. They taught me to smoke. After two days of smoking cheap cigarettes, I took sick. That ended my interest in the assumed pleasure of smoking for a lifetime.

My friendship with these older boys abruptly ended, as did my sharing of cigarettes, when one day my mother saw me walking with them. She called me into the house, where a lecture followed.

"You are not to be friends with those boys," she said in a earnest voice. "They do not come from good homes, and will certainly not amount to anything. They do not like to study, are disruptive in school, and are a bad influence on you. They could ruin your life."

Her admonishments were firm and serious. I would never think of disobeying her, so my friendship with the older boys had to stop. My stepfather, who seldom said anything about school or my friends, did not get involved this time either. My stepbrothers did not pay much attention to me, but that didn't seem peculiar. They didn't care much about school, and spent most of their time in father's business.

They might have become good businessmen, but life spun out of control for them too, in the sequence of events that was taking shape in Poland.

Dynów lay nestled at the foot of the Carpathian Mountains, overlooking the banks of the San River. Cool, deep woods covered the slopes. Clear streams gushed over stones and pebbles. In the deeper pools that formed along the river, we often splashed and tested our swimming, stretching out afterwards on the river bank to feel the sun warming our bodies.

Surrounding the town were fields farmed by peasants who worked small parcels of land that barely yielded enough for their living. Every Thursday, the day they called Jarmark, the peasants came to Dynów to sell the produce from their fields and orchards to the townspeople. North of the Rynek, a square in the center of the town, was another little square, Targowica Miesa, where the peasants sold livestock and meat products: kielbasa, ham, bacon. Some brought cattle to the town's two slaughterhouses, one kosher and the other non-kosher.

After the peasants sold their goods, they visited the stores in town to buy clothing, shoes, headgear, pots, and pans. They purchased kerosene for their lamps, as well as sugar, flour, beans, and other groceries. They got haircuts from the town's two Jewish barbers.

In fact, most of the merchants in Dynów were Jewish. The sawmill and the shoe-tree factory were owned by Jews. My uncle Lemel Silber owned the soda-bottling factory. My grandfather, Leib Kasser, was one of the town's most important merchants. He owned a factory that manufactured candles, the largest grocery store, and a flour mill, and was the local distributor for kerosene, sugar, and products from other countries. My parents were distributors of grain, farm equipment, and imported fertilizers.

These were respected, affluent people. Leib Kasser was the family patriarch. He had four daughters and two sons, all proud to belong to the Kasser family. The family's life centered around Leib Kasser. Everyone looked to him for counsel.

Family, by extension, meant all relatives. Saturdays and holidays the whole clan would gather in my grandfather's house. My great aunt Serkala, her husband, daughter, and two sons, followed by their own children, filled grandfather Leib's house. Stroking his beard, grandfather Leib, a pious man strictly observant of Jewish law, would sit in his large chair presiding over the family. Conducting the gathering with tradition and ceremony, he made these days very special for everybody.

The family prayed together, feasted together, and exchanged news and gossip. They felt protected by his patriarchal love. The knowledge that he was always there for the family, like a solid rock, inspired confidence and safety. Every event in our lives was centered around the importance of Jewish law and practice.

Custom required that Jewish children, particularly boys, go to cheder, a one-room school, where they were introduced to the teachings and ceremonies of the religion. When I was three years old, I was dressed up in a suit, given candies and sweet cakes, and taken to the cheder. There my mother instructed me to share the candies and cakes with the other children. I was making new friends in a classroom where I learned new songs and stories, the folklore of my people.

I was a good student. I liked the Bible stories. I was amazed by the heroic endurance of a people that had suffered through so many trials. The exodus from Egypt, where we had been slaves, inspired me. I felt pride in the courage of Esther and Mordechai as they faced Haman. I felt a joy at the lighting of the candles at Hanukkah and the recitation of the story of the heroic Maccabees, who had fought for freedom against overwhelming odds. Even though the melamed (teacher) carried a kanchig, a stick with a leather strap attached, to use on students who were disruptive or did not pay attention, I did not fear him so much as revere him for his knowledge. I wanted to peer into that mind that stored the history of the Jews. I wanted to put those symbols that formed the Hebrew alphabet into recognizable words and associations. And it was not long before I wanted to know why Jewish boys and girls were called *Zyd*, more or less equivalent to "lousy kike," when they had such a glorious history.

Strangely mixed in with these glorious tales in the cheder were stories about ghosts dressed in white sheets who appeared at night. The biblical heroes whom I summoned to wreak vengeance on these ghosts were apparently ineffectual, because the ghosts invaded my slumber and were hostile enemies to my sleep. Such monsters are frightened by light, but we only had brief hours of electric light in our town.

The electricity was on for only a few hours at night, from the time darkness set in until midnight. I feared going to bed in the dark because the ghosts would enter my room. I insisted that Hania, our Polish maid, come to bed with me. She stayed with me until I fell asleep.

If I woke up in the middle of the night to find she was not beside me, I went into a terror, a panic that the ghosts would torment me. Somehow, pulling the blankets over my head kept them away, but the fear I felt was a precursor to the terrors we would know in the rampage of political change.

Conditions in Poland were rife with tension. Foremost was the envy of the Christian peasants, based on the impression that the Jews had wealth and comforts denied them.

Events are measured on a personal scale. Serene one moment, shattering another. One moment ripped asunder by the other.

The signs of discord were apparent in Dynów, but for me, eight or nine years old, there were secure daily routines. I attended the Polish *szkola powszechna* (public school) from nine o'clock in the morning until one in the afternoon. I spoke Polish very well, and loved reading the literature, history, and geography I was assigned in school. Afternoons, I went to Yiddish school, learning the language, lore, and traditions of the Jewish people. Homework assignments from the Polish school occupied the evenings.

While the student body of the Polish school was predominantly Catholic, many Jewish boys and girls attended. But there were undercurrents of antisemitism in the school. It was not unusual to hear coarse, chiding voices at your ear, "*Zyd*, do you have the answers to the arithmetic problems? *Zyd*, where did you get that hat?" or " *Zyd*, why don't you go to Palestine?"

The more incompetent the student, the more antisemitic. The poorer he was, the more ignorant, the more flagrant his antisemitic outbursts.

The girls were just as bad as the boys. Christian students didn't mingle with the Jewish students. The teachers did nothing to abate the hostile remarks. Some were openly antisemitic themselves.

The proximity of Jews and Christians was part of the picture of Dynów. At one end of Mickiewicza Street rose the many-storied tower and compelling spire of the Roman Catholic church. The church had a large estate, called Plebania, where the priest resided. Beyond the church lay rich agricultural land tilled by the Polish villagers. On Mickiewicza Street, there was a large Christian store, the Kólko Rolnicze (Farmers' Circle) which sold produce and other groceries. Right next to it was my grandfather's store.

At the other end of the street was the Orthodox church with its spiked onion domes. At the head and foot of this main roadway were the Christian bastions of the town that was my home. The Polish gibes at the Jews were a minor itch on a young boy's skin. When I walked the unpaved streets of the town to the Polish school, or took the road toward the synagogue located in Rynek Square, I searched the faces of the Christians for signs of friendliness. Instead I saw them avert their heads.

I asked my mother about this. She said that the Catholic priest, Smietana, would not walk on the same side of the street as a Jew. He would not look a Jew straight in the eye.

"He is the biggest antisemite," she told me, "he preaches hatred of the Jews."

My pained expression did not temper her bitterness. "What do the peasants know?" she continued. "Only what the priest wants them to know. That Jews are Christ-killers. Their day will come."

These hurtful remarks dug deep into the mind of a growing boy. I became more and more aware of the insults doled out to us Jews.

Security and consolation were to be found in my Jewish family, in the Jewish community. I noticed the differences even as a young boy, and I identified with my people. I adhered to the rules and policies, sure of my place, becoming part of the scene.

Usually, after dinner and individual tasks, the family would gather at Zeidah Leib's house to discuss local affairs and politics. I liked to listen to their conversations. I remember Uncle Hertz reading from the Jewish newspaper *Haynt* ("Today").

One evening, reading about economic conditions, they spoke of a Depression. My stepfather, Joseph Wenig, called Yoshe by the family, spoke about his brother in New York and was concerned about the effects of the Depression in the United States.

Closer to home were the changes in Germany resulting from the economic hard times, with the reports of a new political party there. For the first time, I heard the name Hitler mentioned.

"We are hearing openly antisemitic remarks now," my uncle said. "Times are not good in Poland either, and they blame the Jews."

My grandfather's forehead wrinkled with concern. "As long as Marshal Józef Pilsudski is in power, Jews have nothing to worry about here."

I was learning the names of the powerful. Pilsudski, the prime minister of Poland; Wincenty Witos, the leader of the Polish Peasant Party.

"As long as Wincenty Witos lives, the peasants will not do anything to hurt the Jewish people," my grandfather assured us. "He is the one who can control them." The year was 1932.

Unfortunately, not long after I first heard his name, I heard that Witos had been banished somewhere in the West. That made me worry about whether he would still be able to influence the peasants not to hurt us. Lingering in my mind were the threats and insults we endured from the Christian children when we went through their fields for a swim in the river San during the summer. I remembered the jeering as we slogged through the rain-soaked muddy streets of Dynów in the fall. The hard-packed snowballs thrown by the Christian boys at our heads and shoulders in the winter. It was difficult enough to plod through bitter-cold snowdrifts to and from school. Having to avoid the curses and snowball attacks just added to the strain. As winter drew on, rumors and clouds of anxiety drifted into the quiet town where I was born, where most of my family lived, where our circle of friends and neighbors made Dynów our home sweet home.

Now people anxiously grabbed the national newspapers that arrived daily by bus from the nearby larger city of Przemysl. Sharing the news reports, every nuance of the latest events in Nazi Germany was analyzed. At family gatherings, the mood was grim. Where once there had been laughter and gaiety at our family meetings at my grandfather's, now somber political news was exchanged. My relatives wept over reports of the brutal treatment of the Jews in Germany.

One evening, my uncle Chaskel Berkowitz began to sing a song about the Jews of Spain. The words were perplexing. I asked him to explain.

"Jews once lived in Spain," he said with a sigh, "but then, at the insistence of the Catholic cardinal, Tomas Torquemada, the king expelled them from the country. They became refugees from the Inquisition, dispersed in many lands."

That night I could not sleep. My heart filled with fear, thinking of all that hatred and horror. I could not understand the rancor and cruelty in the hearts of the people who persecuted the Jews.

In my mind, history conjured up the ghosts of folklore giving me nightmares. Ghosts swirled around my room. They drove toward my pillow. They lurked in every fold of the curtains. I had always found stories of ghosts frightful. In my younger years, the ghosts had been dispelled when Hania, the Polish maid, slept with me to soothe me when I was frightened by night-crawling monsters, but now I was too old to call out to her. Who could I call on now to ward off the growing Catholic hatred of Jews? Who would help the Jews in Germany?

That week, I put these questions to my teacher in the Jewish school, Moishe Lazar.

The Messiah, he told me, would come in due time, and when he did, the bodies of the dead would roll underground, rise from their graves, and return to the Jewish homeland.

That homeland, Palestine, was frequently mentioned in the conversations I heard at my grandfather's. Palestine was a name associated with hope. I listened joyously when my great-aunt Serkala Heilman told us how happy she was that her son Chanoch was a chalutz (pioneer), safe in faraway Palestine, where he was helping to build a Jewish state.

I listened but was confused. What about the Jewish state that would arise when the Messiah came? But they were not talking about a Messiah. For the first time, I heard about Dr. Theodor Herzl, who had told the Jews to go to Palestine and build their own country there. Was he the Messiah? Would all Jews go to Palestine now, I wondered.

I tried to concentrate on my Polish schoolwork despite feeling misplaced, like an outcast, scared by the changes Jews were talking about. Because so much was happening politically, the curriculum was extended to include world geography. I associated the names of strange countries with the tales Jews exchanged, identifying them with places where our people were being persecuted. I read the books, studied maps, memorized the names of the capitals of all the European countries as well as the countries of other continents.

My geography teacher, Pan Bielawski, noticed my keen interest in this subject. A Polish patriot, he silently admired the fascist movements in other countries. He marked every military affair and advance on the classroom's big map. He considered Poland a strong military power. His enthusiasm was contagious, and he noticed my fascination with the geography and history he was presenting. Although I knew him to be an antisemite, I reveled in his attention to my questions. He discerned my interest in world affairs, nodded approval to my comments, and spoke well of me to the school's principal, Miss Wojnerowna. Pan Bielawski often waited to walk with me on the way from school, to talk about shaping events. He put questions to me that seemed oddly connected to the classroom lessons.

"What are the Jewish papers writing about these days?" he would ask sarcastically. "Are they discussing foreign affairs?"

I proudly told him that the papers were covering daily events in Poland, and that Jews were concerned about Poland's fate.

"What they should be proud of is Germany's respect for the Polish army," Mr. Bielawski retorted. "Germany is Poland's friend."

He would then talk about the Italian invasion of Abyssinia or the civil war in Spain. He admired Mussolini and General Franco. He despised the Soviet Union. I had little knowledge of the Soviet Union and listened eagerly.

I liked walking with him, talking to him, hearing him say that I was a good student. I knew I was a good student. My math teacher, whose name was Cudziewiczowna, often called me to the blackboard to solve math problems. She even told the Christian students to learn from me. I was proud of my good grades in public school and the Jewish school.

My grandfather, short but of a portly bearing, received my report cards and praised my work, always saying a few words to guide me toward scholarly work in talmudic studies. I had already reached the highest level that could be attained in the cheder where I had begun my Jewish education, and was now enrolled in a higher grade in the cheder of Pinchas Schechter, where I was to study the most advanced talmudic tractates as well as the Mishnah.

My mother was pleased, but she had more secular, modern views and felt I should be prepared for a worldly life. She emphasized the importance of my studying litera-ture, poetry, history, and math. She liked to hear me recite the different poems I had to memorize each day. I couldn't help wondering whether her praise for these studies might be connected to her feelings for my natural father.

Whenever I thought my life had become stabilized, something shattered the calm. It was when I was twelve years old. My family had just finished celebrating the Sabbath, and my beloved grandfather went to bed. No one was able to explain the cause, but he never awakened from that sleep. Solace if any, in our bereavement, was that the patriarch died like a Zaddik, or Righteous Man. It is said that a Righteous Man is one who dies on a Sabbath or holy day. Leib Kasser the Zaddik, the wise man, benefactor of our family, was deeply mourned by all who knew him.

I too mourned, for my bulwark, my counselor, my idol, my beloved grandfather. When rich and poor gathered at his funeral, I quickly understood that he had been a leader of his community, a benefactor of the poor, helpmate to workers, advisor to business associates.

He gave tzedakah (charity) generously, quietly. He supplied the poor with Sabbath and holiday meals. He provided dowries for poor brides and often paid for their weddings. For him, all Jewish people were part of the Jewish family.

At his funeral, the poor justly wailed, "What will happen to us now? Who will help us?"

So vast was the gathering at his funeral, it seemed as if the whole town had closed down to attend the services and pay final tribute to this stalwart. Even many Christians were there to mourn the death of the honorable Leib Kasser.

In the peaceful years of my childhood, when the undercurrent of racial slurs was the only disturbance to the amity of home and friends, my grandfather considered Christians to be congregants of mankind. His help to the poor and helpless was without prejudice.

His carved high-backed chair was now empty. His voice was silent at Sabbath prayers and family communions. His adoring eyes no longer sought mine to hear my daily Hebrew recitations. He was no longer there to guide me through interpretations of confusing passages in my talmudic studies. His embracing arms no longer drew me close. I needed solace. I needed to recapture, sustain what was the spirit of him. I needed to wallow in a pit as animals dig, in which I would be suffused with his breath, his inspiration, his goodness and humanity.

I found it in deeper religious observance. In my yearning and sadness, I saw the joyous outflow of Hasidic Jews as a respite from sorrow. I envied their triumph over despair, their rapture with Hebraic lore, their ecstasy in song and dance, their mystical ritual rites that procured wonder for them. Such worship, a contrast to the solemnity of the synagogue, lured me. They could pierce the veil of sadness with their song. Why not mine?

I joined them. A proselyte, I went to the Hasidic services of a rabbi in the neighboring village of Rabitichow. I began to grow side-curls. Except for my grandmother, in whom I confided, I shared my participation with the Hasidim with no one. I concealed my own delight in their congregation. My grandmother helped me get the proper black hat and garb of a Hasid. I kept the clothes in her house, putting the cloak on before making my way to their prayer house, shedding the clothes before returning home, trusting my secret of this subterfuge only to my grandmother.

I knew my mother to be more secular-minded than her parents. She continually encouraged me to learn the cultures of the world. I knew she would berate me for immersing myself in reverential rapture of a millennia-old religion.

Boys have their chums and their secret meetings. They think they are so cunning—that they can hide their private thoughts from the adults. I had my secrets. I had my wide-brimmed hat, side-curls, and cloak. That was my masquerade. No one could identify me in that garb as Eliezer Wenig. Least of all my mother, who sat in the balcony of the synagogue, the separate section designated for women. If she looked down, all she would see would be the habitual garb of a Hasidic boy, I believed. But I underestimated my discerning mother.

When I came home, back in my conventional clothes, she berated me for trying to deceive her.

"I don't object to your orthodox prayers," she would state, looking deeply into my eyes, "I even understand why you want to say what you think are the deepest prayers and ceremonies that would honor your grandfather, but I do not want you wearing Hasidic clothes. That is not what I want for you. I want you to grow up learning and knowing what is going on in our world. You cannot hide in religion. We Jews are facing crucial times. Do you understand me?" she asked.

I loved my mother. I respected her. I wanted to obey her in the full meaning of the commandments. It was not easy for me to give up the joy of participating with the Hasidim. When she took me to the barber to have the side-curls cut off, and disposed of the Hasidic attire, I ached to tell her that she was cutting me off from the cosmos where I had found sanctity. But expressing my thoughts, I believed, would mean disobeying my mother. That I could not do. I continued going to our synagogue regularly, but with a sense of loss.

I soon had reason to respect her views, though. The tension in the Jewish community was intensifying. Everyone was talking politics. The arrival of the national newspapers from the city of Przemysl produced frenetic excitement. Groups assembled, sharing news about Mussolini and the Italian invasion of Abyssinia, Franco and the Civil War in Spain, the effect of these campaigns upon the Soviet Union.

Mostly people would gather to discuss every nuance of the
reports from Nazi Germany and their cruel treatment of
the Jews.

The apprehension became even greater after the sudden death of the prime minister of Poland, Marshal Józef
Pilsudski, a statesman considered friendly to Jews. After
his death, in 1935, the Polish conservative and nationalist
parties became more powerful and more antisemitic. Their
leaflets proclaimed the Jews enemies of the Polish state.
They called for the expulsion of the Jews from Poland.
Although Poland was not totalitarian, tendencies in that
direction were strengthening. The Polish foreign minister,
Józef Beck, enamored with Nazi Germany, thought he
could ally Poland with Hitler. Among his cohorts was
General Edward Rydz-Smigly, who led a clique of colonels
brandishing their antisemitic banners.

The fervor was felt in the Polish school, where the
Christian pupils proclaimed their loathing for the Jewish
people. One daring leader of this gang dramatized his
intentions by slicing his hand across his neck, saying,
"Now that your 'Uncle Pilsudski' is dead, we'll take care of
you in our own way."

Fear crawled into bed with me. Like a mist that seeps
into the bones, so it was for the Jews of our town. Fear slid
into their dreams, awoke with them, slipped into their
clothes with them, occupied every pocket, and clung to
every handshake or daily exchange. My mother's beautiful
blue eyes were heavy with worry. The family spoke of
plundering, destruction, degradations they were aware of.
They told stories of Jews forced from their homes and businesses, herded, marched through Europe to unknown destinations. Fear is the ally of the bully, something a boy
learns when he is young. Fear is the ally of the powerful,
something adults sense. The attacker knows that fear cre-

ates panic. Young or old will flee from it; sometimes fear will make them crafty, aggressive, and in some cases, it will leave them helplessly stranded. I was seeing all this happening.

Any hope of living in Poland was slowly dimming. In every Jewish home, families talked of emigrating. Some wanted to go to America, but their hopes were slight. In the United States, where a strict quota system was observed, aggravated by the Depression that had gripped the country, Jewish immigration was incredibly limited.

Zionists rallied with enforced bravado, spurring each other on with plans of going to Palestine to help build the Jewish state envisioned by the Balfour Declaration. I, too, was caught up in the Zionist euphoria. I stopped attending my Jewish religious school and enrolled in the recently opened modern Hebrew school, called Tarbut ("Culture"). This was not like the talmudic school I had attended. Its purpose was to prepare people for life in a Jewish state in the land of Palestine. We were taught to read and write in modern Hebrew, converse in Hebrew, sing nationalistic Hebrew songs. We had courses in Jewish history, the geography of the proposed state, and the martial arts, should resistance to establishing the Jewish state of Palestine confront us.

I imagined myself in this territory, training my body and mind for this possibility, particularly to be ready for combat. I searched out the books on military formations, maneuvers, engagements, prowess. I read all I could get my hands on about arms and weapons. I wanted to be ready, seeing myself already grown up, posturing as an adult, engaged in battle.

The boys I played with and went to school with noticed the change in my bearing and my conversation. I was breaking the habits and code of their circle, breaking up their team in play, and it alarmed them. They teased me as I drifted into the company of the older boys and girls at my new Hebrew school. I was making new friends who included me in their circle, who shared my goal. They made me feel important.

This crisis in my life was remarkable not only for my popularity among the older boys but with the girls as well. My sweetest memory of those times is of being in the company of Mania Frankel. Three years my senior, she flattered me with her compliments about my studious mind. She told me she liked talking to me, that I was not foolish and flirtatious, that I talked sense about the crucial situation. She was comfortable with me. Oh, how my adolescent mind lapped that up. One day, as we talked, she invited me back to her house, where we continued locking our minds into each other's thoughts about the present and future of our lives. There was a warmth, a congeniality, between us, a feeling that the prospects for the future would emerge from our mutually shared thoughts, that we could make a better future. A flurry of sensuality flared in which our energies merged and from which consequently emerged a bond of hopefulness. Her dark eyes were lively, twinkling with approval, fetching, conveying, while attracting and pinning my eyes to hers. In the magical moment that makes such things possible, she drew my face toward hers, clasped her hands on my ears, and kissed me. A long kiss. A searching, sharing, ecstatic kiss that revealed the Garden of Eden where innocent love and discovery roam.

Those were days of young love when I came early to class, lingered in the halls after class, where, by some private signal that nature provides, we would meet. When she greeted me, her smile, her blossoming body, her luxuriant dark braids that lent teasing shadows to the soft skin near her dancing eyes, made me feel as if I were on the crest of a mountain peak.

Being with her, talking with her, being drawn toward upper classmates with her, gave even more importance to student meetings. Meetings about the providence of Polish Jews. Around us, the antisemitism was intensifying. Zionism was its counteraction. The young people were talking about Professor Chaim Weizmann, their hopes raised by his formula for a Jewish state. Many joined, as I did, the faction of the Polish Zionist leader Yitzhak Gruenbaum; others followed Vladimir Jabotinsky's more militant group, Betar. At home, my brothers Mundek and Shmulek chose to align with Gordonia and Hashomer Hatzair's Socialist Zionist movement, which advocated changing the Jewish image from merchant and scholar to laborer and farmer. My mother made no distinction between the movements. She approved our alliance with Zionism as a more secular, more realistic understanding of world conditions. While my father was not indifferent or detached from political events, he kept his hopes pinned to solutions that would not change our way of life. He attended to his businesses. He was our provider. He let mother instruct and influence our activities.

My mother perused the news reports as eagerly as I did. With the same apprehension, we read the chilling reports about the concentrated rearming of Nazi Germany. I fastened onto the details of the weapons, tanks, airplanes, and naval vessels being built there. War fever was high. Contagion spread among the Poles. Our teachers began instructing us on the use of gas masks, not so much from fear of a German invasion as a concern that an aggressor nation—who else but the Soviets?—opposing the Nazis would engage in chemical warfare, spraying poison gas on civilians. We learned how to identify the various gases that might be used.

The Threat of Hitler

A chill went through the Jewish community in 1936 when we learned that Hitler's armies had occupied the Rhineland. Surely the Western nations would react and order him to remove his troops from there. But nothing happened. And then, in 1938, no nation raised a protest or called up its reserves when Hitler's legions were poised to advance into Austria. Austria had an army. Would it fight back? Would the Austrians resist? What fear was paralyzing them as their country faced this ultimate threat?

We gathered in the streets, in the squares, beating each other with questions, venting our anger over violations of borders, exchanging views on strategy, but our voices petered out under the oppressive blanket of our fears. However we projected events or analyzed them, we were left with our own uncertain future and fate. If a nation like Austria allowed itself to be taken hostage without lifting a sword, what chance was there for Poland? Or for us? The final infamy was the resignation resonating from the radio address by Chancellor Schuschnigg of Austria, who sadly ended with "God protect Austria."

Shaken, our family gathered one Saturday afternoon in my grandmother's house to talk about the impending threat to our safety.

"What's to be done?" my uncle Chaskel Berkowitz asked.

"Where can we go?" pleaded my aunt Rachel Zeiger. "Tell us," they asked. They were so used to my grandfather, the shepherd, leading and giving them cohesion, but he was no longer there to counsel. "Tell us what to do," they demanded of the spiritual presence of my grandfather.

My uncle Lemel Silber, worried about abandoning his soda factory, asked, "How can we abandon our business, our homes? How do we protect our properties, our money?" The questions flew like chicken feathers under the cook's plucking fingers and similarly soundlessly fluttered to earth. Nobody had an answer. My father raised serious questions about being allowed to leave with possessions and money enough to set up homes somewhere else. The somewhere else was as vague as the answers. Who would take in Jews?

Then I heard my father test his own possibilities.

"I should write to my younger brother in New York. He is a metal manufacturer with a good business. Maybe he could vouch for us. But I do not know what our chances are. They're not letting people into the United States. I don't even know how his business is going in that depression."

"You should contact him," urged my uncle. "For us there is no such hope. We can't go anywhere. No one will take us. Not even Palestine."

I went home with their terrified voices drumming in my ears. I dreaded the weeping and despair that was counterpoint to every bulletin heard or read. From a bureau in our dining room, I withdrew the pictures of Uncle Irving, Aunt Ruthie, his wife, and their two children, Norman and Jerry. They had faces resembling my brothers and my sister. All I knew of them was what came in letters. And now the fate of my family seemed to hinge on their largess, their influence. I replaced the pictures, my father's pessimistic tone flooding my thoughts.

What further chilled our hopes of finding a refuge was the news that the British were enacting severe restrictions on Jewish immigration to Palestine. But there was a surge of determination among the Zionists to resist the edict. Aliyah Bet, a clandestine Zionist organization, became the rebuttal. With nothing but wit and fervor, they sought to circumvent the restrictions by bringing in immigrants illegally. These were young people acutely alert to the gathering storm of persecution. Determined to force their way into Palestine, they rented small vessels and hired crews to smuggle hopeful settlers into the proposed homeland.

Many were caught and sent back to their country of origin, most often Poland. But we rejoiced when we heard that Samuel Grunes, the young man betrothed to my cousin Gonia, had made it. Before he began this hazardous secret journey, Samuel vowed to reunite with Gonia in Palestine. She was to apply for entry under the quotas imposed by the British White Paper restricting immigration into Palestine. Aunt Bucia Silber and Uncle Lemel were already beginning to weep over Gonia's impending departure. Gonia was preparing to hazard the journey, as were others. Sadness over such separations seeped through the town.

Wherever I turned, somber faces stared with disbelief at the news reaching our small town of Dynów. A family that owned a radio, one of the few in town, set it up on a window sill to facilitate the spread of newscasts and official government broadcasts. Townspeople gathered under the window to listen and exchange opinions. One family, which had a shortwave radio, shared international news with its neighbors. I was often glued to these reports. I was bewildered by the furious rise of enmity among nations, frightened by the blame heaped on Jews for the economic depression that was gripping the Central European countries. Threats and abuses to Jewish businessmen were becoming more intense.

I tried to fathom how my father or my uncles or any of the tradesmen in Dynów could be responsible for unemployment, or low wages, when they were so central to the livelihood and welfare of the community. Horror stories were being exchanged at every stall during market days in Rynek Square. Jews returning from the synagogues after prayer clustered outside the shops. Women, visiting their neighbors' kitchens, shopping for groceries, or hanging wash on the clothesline, were drawn together to share their anxieties. I heard the tremor in their voices. I saw shadows under their sagging eyes weighted with worries. I read avidly, anything that analyzed the economic and political situation, talked endlessly with my Tarbut classmates about the prejudice igniting around us. My nights were filled with thoughts of my family. I saw them as victims caught in the talons of cold-blooded buzzards chewing at their faces and dismembering their bodies.

With troops massing and threatening, I needed desperately to steady my world. One evening, I sought the seclusion and privacy of the movie house, the only one in Dynów. I went hoping to curl into the seat to watch a swashbuckling adventure, ready to abandon myself to the rescue of a fair damsel from the hands of the pirates. In a gripping story, no borders exist between imagination and reality. For a brief time, I could believe myself combing the seas, chasing a bold buccaneer who dared to raid colonial coasts and claim ransom for a tearful maiden.

But before the feature movie started, a newsreel went on showing Nazi stormtroopers, arms upright like pointed bayonets, goose-stepping to the strident shout of "Heil Hitler." Enlarged to fill the screen was the frenetic face of the Fuhrer, shouting contempt for Jews. The throngs listening were hypnotized by his oratory. Men and women, young and old, cheered to his cues, shouting "*Ein Volk, ein*

Land, ein Führer" ("One nation, one land, one leader"). Over and over, like a phonograph record stuck in a groove, they shrieked, *"Deutschland ist Hitler und Hitler ist Deutschland"* ("Germany is Hitler, and Hitler is Germany").

A masterful orator, he mesmerized mobs with his accusations of Jewish complicity in their troubles. Then, with theatrical showmanship, he led them in chorus after chorus of one of the Nazi's favorite anthems: *"Wenn Juden Blut von Messer schprotzt"* ("When Jewish blood pours from the knife, it is so good for us"). I cringed, I shuddered. This was visual, this was no editorial, this was no fiction. This was the real thing, straight from Berlin. The power provoked, the hate evoked was trancelike. That impassioned crowd would obey any order their Fuhrer gave. And I, an object of this rancor, felt like a calf corraled for the butcher's cleaver. I could not watch or listen to more of his virulent antisemitism. I no longer had the heart to stay for pirates, for fantasy.

I went home, trying to wrench justification and meaning from what I knew of the Jewish religion. Nothing in the tomes I pored over with my teachers taught treachery, plundering, brutality. Jews wanted to live in peace, earn their bread, observe their holy laws.

I began to spend sleepless nights dreading the next day's bulletins, which would have more frightening news. I took to reading at night. I had this intense drive to find explanations for the mass hysteria of the population that believed the accusations Hitler hurled against us. I read and brought home newspapers and books that were not part of my school work. It was not long before I began to hear my mother scolding me, "You can't keep the lamp burning all night. You have to go to school in the morning. You will not be able to keep your eyes open in school. Go to sleep."

How could I tell her of the nightmares I was having, of the stormtroopers surrounding me, their weapons pointed at me. Awaking startled, my body bathed in sweat, I could not shake the image of them stepping forward to thrust their bayonets into my body. Surely I must have screamed out.

Not wanting to share these awful dreams with my family, not wanting to hear my parents scold me, I started to spend nights in my grandmother's house. I slept in the room with Uncle Jankel, my mother's younger brother. I liked to talk to him because he too was interested in history and current events. We talked late into the night, twisting and turning the details of the news. After a while, he would turn over and go to sleep, not minding if I stayed up. Reading far into the night, I would sometimes hear him stir, asking what I found so absorbing in the book. One of the many at a time I brought home from the library. Between those covers were the mysteries of the world, the marvelous minds of the world, the chronicles of man's life in the world. One time it was Josephus Flavius' *The Jewish War;* another time, my first glimpse of Russian culture in Sholokhov's *And Quiet Flows The Don.* Everything was fodder for my eager mind.

I fought the enfolding cloak of sleep with a gimmick I had read about, used by the Polish hero Tadeusz Kosciuszko, whom they had honored in the United States by naming a New York bridge after him. Kosciuszko, an avid reader, reading by candlelight far into the night, was said to have tied a rope from his leg to the leg of a chair. Should he doze off, the slightest move he made would tip the chair, arousing him. That impressed me. I tried it. It worked for me, and my uncle, if anything, was amused, leaving me to my nocturnal reading. My grandmother, sleeping in an adjoining bedroom, never complained.

Rather, she was pleased that I wanted to sleep in Jankel's room and share a close relationship with him.

Jankel was there to subdue my terrors, as I may have been for him as well, particularly when a political crime took place in our little town. Crime, even petty crime, seldom happened. In such instances as it did occur, we had our police station, police commandant Jan Kunik, and policemen Michalak, Mac, and Flisak.

Commandant Kunik's daughter was one of the top students in my class. We would exchange ideas, check homework together, particularly history, discuss solutions to math problems, or just look at each other approvingly as good students do. But we never had any social exchange. Her respect for me didn't go past the barriers of her antisemitism.

If her father, Commandant Kunik, held such views, he kept them in check during the years 1929 to 1935, when Dynów was considered a city, and its *burmistrz* (mayor) was Jozef Gosecki. Even when the local government was downsized to a town, it was under the jurisdiction of Alexander Krasnopolski, the *wójt* (district administrator). Both men appeared friendly to the Jewish population. In fact, Alexander Krasnopolski's father, who owned the bakery across the street from my father's store, purchased flour from my father. They got along very well. In the next few years, as antisemitism became more flagrant, he was courteous, but there were subtle changes in the way he talked to the Jews. Eyes averted, an extended hand in greeting ignored, no longer lingering when he came in to purchase provisions in the Jewish stores. Still, Commandant Kunik kept order in Dynów. We did not question his politics.

By 1939 political storms were raging throughout Europe. When Commandant Kunik and Officer Michalak, visiting a flour mill in a nearby village, became victims of a crime, it may very well have had political implications. Noticing two strangers whose behavior aroused their suspicion, they approached and asked for their identification documents. The two young outsiders drew guns from their pockets and murdered the commandant. Michalak was injured and unable to pursue the gunmen.

The incident terrified the townspeople and provoked the county authorities to ask the national government to assist in finding the killers. A special security force of about two hundred men from Komanda Glowna (Central Command) streamed into town, sirens blaring on their trucks, to search for the criminals. The soldiers were armed with rifles, but I for one was disappointed, having anticipated a display of heavy weapons from this elite security unit such as I had been reading about. They set up only one light machine gun with a sparse pack of ammunition. The only show of military might was in their strutting and their brisk voices, which resounded on the cobbled streets. They were ineffectual. They did not catch the perpetrators of the crime. About the only impact their presence made was speculation about the efficacy of Poland's army. Beyond that, there was no end of talk about the identity of the two gunmen who had escaped the law.

The most likely explanation was that the unidentified men were members of the *Ludowcy*, the Peasant Party, vengeful because their leader, Wincenty Witos, had been sent into exile. The contagion of the Communist Revolution in Russia had spread to neighboring countries where peasants worked the huge tracts of lands owned by the aristocracy. In Poland, the families of Czartoryski, Lubomirski, Radziwill, and, closer to our town, Count Potocki owned many thousands of acres of arable land, tilled and harvested by peasants who received little reward for long, hard hours in the fields. What small parcels belonged to the peasants for their own farming yielded little to sustain them, making them dependent upon the largess of the landowners, who made it seem that they were giving out favors to those they hired on their lands.

The Peasant Party goaded the discontent by telling the peasants they were being exploited. For labor leader Witos and his followers, the times were ripe for change. Agitating for more land for the peasants, an idea borrowed from the Communists, for redistribution of land, they ran smack into the power of the aristocracy, which was more clever, more wily, more worldly than peasant agitators. When the peasants, incensed by the party leaders about the injustice of the system, marched through the Rynek, the town square, demonstrating for the return and release of Wincenty Witos, the champion of their rights, the right-wing Endeks, henchmen of the aristocracy, handed out antisemitic leaflets blaming the Jews for their problems. Clearly, this was a ploy to divert the peasants' attacks from the aristocrats and on the Catholic Church, also a large landowner. These two powerful despotic forces controlled the system. And the Jews were convenient scapegoats for the workers' and peasants' grievances. They branded all Jews communists. They eagerly told the peasants that the communists intended to confiscate the land, take it for themselves, and use it to add to their wealth and power.

Not surprisingly, many Jews were attacked, beaten, robbed of possessions. Not surprisingly, people were blaming the Peasant Party for the murder of the police commandant. I began to hear reports that the Polish army was conducting a campaign against communists. I found my interest aroused about this second movement sweeping through Europe. I knew little about the Soviet Union. My classmates or teachers had never mentioned Karl Marx or his ideas. I had much to learn and understand about the rival movements, especially since Polish speculation avoided reference to German Nazi agents in the murder of our commandant. I had heard suspicions of Jewish complicity directed as a possible explanation. Even in my young mind, I sensed that the Poles were willing to embrace and forgive Nazi transgressions for the sake of antisemitism. The Polish government, headed by Prime Minister Slawoj Skladkowski and Minister of Foreign Affairs Józef Beck, felt comfortable with Hitler's Germany. I would soon become aware that Colonel Beck was a political career man who had his own biases. England was cynical about his alliances.

Poland had a history that lent itself to an alliance with Germany. This was because Poland faced a serious geographical dilemma. On her western borders, Germany was her neighbor. On the eastern border, she had Russia. Each of these ambitious giants coveted access to Poland as a corridor to attack and invade the other. In the eighteenth century, in just such an aggression, Prussia, Russia, and Austria had each taken part of the country, divided the spoils in a series of massive partitions that ended Poland's existence as an independent state.

Poland regained her independence in November 1918, at the end of World War I. But painful impressions lingered. Poland remained more fearful of Russia. Hence, Nazi Germany was less threatening than the Soviet Union, and Hitler, rather than Stalin, was the choice for an alliance.

I wanted to know everything about Adolf Hitler. Everything was not what Hitler was going to reveal. Soon enough I found that references to his background were shunted to his strategy rather than to his credentials for leaping to the position of head of state. I heard older pupils in school talking about *Mein Kampf,* a book he had written while a political prisoner back in 1923. All I knew was that the antisemitism he spouted in those pages gave ignorant peasants and workers an excuse to hurl insults at the Jews. Open threats to harm and strip the Jews of property surfaced. The news was filled with Hitler's speeches and his rising power. The fear of his evil influence was capturing us. It was like a cosmic rain showering the earth with pellets that threatened to crush our community.

In my own way, I was mesmerized by his activities and speeches. When I heard that Hitler was going to broadcast an important announcement, I joined the many who gathered to listen under the window of my math teacher, who owned one of the few radios in Dynów. Despite the poor reception, we who knew Yiddish, an offshoot of German, understood his words. In a loud, booming voice, he vilified the government of Czechoslovakia for abusing the Germans who lived within its borders. Czech protests about Germany's encroachment of their borders simply fueled his fiery oratory. He demanded that the western part of Sudeten Czechoslovakia be ceded to the German Reich. What I heard confirmed what I had read in his book: he was hell-bent on leading Germany to glory. He meant to overrun Europe, enslave it, dominate the world.

A shiver ran through the crowd. They huddled but found no words to express the terror seizing them. Heads shaking in disbelief, eyes seeking help, they found no hope forthcoming. Even the Poles were fearful. Sadly, filled with disquieted feelings, they dispersed.

I had my own feelings. Surely the Polish government would stand firm against an invasion of its sovereign rights, I thought. I looked for signs confirming this in the faces of the adults, but there were none.

I looked for encouraging signs in the newspapers.
Dynów did not publish one, but the papers came to us on
the bus from Przemysl. I rushed to meet the bus on delivery days, waiting for the bundles of newspapers to come
in. There were never enough copies for the now-escalating
demand. Others like me, eager to get their hands on a copy,
dogged the distributor's steps, following him to the store,
holding out the payment with one hand as the other
grabbed a copy.

I held my breath as I searched through the pages for the
international news. Looking for hopeful signs of strength
and determination among Polish officialdom to thwart the
·Fuhrer's aggression. We Jews assumed that the Poles were
sympathetic to the Czechs; we thought they respected
Czechoslovakia's democracy and cultural achievements. We
knew that the past president of Czechoslovakia, Thomas
Masaryk, and the current president, Eduard Benes, were
friendly toward Jews. Surely Poland would side with the
Czechs to resist Hitler. Surely England and France, the great
powers of the continent, would respond to this threatening
conqueror. According to the newspapers they were rearming. They would use their military forces to repel the invader. They would not permit Hitler to gobble up the smaller,
weaker Czech nation. Surely the United States would take
action to clip Hitler's appetite for territory.

I pored over every report of military preparations. I followed every plan and maneuver. I was fascinated by the
growing effort of the European nations to build up their
military might. I had the same faith as the French, who
were reinforcing the Maginot Line with heavy guns, believing, as they did, that this fortification was impenetrable.
That was the western front. How were the nations east of
Germany preparing for war? And the Soviet Union?
Wouldn't they stand firm to protect their borders?

We had very little information about the Soviet forces. Polish censors controlled what was published. They had no respect for the Red Army. We believed them when they said that the Soviet Union's military forces had been weakened by Stalin's purge of the generals. We believed their reports that the Soviets had few modern weapons. We believed there was no threat from Russia. But then we heard contradictory rumors from people who were sympathetic to the Soviet Union. The Soviets, they told us, were very powerful, with a huge arsenal of tanks and aircraft to rival the Germans.

"Why," said one bearer of these tales, "they've invented an airplane made completely of rubber. It's so maneuverable that it can hit any target and get out of range of enemy fire before you can blink an eye."

"In fact," offered another socialist sympathizer, "this plane is so far advanced over anything other nations have that the Russians have put over eighty thousand into production."

These were no small details. In my mind, war was inevitable. I acted as if that were the case. I talked to anyone who would listen about armies, weapons, strategy. They began to call me the Jewish Marshal. I enjoyed the popularity. It gave me a feeling of power which I thought I shared with my nation. After all, Poland was also rearming, somewhat like the Soviet Union. Poland's Cigelski factories produced heavy artillery and was pumping up production.

Such rumors spread like wildfire. Of course, we in Dynów believed in Poland's military strength. We believed its army was well trained and bold. We trusted its soldiers to defend our country. We trusted them to unite with other nations against Hitler.

Instead, the Polish government offered no protest when Hitler gobbled up the Sudetenland. Moreover, inspired by Hitler's bold demand, it forced Czechoslovakia to cede Cieszyn Silesia to Poland, thus taking part in the destruction of a friendly neighboring country. Hitler supported the Polish claim. I pictured Hitler and Beck as banded hunters bending over a carcass, fingers dripping with blood as they tore pieces from it, greedy mouths chomping away.

I imagined the leaders of the two countries drooling over their acquisitions, Hitler's trophy the Sudetenland, Poland's army ready to march into Cieszyn Silesia. My impressions were enhanced when martial music blared over the radio, the tunes of these rousing marches pounding in my head, the words hammering my ears. An outburst of patriotic song and flag-waving that should have increased my military ardor and pride in Polish valor.

But something about the words to the song chilled my enthusiasm. The song *"Nikt nam nie zrobi nic, bo znami jest Rydz-Smigly"* ("No one can do a thing to us because we have Rydz-Smigly"). It was not that I had no faith in Rydz-Smigly, the commander of the Polish army. But it sounded like hollow praise for helping to dismember the Czech nation. Also, I could not dismiss the horror in the Jewish whisperings over the fate of a people they liked.

Many nationalist Poles proudly demonstrated, gleeful over the acquisition of Cieszyn Silesia, even bragging that Adolf Hitler would help them get colonies in Africa. We Jews, however, were fearful of Poles so willing to jump on the Nazi bandwagon. With good cause. This alliance unleashed stronger, more scurrilous antisemitism.

Now, when the neighbors saw me, irony dripped from their teeth.

"Marshal Wenig, what do you say now? Still so interested in armies and armaments?"

I wish I could have said yes, but with some conviction that our country and its army would help the Jews.

"Marshal Wenig." My pride in the title dimmed. Emboldened by my familiarity with Polish history and the monarchs who had ruled Europe, I had been only too willing to recount the diplomatic strategies and military conquests through which borders and power had shifted over the centuries. I retold stories I had read, finding in myself a storyteller's mystique to hold an audience. In early evenings, my young cousins and friends called to me, "Are you coming out? Tell us another story, a war story, a story about Poland's glory."

They would gather round, and I would tell them about the Golden Age of Poland: the fourteenth, fifteenth, and sixteenth centuries, during which art and science had flourished. I told them of the sadder centuries during which the partitions had resulted in the disappearance of Poland from the map of the world. I spoke of how the Poles had been cheered by the rebirth of an independent Poland under Józef Pilsudski, and of his great victories in the Russo-Polish War of 1919–20. Because I had become so engrossed in military affairs, they wanted me to describe every battle, every triumph, every detail that enriched Polish history. I had pictures in my mind of uniforms, of military formations, of weapons and battlefields—all of which I brought to life for them. I was especially interested in the rearmament going on in our own time, as the nations of Europe girded for war, describing each nation's fighting forces and state of preparedness. The little faces, upturned, listened and watched as if I were a cinema screen where they saw battles enacted. They moved close to me, little bodies rammed against mine. One little boy trembled.

"I'm afraid of the big noise," he complained. The rumblings in the distance scare me. "It's like thunder. Will it come here?"

He hid his head in my lap and I knew how he felt. I had crushed my body against Hania's in my younger years. I knew the comfort of her body in the bed. I had told my friend about my fear and Hania's cuddling presence in my bed. Instead of understanding my confidence, my friend wanted to know if Hania had touched my private parts.

"You know," he whispered, as if I would reveal something obscene that would relate to his own sexual mysteries, "down there. Did you touch her? Did you feel her tits?" He misconstrued my confession of fear. Touching was not what I had sought in her protective arms. Power to dispel my fears was there. In a parallel way, I tried to tell my younger listeners that military arms, power, would protect Poland. By reassuring them, I was trying to subdue my own fears.

I was a reporter as well for the adults. Whenever I brought the newspapers that came on the bus from Przemysl, they asked me for the latest news. They wanted details, too. They wanted to hear every last word of Hitler's demands and military thrust against Czechoslovakia. They wanted to hear that the people would not give in to Hitler. They greeted news of opposition to Hitler in the Western press with hope.

Their hopes were dashed by reports out of Berchtesgaden and Munich, where Mussolini, the dictator of Italy, Chamberlain, the British prime minister, and Daladier, the French premier, met with Hitler to resolve the Czech situation. Many expected that the great powers would deliver an ultimatum to Hitler, a strong resolution that would halt his aggression by showing their commitment to the preservation and integrity of the Czech nation. Groaning in disbelief, I read the communique aloud. Far from making Hitler back down, the great powers had agreed to his demands. Czechoslovakia had to cede the

Sudetenland to Germany. This concession was based on Hitler's promise not to make any further territorial demands on other countries. Prime Minister Chamberlain's picture was on the front page of the newspaper, showing him waving the treaty signed by the German Fuhrer and announcing, "Peace in our time."

Poland, allied politically with Germany, shared Hitler's triumph and spoils. Poland was awarded Cieszyn Silesia. Polish officers led the celebration of this acquisition. They boasted of this acquisition and their approval of Hitler's action. They had chosen to align with the powerful conqueror of the twentieth century. How smart. Ignorant Poles drank the wine of conquest, danced and sang patriotic songs promising greater glory to Poland.

The Jews of Dynów heard the voices swollen with grandeur. Their hearts and minds fastened on recollected history, in which power always raised the specter of persecution. The signs were already there.

When I heard the familiar question, "Marshal Wenig, you have such a head for politics. What do you think about this news?" the voice was not derisory. Too much sadness for that. And I, who was so drawn into the historic array of soldiers girded for battle, was hearing that such power had its duplicity. It could conquer nations but could also annihilate within its own nation those of differing blood and religious belief.

"Marshal Wenig, what now?" they asked.

My answer, based on the ominous reports in the international press, was, "I predict that war is just around the corner."

The War Is Upon Us

With the declaration that Germany must be *Judenrein* ("free of Jews"), thousands of Jews were expelled from Germany. Their savings confiscated, dispossessed of property, stripped of belongings, they fled to the Polish border. With the clothes on their backs, a few salvaged possessions of little value wrapped in shabby bags, they faced unwelcome signs wherever they sought refuge. Thousands arrived in Poland seeking refuge with kinsmen who took them in with aching hearts, made room for them in their homes, and shared their bread with them.

Hitler cunningly assessed the reluctance of Europe's statesmen to take action against him. He cleverly covered his intentions by soothing and baiting the rulers of Poland with a chunk of Czech land. He knew them as a hunter knows his hounds, holding out a bloody scrap of meat to lure them to the kill. In their greed, they were blind. They ignored the omens. They did not see that the acquisition of the Czech arms industry, the great Skoda Works, would increase Germany's growing military might. They were heedless to the rumors of Hitler's designs for Poland.

Following the shattering news that Nazi boots were tramping across Czechoslovakia, crushing a Slavic democracy, yoking its people to the Nazi war machine, were signs that Hitler meant to claim the independent city-state of Danzig. This would give him a corridor through the province of Pomorze (Pomerania) in northern Poland to East Prussia. Pomerania had been taken from Germany after World War I in order to provide the new state of

43

Poland with access to the Baltic Sea, but as a result East Prussia had been separated from the rest of Germany. Hitler saw it as his mission to reunite the two.

Panic spread through Polish villages and cities. For Jews, the danger was twofold: country and creed were endangered. There would be no homeland, no escaping the Aryan inquisition. The Jews had already seen newsreels showing Hitler's armies marching into the Sudetenland and the sobbing of the Czech people. The roads to Poland were cluttered with displaced Jews. Three and a half million Jews, about one-tenth of the Polish population, trembled at the implications of a fate like the one that had befallen the Jews of Germany.

I searched the papers daily for some indication that Britain and France would stand up to the Nazi menace. I listened to every newscast. I found myself whispering with my friends about our parents' fears. What if, as they were saying, we had to join the nomads we were seeing on the roads? We could not go westward. That way lay deportation to German labor camps. Eastward lay the uncertain paths toward the Soviet Union. We could not go south, where Hitler had trashed Czechoslovakia to link up with Mussolini, who had his own territorial ambitions and his own alliance with Hitler in a so-called Pact of Steel. The papers spoke of the fascist Axis powers and the Allied Western nations, already drawing battle lines, with the Soviets as an undefined factor. Such was the dilemma for Jews. Such was the dilemma for Poland.

Poland was caught in the German vise. If Hitler moved into Polish territory, Poland would have to turn to England and France for help. Chamberlain and Daladier, in turn, started feverish negotiations with the Soviet Union to join forces against the common menace, Nazi Germany. Poland was finally seeing that Hitler fully intended to conquer, piece by piece, all of Europe. He intended to take on the world. When news reached us, in August 1939, of Winston Churchill's suggestion that England and France send a military mission to Moscow to negotiate a alliance, my hopes rose. Did not England, with its colonial empire, control one-fourth of the world? And was not France renowned for colonial and military strength? They were powerful enough to hold Hitler in check.

The hopefulness was short-lived. Instead of a pact with the Allies, Stalin signed a nonaggression pact with Hitler. The Polish government issued mobilization orders to the reserves. A shudder went through Dynów. Tensions ran high. It did little to assuage our anxiety to hear Prime Minister Chamberlain announce that England and France guaranteed Poland's independence.

Along Mickiewicza Street, our town's main thoroughfare, grave faces appealed to others for news reports. People offered and shared ideas on military tactics. Everyone became a general. Everyone pictured himself on the general staff.

"If I were . . ." one heard people speculate. Every head had two sets of ears. One to listen to an authoritative voice, the second to eavesdrop on a neighboring voice with another point of view. Nothing was learned that the early cavemen did not know: everyone was a target for the enemy's arrow, and huddling was a momentary delusion of safety.

The Jewish women had their own response to anxiety. They made visits to the cemeteries, praying, beseeching the dead to talk to God, to plead with Him to protect and guard their families if war broke out. In the synagogues, they wailed and implored God to hear their prayers for salvation. I looked up at their sorrowing faces and their humble bodies and wondered why such evil had been unleashed on the world, wondering where we could hide from the frightful Fuhrer.

I joined the men in prayer, but when I came out of the synagogue I wanted my thin body, now getting taller, to shrivel, to fit into the bark of a tree, to shrink and drain into the roots, into the soil, to be no part of this human race that could cause such suffering and cruelty as we were beginning to hear of. Families were being forced out of their homes. Herded and carted off to labor camps. Or else, while fleeing from one unknown fate, they became victims of another unknown fate. What horrors awaited them?

Adults kept asking my opinions: "Lusiek, in your fascination with weapons, did your mind ever conceive such instruments of torture and revenge?" The martial songs taught in our school kept drumming through my head. Only for me they were not songs of patriotic fervor but war chants against the Jews.

Ever since March 15, 1939, when Nazi Germany had invaded Czechoslovakia and then had demanded Danzig and the so-called Polish Corridor to East Prussia, we had been living in a state of preparation for war.

On the way home from school one day, preoccupied with what we had just learned about pasting paper strips on our windows to prevent the glass from shattering in case of an air raid, I ran into my geography teacher, Pan Bielawski. He came over and engaged me in conversation, something he hadn't done for the past year. He wasn't bragging now about Poland's alliance with Germany, but expressed concern about the danger Poland was facing. "We should talk like this again," he said.

We often took walks together after that. "Poland is strong," he said, "Poland is rearming. You'll see, we have no reason to fear the Germans." He was doing more to bolster his own hopes than mine. But I soon found that it wasn't my affirmation he wanted but information.

"What are the Jewish newspapers saying? What are the Jews planning to do about the persecution in Germany? What will they do if Poland is attacked?"

His interest in my opinions flattered me. I willingly believed that he had sought me out because I was known to follow the news so avidly. I even believed that he respected my analysis of events. I was not so wise as to suspect him of prying in order to get information that could be used to harm the Jews. Even the older people who saw us together were impressed by the teacher's interest in me. When they asked, I told them he wanted to know what the Jewish newspapers said about the dangerous events unfolding. They thought that he, like the rest of us, was searching every publication for a glint of hope.

One day, after walking with him, I went to get a haircut. We had two barbers in town. I went to Adolph Bieber on Mickiewicza Street. The conversation there was very much the same as in the streets. When Michalak, the town policeman, came in to get a haircut, the barber put the same question to him as to me.

"Well, is there going to be a war?"

"Yes," Michalak answered.

"How can Poland fight such a powerful nation as Germany, especially with its air force, the Luftwaffe, as strong as it is?" I wanted to know.

"I can tell you," Michalak said; "I know from a reliable source that England has given Poland the *Zenitowka,* the ultimate anti-aircraft gun."

Forming a pyramid with the palms of his hand to suggest the base of the gun, from which the shells would be fired upward, he exclaimed, "Zoom! Pow! Any German plane that flies over the area would be destroyed immediately. With this super-gun, Poland has nothing to fear from the Luftwaffe."

"Is that a fact?" Mr. Bieber, the barber, was incredulous.

"Absolutely, Michalak insisted. Not only was Great Britain sending Poland the anti-aircraft guns, but they were sending black soldiers from their African colonies to Warsaw to operate the guns.

But Mr. Bieber had his doubts. "Do you think Poland can hold off a major attack by the German army? Look how well they did during the Spanish Civil War," he argued.

"Are you kidding, can you imagine what is going to happen to Germany when our cavalry gallops into Berlin," Michalak beamed. He was quite serious. Like so many ignorant Poles, he believed that Poland had tough troops.

Mr. Bieber and I did not share his confidence. Mr. Bieber winked at me. He knew I was not taken in by the braggart. We both knew Michalak's reputation. Behind his back, he was called Michalak Bezputski, meaning "dickless," or more literally, "without a putz." Word had gone around that his penis had been shot off in a dispute. Being privy to a jest with sexual implications in the barber shop was tantamount to being admitted to adult society.

Friday, September 1, 1939, was a beautiful day. The late summer sun touched the trees and flowers. The shadows cast by the trees changed with the gentle breeze. My mind played games with the shapes of the shadows, benign and friendly. Those were the inventions and the humor of my childhood. The smells of chickens and geese roasting, potato puddings, and rendered fat drifted from the windows. Rugelach and strudel, brown and white dough balls that we called lekach set out to cool, gave off their own aroma of honey and spice. Inside the house my mother was preparing for the Sabbath. In our garden and home, the bustle and preparations for the High Holy Days, just a few days ahead, quickened our hopes for a better year to come.

We were thinking, too, of the joyous holiday of Sukkot, when we would string fruits and cut out paper palms, painted green, to decorate the sukkah. Changeless tradition. Hella, my little sister, was sitting at the kitchen table making colorful paper chains, decorations, and cardboard cutouts. There were cutouts of Moses with the tablets, there were stars, that she would hang on the walls of the sukkah.

It was Friday, September 1, 1939. As in the past years of my childhood, I anticipated a warm holiday season centered on family, the synagogue, and greetings for the new year to come. Instead, the forenoon peace was interrupted by an urgent announcement. *"Uwaga! Uwaga! Przelecial koma trzy"* ("Attention! Attention! Overflew coma three"). The radio announcer repeated these very strange words three times. The words were "Overflew coma three" but what did that mean? A military code mistakenly was aired on public radio?

Momentarily this army signal added to my fascination with things military. I was getting a privileged peek into how the army did things. That peek, however, had imperative implications that threatened to shatter the remnants of peace. I tried to make sense of it while my stomach churned with its own mixed signals of awe and dread.

I looked at the faces around me to see if anyone else had heard and understood the words. I walked past the stores on Mickiewicza Street, oddly vacant, the sidewalk ominously empty and quiet, a hush before the sudden booming noises overhead. I looked up, there were no signs of a storm. As before, an eerie silence settled as if this disturbance had been something imagined. It was my foolish response to war talk but would not affect life in the little town. Shake it, I told myself, as I looked down the vacant street.

I walked back toward the neighbor's house where the radio was turned up and now saw consternation on the faces of the listeners. My friend Dufciu, usually stirring up comments about the news, was standing still in the small cluster, like myself keenly intent on the broadcast.

"The president is going to speak," he whispered as he motioned for me to listen.

President Ignacy Moscicki's voice was tense. "In the early hours of the morning, the German army invaded our country. German bombs were dropped on military installations, on areas of concentrated civilian population. This is a brutal attack on our country."

He then went on to appeal to the people to stay calm in this difficult hour, to stand by their leaders and await further information. Strangest of all was his appeal to soldiers to show restraint and save ammunition.

"Why did he wait so long to tell us about the invasion?" I wanted to know, but my question received no answer.

Obviously it was German planes flying overhead that explained the rumbling we had heard. I persisted with my questions. "Why don't they use their anti-aircraft guns? Why should the army save ammunition? Doesn't Poland have weapons and bullets to fight off the attack? They have to put up a fight." Quick flashes of air raids and ground fire were the responses to my questions. Nobody spoke. I was left looking at shock and hopelessness.

I ran to my father's store. My brothers Mundek and Shmulek were there. My mother left her kitchen to the care of the maid and rushed there too, with Hella my little sister weeping at her side. They asked me what I knew.

"Is Hitler going to conquer all of Poland?"

Although I was only fifteen years old, they gave credence to my opinions. They knew I followed current events avidly.

"I can't tell you more than I've heard. If Germany dropped bombs, it means war."

I looked at Hella clutching my mother's arm, her eyes blinking with fright because she could not fathom the meaning of the word war. I tried to explain it to her, but doing so increased my own agitation. I had to find someone who could explain the implications of this attack.

Uncle Lemel was a very religious and well-informed man. I went to see him in his candy store. He was not there. I went to his soda-bottling factory, another of his enterprises, and found him as shaken as I was. I started to blurt out the news, thinking he had not heard anything. Stroking his black beard, he peered at me as if he were looking at a stranger. He lowered his eyeglasses so they rested on the tip of his nose, his eyes full of fury. His ruddy cheeks quivering feverishly, he shouted, "You wanted a war, now you have one!"

I had gone to him because I liked to talk to him. He had always been a good audience for my accounts of the newest weapons and tactics used by Franco's forces in the Spanish Civil War, and by Mussolini's in the conquest of Abyssinia. He was accustomed to seeing me pantomime war engagements. At such moments he had always praised my intelligence, now he was condemning me. I could not believe he thought I would be elated over this string of events.

Hurt by the way Uncle Lemel had treated me, I walked back down Mickiewicza Street, which was now a sea of people. The shocking reality of the news had brought them out to commiserate and seek solace from one other. Storekeepers joined the crowd, leaving shops unattended. Even my father, usually reserved in manner, was in one of the clusters, wildly concerned abut the fate of Polish Jewry. Insisting on the right of Jews to be protected because so many had served in the Austro-Hungarian army, he boasted of his own service as an artilleryman on the French front in World War I.

"We had the heaviest guns in our arsenal then, a forty-two-centimeter gun known as Big Bertha," he proclaimed. "That gun was manufactured by Krupp in Germany. It took fifteen men to handle it."

The people clustered to hear further broadcasts, but none offered more information. The Polish authorities were suspiciously quiet.

The bravado that had accompanied earlier reports about General Rydz-Smigly and his battalions was missing. The people, heavy-hearted, disbanded and shuffled off to their homes for the Sabbath meal.

The mood was somber. My father made the blessing over the wine, then asked each of us, Mundek, Shmulek, and me, to recite the Kiddush. We ate quietly, preoccupied with concerns about the recent events. Usually a joyous song, the "Sabbath Bride," would accompany our Sabbath meal. Now we all were muted and sad.

The next morning, September 2, at the Sabbath prayers, the women were admitted to the men's sanctuary, highly unusual except in the most extraordinary circumstances. Their heads covered with shawls, they approached the Torah Ark and beseeched God for help. Their keening voices brought tears and cries from the men. The scintillated prayers of the men swelled and seemed to hurtle against the walls of the synagogue. Surely God would hear their supplications, they hoped.

On September 3, England and France declared war on Germany. A fact after the act. The news did not lift the despondence that pervaded the Jewish community. Little was said of Polish resistance to the invasion, leaving the impression that nothing could be done to stop the Nazi onslaught. For us in Dynów, it was only a question of when Hitler's army would enter the town.

On September 5 came a mass of refugees from the western part of Poland. Some entered the town on horse-drawn wagons. Most were trudging on foot, their feet swollen, hungry, weak, and exhausted from the travail. They clutched their belongings as if the contents of their few bundles maintained their human grace. From them, we learned what was happening beyond our town.

With their outdated guns and limited supply of ammunition, the Polish cavalry proved ineffectual against the German tank battalions. To add to the misery, they did not even have enough food. All this was unthinkable and became more so when the refugees told us of German Stuka divebombers machine-gunning Polish army columns, training their guns on civilians who ran and scattered for safety. Suddenly, help had seemingly descended from the skies in the form of fully armed Polish paratroopers, attempting to stem the German blitzkrieg.

"Ah, look up there," they cheered and shouted. "Poland does have a clever defense against these devils."

The horror was that this was a deceptive ploy. The paratroopers were German soldiers dressed in Polish uniforms infiltrating and massacring their enemy. The German army not only seemed invincible, they appeared to be brilliant strategists who were able to anticipate every move the Polish generals planned.

"Don't be naive," the refugees told us. "Germany had plenty of spies, Polish Nazi sympathizers who fed them information."

The Germans, coming from the air and on the ground, were creating havoc. The Polish army was in disarray. Civilians fled, appalled by the inept and gullible army, knowing they were in danger.

Dynów was in the path of escape. Christians and Jews streamed in, were given shelter, food, and warm baths to tend their tired feet.

Charity is second nature to Jews. From an early age they are taught to give tzedakah. Good deeds are not meant to be rewarded, but every Jewish heart has some remnant of mankind's pagan history. This was charity. It was an offering such as primitives might give to angry gods, an offering to stave off a similar crisis for themselves. God would hear their prayers, see their offerings, record their compassion. He would reward them, provide salvation for them.

Perhaps the clouds were too thick with gun smoke for God to see the earth's surface, because no help came from the heavens. Help was a word invented for human needs. Help was what the people of Dynów had to extend to an even greater degree when retreating soldiers began to stream through the town. Pitifully dragging their feet, disheveled, unshaven, defeat etched in their dusty faces, they avoided the questioning gazes of the onlookers.

Along with them were the sounds of horses' hooves and creaking farm wagons carting the wounded. Rough blankets barely covered gaping wounds. The sobs and calls for help were heart-wrenching. Although they were not trained for it, many young girls in town offered to nurse the wounded, who were taken to our school, now converted into a hospital. There were beds, but no medical equipment or medical supplies.

Wounded soldiers confirmed the gloomy reports we had heard from the refugees. Transported in peasants' carts to the battlefield, they were poorly equipped, lacked food, boots, ammunition. Their units were decimated by the German air force. But they wanted us to know that they had put up a strong resistance. The pathetic remnants of the Polish army blamed their defeat on short-sighted generals who had believed Hitler's promises to Poland.

We were no less short-sighted. We dared not concede Hitler's next move, driving his forces east. We could not believe that our town would come under siege. If the Nazis intended to come through Dynów, wouldn't we hear the thunder of tanks, the booming of bursting shells, the war whoops of modern warfare?

They took us by surprise. It was September 12, 1939. The German soldiers did not come from the west, as would be expected. Through a diversionary maneuver, they came from the north, from Lubna Gura, and entered from a side street, off Mickiewicza Street, riding on bicycles. One bicycle had a machine gun mounted on the handle bars. The other riders had rifles slung on their shoulders. They stationed themselves across the road, staring, barricading entry or exit. They gestured to the pedestrians and ordered them to lie down with arms outstretched.

Terror either stuns or triggers flight or reflexively makes man strike back. The latter two are animal responses. The first is human. The adult human knows what a bullet can do. He feels hopeless and helpless. Most responded to the order. But while machine guns clattered and rifle shots cracked the awesome stillness, a few of us bolted and ran to a side street. We were still responding to animal instincts, scurrying to safety.

On that day, September 12, 1939, I sought shelter. The nearest doorway was to Grossman's bakery. I hid there while the shooting went on. My heart pounded, my stomach churned. My head felt as if my hair were separating from my scalp. I looked at the baker, Moishe Grossman, whose shaking hands were clutching his face. His body was moving convulsively as if pushed and pulled to make a decision. Retreat to a cellar that might or might not be a haven? Then the shooting stopped, only to be followed by the rumbling, ground-crunching sounds of trucks entering the town. Braving a peek down the main street, I saw German soldiers riding in huge trucks pulling artillery. Some of the trucks stopped to discharge soldiers and equipment. Others moved on toward Przemysl.

I ran home, where my mother grabbed me, patting my body as if checking to see whether I was injured. Her face contorted with fear, her hands shaking, she kissed me violently, anxiety having taken over her total being. Looking around, and not seeing my two older brothers, Shmulek and Mundek, I too became nervous. I knew they had been on Mickiewicza Street when the German soldiers came into town. My mother, unable to control her tears, collapsed onto a chair when the door opened, and she saw father flanked by Shmulek and Mundek enter. With cries of relief we hugged each other. Disbelief and gratitude filled our hearts to see the three of them unharmed by the flying bullets in town.

With alarm-filled eyes, mother listened to Shmulek's story.

"We were ordered to lie down on the ground. I stretched out my arms, just as they told us to do. There were Polish soldiers on the street, but they dropped their weapons and offered no resistance. Then came gunshots. We thought we were all being shot, but they were firing into the air. They were signaling their forces on the western outskirts of town to move in."

We all thanked God that my father and brothers were alive. It was enough to confirm one's faith in prayer.

That first incursion was followed by more German movements as truck after truck loaded with German soldiers passed through Dynów on their way deeper into Poland. We watched them from the windows, and when we were sure they had all passed, we walked out into the street. There we saw the gray uniforms of the Wehrmacht, the German army. A cluster of curious Polish children surrounded a group of soldiers. Jewish children would not dare get that close.

Everything had happened very fast, but already there were signs of the German occupation. Hanging over the

Kólko Rolnicze, the large food and agricultural supplies store owned by the Catholic Church, was a sign which read *Arisches Geschäft* ("Aryan Store"). Apparently seeking to curry favor with the Germans, the pious priests were demonstrating their sympathy for the Nazis and their anti-semitic venom against the Jews. It should not have surprised me, knowing how the Catholic Church preached anti-Jewish hate-sermons, but it turned my stomach to see how quickly and easily they had begun to court the enemy.

I watched the German soldiers entering the Aryan store. Aware that conquering soldiers seek booty, I expected to see looting, but they came out empty-handed and headed for my late grandfather's store instead, a mini-supermarket. I inched up to the store, took a few steps inside to see what they were doing. No one dared to stop them as they brazenly climbed ladders and took down choice condiments. Then, surprisingly familiar with the premises and the stock, they went to the secret cellar located in a passageway between my grandmother's house and our house. They lifted the boards disguising the concealed entry, climbed down a ladder to the cellar, and took boxes of very expensive chocolates and other items. Carrying their loot, they walked out without saying anything to the family.

The ease with which they had found the storeroom was not hard to figure out. Our trusted employee, Jasiek, was the only one, outside of the family, who knew about the secret cellar. Always thought of as a reliable employee, he had been with our family for many years, and his loyalty had never been questioned. Now he had betrayed us. Our faithful servant was a Polish Catholic born and bred. Obviously, his first loyalty was to the church, the very church that fomented so much antisemitic hatred. Unquestionably, our fine-looking employee with the quiet blue eyes was a private eye for the Polish patriots. He had given confidential information to the holy Aryan store-keepers, who in turn had invited the German soldiers to help themselves to our costly merchandise.

My grandmother and my uncles watched in horror as the ransacking took place. Afterwards, I did what I could to help tidy up the store. In hushed tones, they talked about omens of the future. Their fears were like spiders crawling on my skin. From the dark corners where the scents of spices and fruits clung to the walls, I could see no refuge against the portended dangers. I needed to get out into the sunlight, breathe the late summer air, before I could feel that I would live, that my parents, my relatives would not be harmed by the invaders.

Binding my phylacteries on my head and my arm, I prayed fervently that no harm would come to us. The leather on my skin seemed infused with God's power. I felt the spirit of God in my body. I communed with Him. My belief in God and His power was unshakable, it gave me hope. God would not abandon me.

Still, I knew, our daily life was now overshadowed with grave threats. Hitler's insatiable appetite for conquest had long been evident. Czechoslovakia flanked Germany on the south and Poland on the east. From there, his sights were set on Lithuania, our northeastern neighbor. That would take Hitler to the borders of the Soviet Union. I hung onto every news report, arranging in my mind what was happening on all sides of Poland. I walked around with a map in my head, shading with different colors the areas where Hitler was brandishing his power.

With portents of war and silent prayers swarming in my thoughts, I walked out of my grandmother's store just as Tonia Grossman came hurrying around the corner. Her head kept turning, her eyes shifting to both sides of the street as if she were being followed. Tears choked her voice. "Lusiek, something awful has just happened."

I walked beside the young girl toward Grossman's bakery down the street, where Tonia's family occupied the upper floor. I wanted to calm her, see her safely home. "Tell me what happened."

"I was going home when I saw German soldiers on the street and ran away from them. One of them, he looked older than the others, chased me and asked why I was running away. I told him I was a Jewish girl and was afraid of German soldiers."

"What did he say to that?" I wanted to know.

"He said I didn't have to be afraid of German soldiers, but that he felt sorry for us Jews when the Gestapo arrives. That made me even more afraid. And then he said there are too many Jews in this town. What does he mean by too many Jews, Lusiek? I'm so frightened."

I couldn't tell Tonia that his words frightened me too. I held her hand until we reached the bakery and watched her go in.

The events of the next few days, coinciding with the preparations for Rosh Hashanah, the first of the High Holy Days, which began on September 14, were heightened with terror. This should have been a joyous time of prayer in preparation for the new year, but on the street there was uneasiness, tension, fear. People clustered together, whispering urgently about the latest tidings from Warsaw and Lwów. The Germans had cut off the usual modes of communication with these cities by confiscating all Jewish-owned radios and imposing travel restrictions. Nor did any newspapers come in on the bus from Przemysl, as in the old days. Rumors were now our only source of information. People were hungry for reports of what was going on. They groped for something hopeful to say. They kept repeating what everyone already knew and listened carefully for anything new.

When the holiday arrived, everyone went to services. The three synagogues were filled. We were all eager to participate. Even those who were very ill or infirm hobbled along. They too wanted to add their voices to the praying congregants. The cantor's tearful voice, beseeching God to intervene, reached into their hearts. Heads bent and bodies shackled, they swayed in rhythm, pronouncing the ancient chants. Quiet tears flowed as inner voices cried. Bonded by the power of prayer, they felt safe in the synagogue, until they noticed the German soldiers stationed at the door. Their presence was that of an intruding, unsettling onlooker with no good intentions. The cantor, disquieted, was faltering, not at the words but because of the uneven beat of his own heart. Tremors shook us all. Slowly, without speaking, and communing only by eye contact, the people filed out of the synagogue.

At noontime my family went home to a well-prepared holiday meal. The dining-room table was covered with a richly brocaded tablecloth. In the center of the table was the golden twisted challah on a silver tray; there was a highly polished baroque candelabra at each end, the crystal decanter of wine, the silver goblets, holiday china with its festive floral borders, all set out as if this yom tov (holiday) were going to be spent in the usual manner.

The holiday roast, the potato pudding, the sauces, the gingered fruits, the cakes, all were solemnly passed around. Nothing tasted good, I had no appetite.

Restless, anxious, we left the table and walked out into the street. Many others were milling around, eyeing the soldiers posted there, wondering what was going to happen next.

A sudden rumbling was heard. Large trucks zoomed down Mickiewicza Street, their sides emblazoned with German posters bearing the terrifying words "Kill the

Jews!" The trucks slowed down to discharge black-uniformed soldiers. Instinct told us that their arrival meant
trouble. We scattered in every direction. I jumped into the
closest building, one owned by my uncle Lemel Silber.

Uncle Lemel was a good man. He was sheltering ten
Jewish refugees who had run away from the advancing
German army. Unable to run any further, they had
remained in Dynów, welcome in the shelter of my uncle's
house. My aunt Bucia, like my mother, who was her sister,
was gentle and kind. I loved to be with my cousins Gonia,
Escia, Hella, and their brother Shmulek.

I thought I was safe with them, but Uncle Lemel saw
those black-uniformed soldiers through his window.

"Quick! Quick!" he ordered me, his son Shmulek, and
the sheltered men, "Up to the attic!" He pulled down the
ladder for us to climb to a secret attic, then pulled the ladder up after us. There were thirteen of us in the attic. We
took turns peering through some cracks in the wallboards.
We saw the black-uniformed soldiers in front of the stores
and dwellings. We heard their coarse commands, "*Juden,
heraus!*" ("Jews, out!"). Their faces full of contempt, they
dragged Jews from the buildings.

Not more than an hour later, they approached Uncle
Lemel's house. At their heels were snickering Polish patriots, among them our neighbors, who pointed to the attic.
They entered, knocking at the boards, shouting for us to
come out.

All thirteen of us climbed down the ladder. Uncle
Lemel, Shmulek, and I were the last to emerge. Our hearts
sunk with each descending rung of the ladder. As we came
out into the open, Uncle Lemel nudged us. "Run for it!
Don't let them take you."

Uncle Lemel, Shmulek, and I broke from the group,
jumped the fence next to his house, the three of us running

in different directions. Of course, the soldiers shouted at us to halt. We ignored them, running as fast as we could. The others were undoubtedly captured.

I ran to my grandmother's house and hid behind a door. When I heard my mother's voice from the back of the house, I ran to her. She grabbed me, gave me a hug, and, choking on tears, tried to tell me she did not know where my father and brothers were. They had run from the house just before the soldiers broke in. She had told Hella, my sister, to hide.

Formidable in their black uniforms, the soldiers had stood before her. "*Frau, wo ist ihrer Mann?*" ("Woman, where is your husband?").

She surprised them by answering in German. This small woman was gutsy. She held their gaze as she slipped off her wedding band. "*Ich habe keinen Mann*" ("I have no husband"). She held out her hand so that the soldiers could see her bare finger and believe her unmarried.

When they left after finding no men in the house, my mother had taken Hella by the hand and gone to my grandmother's house.

Then, as if remembering that she was embracing me, she cautioned, "It isn't safe for you to stay here. Go to the Grossman house. They'll find a place to hide you."

It was still early afternoon, the first day of Rosh Hashanah. I was afraid to go back to the Grossmans', but she insisted. I ran, dodging in and out of yards. The atmosphere in the Grossman house was tense and worried. Several members of the family were missing.

As the afternoon faded, neighbors, aunts, cousins sought news and comfort at the Grossman house. The absence of the men was like the long silence that hangs in the air before a storm. Eyes beseeched other eyes for hope, for belief in prayer. Their sadness was so overwhelming, they could not restrain the cries, the moans that reached into every heart and brought on more laments. We wept and wondered.

In the Grossman bakery, behind the ovens, were some rooms used by the family. Their bedrooms were on the second floor. The cellar had nooks and cubbyholes where I could easily have hidden, but they took me to a small room upstairs. How like them to think of me as a guest, offering me a comfortable place.

I sat on the bed, my heart hammering, my fright drilling holes in my brain so that I could think of nothing but cold blue eyes and black uniforms. I shut my eyes. The blackness did not shut out the images of slashing bayonets. I opened my eyes. Blue eyes under black visors stared at me. I shut my eyes. A wall of black uniforms confronted me. Shadows squeezed through the chinks in the plaster, one a grim accuser capable of flinging me into a truck. I tried to pray. Nothing came to mind. Not the ritual prayers for safety. Not the traditional prayers committed to memory since my Bar Mitzvah. Even the memory of that event was blocked by black uniforms and marred by pain.

I found myself thinking of physical pain. I touched my nose. It was crooked. A fluke of an accident on the volleyball field. The net had come loose. I had tried to tighten it, cranking the handle, but it came loose and flipped out of my hand, hitting and smashing my nose. The doctor had set it, but it was never straight afterwards. The pain had lasted for weeks, right through my Bar Mitzvah celebration. My mother had planned and prepared a festive table but I could not enjoy the party. My prayers, my speech were impeccably delivered in spite of the grueling pain.

What I was now experiencing was bitter pain. A pain that gathered in the back of my throat from the coursing fear in my body. Pain that had black tentacles and threw shadows around me and pulsated like lungs, drawing in and exhaling breath. It had seemed appropriate to suffer pain at the time of a simchah (celebration) like my Bar Mitzvah, for Jews cannot have pure joy. Suffering is their history and their destiny. I wanted to tell God I was suffering now, on the holiest of holy days. If he would make the Germans leave our town, I would love and respect freedom as long as I lived.

That Rosh Hashanah night was a sleepless one for all. We walked about, looking at one another as if this would be the last imprint of our faces we would remember. Pacing the room, we looked out into the darkness of the night, which had a red glow. We had a premonition of something terrible happening, a danger we did not want to see. The red glow made the rising sun hazy and fiery.

Ordinarily, the bakery downstairs would have been bustling during the early morning hours, but because of the holiday, no baking was done. The baker employed by the Grossmans was a Christian who came in that day to prepare the ovens. He was there to respond to a knocking at the door. When we went downstairs and questioned him, he told us the black-uniformed soldiers had come asking for two shovels. He had given them the shovels, not daring to ask why they wanted them. We naively assumed that they had needed the shovels to dig trenches at the front lines. We were grateful that he had not summoned us to do their bidding.

Hania, one of the young Grossman granddaughters, wiping sleep from her eyes, asked, "Was there a fire during the night?" Strangely, rather than listening, I was admiring this tall, slim, beautiful girl whose dark braids hung on her shoulders. Her eyes had shades of green, like ferns in the forest. I blinked and shied away from my luring thoughts because Moishe's wife's voice, an urgent worrying voice, was pleading with the baker:

"Go find out what is happening. Go quickly, please."

The Polish employee left immediately. When he came back, we did not want to believe what he tried to tell us.

"The three synagogues," he said, "were set on fire by those black-uniformed soldiers."

"All three?" Mrs. Grossman asked, her anguished cries a funereal, tolling wail.

Horror, we cried. Such inhumane horror! Ferocious horror executed by human beings, or were they? Horror so deeply conceived it seeped into the nucleus of every cell in our bodies!

In the shadowy room, I looked at the faces of my neighbors, transformed with my own disbelief. I saw their eyes, noses, lips clogged with sobs from the innermost parts of their beings. My own tears were blurring their features. I felt the wrenching from my face of a veil that had been over my eyes for these fifteen years of my life. I was comprehending evil so deep that I would never be the same.

I was to learn the extent of that first insight into evil when the Polish baker told us that the Jewish refugees inside the synagogues had been burned to death. Those sorrowful displaced stragglers who had sought refuge there. On Rosh Hashanah, when worship was most sacred. On the holiest day in our calendar, our holiday of Rosh Hashanah, the black-uniformed soldiers perpetrated this most heinous crime against humanity. A flagrant disavowal of God. I listened to the evil things they had done. I had a fleeting moment of conflict about the divine dividing line between good and evil that Jewish learning advocated. The line was straining.

On the second day of the holiday, September 15, 1939, we learned that the black-uniformed soldiers were gone, and everyone went to their own homes. Mother, Hella, and I walked home, not knowing the whereabouts of our father

and of Mundek and Shmulek. We stopped at my grandmother's house. There we found Uncle Chaskel Berkowitz,
one of those who had been forced from their homes by the
Germans. He had grim details to add.

"The S.S. stormtroopers," he said, "ordered Jews to
march to the schoolyard. Many were Jewish refugees. Late
in the evening, an officer asked if there were any married
men with four or more children. I was one of those who
raised a hand. They let me go home. The rest were placed
into trucks and driven away. No one knows where they
were taken. They went west."

"West would be Germany," my grandmother said.

"To German military factories," I offered, from a newspaper item I had read.

Another night of anxious waiting for the return of the
rest of our family. In the morning, my father sent a message
to my mother through Jantek Hadam, one of his Christian
friends, a customer, that he was hiding in the village of
Bartkowka, which was on the other side of the San River.
My older brother, Mundek, was with him.

That morning, my other brother, Shmulek, came back
home and told us that he had been hiding on the outskirts
of the town. Nobody felt safe while the soldiers were still
in town. We could see them through the windows. They
were apparently army troops, not S.S., for they wore gray
uniforms. They had a number of trucks with them. Their
metallic voice of command, blasting from bullhorns,
ordered all young Jewish men to come out into the street,
where they were assigned to wash the trucks. My brother
Shmulek too went out to wash the trucks.

All during the day of September 16 the question gnawing at us all was, where had the S.S. troops taken the men
on that first day of the Jewish New Year? One, then another, brought the sorry news.

The men had been driven to a forest near one of the neighboring villages, the forest we knew as Zurawiec. They had been ordered to get off the trucks and stand alongside a pit. Then they were machine-gunned to death.

On September 14, 1939, that first day of the holiday, 198 Jews were murdered in Zurawiec. Another ninety Jews were machine-gunned at the Plebania, the estate owned by the Polish priests, and two more at the Catholic church.

We received this grim testimony from two wounded survivors, who had hidden in the forest for two days, in pain, incoherent, afraid to venture out until they were sure there were no troops around.

These cruel, revolting stories were as palpable to me as if they touched my body and breathed in my face. I could not believe that a government would order soldiers to take innocent civilians and shoot them like animals. They had not stolen anything, they had not killed, they had not been criminals. They had obeyed the law, they had been good people, talmudic scholars, philosophers, and hard-working men who lived ethical lives. Among those so brutally slaughtered were three of my uncles, David Heillman, Hertz Kasser, and Hirsh Zeiger. So too were dear friends and neighbors. Did German ambition and lust for blood have no bounds? Was there not enough killing on the battlefield? Now I understood why the S.S. troopers had gone to the Grossman bakery for shovels.

The grief in town was suffocating. It lay on every shoulder. It bowed every head. The wailing, the keening, was heard in every corner, every house. There was no consolation to be offered as one would give on the death of an ailing or aged person. There were no words of wisdom to lean on. Reason was out of reach. The evildoers were beyond human ken.

Yet no reproach was uttered by our Christian neighbors. No soft words of remorse. They hid their eyes from
us. They avoided talk. But I remembered the vile epithets
from classmates, the recently heard threats, "Hitler will
take care of the Jews."

Why did they hate us so much? We who had given the
world great scholars, scientists, musicians, artists, writers.
We who had made known the grandeur of God, why were
we so hated? What made them so inhumanely bestial? I
knew nothing of nationalism. I knew nothing of lust or
greed or envy. Was this what the world was that I was
growing up into? A world of fear and death? Of flight and
mourning?

In my grandmother's house there was deep mourning
for Uncles Hertzel, her son, and Hirsh, her son-in-law,
slaughtered in the forest. Soberly, tearfully, relatives and
friends held her hands, prayed with her. No casual words
were uttered, no words could offer consolation. There were
only eyes looking into eyes, recognizing their own grief.
Silent grief too full of itself to share.

On September 28, my aunt Etka, my father's sister-in-
law, came to our house; she came to plead with my mother to let me go with her son, my cousin Shmulek, to cross
the river San, perhaps to safety. We knew that father was
in hiding with a Polish peasant family in a village on the
other side of the San. We believed my older brother
Mundek was there too. Perhaps Shmulek, who had run
away after the truck-cleaning incident, had made his way
there also. Men who had escaped the roundup had gone
into hiding. And to add to the critical situation, there was
news that the Red Army had marched into the eastern part
of Poland.

Escape to the East

Poland was already watered with Jewish blood. Poland was not a place to be. Although reluctant to part with me, my mother saw the danger lurking for Jewish men. I went with Aunt Etka to the other side of town, the Rynek section, which was the last I was to see of Dynów.

With a few zlotys of Polish currency in our pockets and the slacks, shirt, and shoes we were wearing, cousin Shmulek and I ran across the fields toward the San River, furtively glancing over our shoulders to make sure that no enemy was trailing us. When we reached the river, we paid a local Pole to take us across in his rough-hewn boat. We saw other Jewish men with the same intent to cross the river.

We had no idea where to go or where to find my father. When we reached the village of Bartkowka, we were afraid to linger there as it was too close to Dynów. Together with some other Jews from our town, we headed for another village. In a hilly area inhabited by Ukrainian peasants, the villagers of Ruski Javornik were reputed to be friendly to Jews. That was enough to direct our steps there. Strange are the ways alliances are formed. The Ukrainians did not get along very well with their Polish neighbors, and this made them sympathetic to the plight of the Jews. "The enemy of my enemy is my friend."

In Ruski Javornik, there was a well-to-do Jewish landowner by the name of Baruch Metz with whom my father was acquainted. My cousin Shmulek and I made his house our destination. Trekking along the road we contemplated the possibilities: would we be welcome, would there be room for us? What a surprise greeted us upon arrival. Among the other people who had fled to the home of this Jewish family were my father and Mundek. We embraced and kissed, so happy to see each other alive, with father immediately pressing questions at us. He wanted to know what had happened in Dynów after his departure.

"There was panic in town," I told him; "we and many other Jews had crossed the river to get away from the Germans."

"First, tell me about mother, Hella, and Shmulek," father asked anxiously.

"So far, the women and children are all right," I said, even though I didn't feel assured about the safety of my mother and my sister. I felt that alarming father more than necessary would be pointless. Father than told us about the Red Army moving into the eastern part of Poland.

"The river San will be the border separating the Red Army from the Germans," father announced. "The village we are in will become part of Soviet-occupied Poland. You might as well know that Stalin and Hitler made an agreement in August 1939 to divide Poland between themselves."

Others overheard him telling us this and a heated discussion arose among the people with whom father was housed.

"Treachery!" some shouted. "Wolves tearing the country apart!"

Was that true, I wondered. Had my running and dodging capture for two days to get here, thinking we would be safer, been only a fantasy? Could the Germans still come across the river and slaughter us here? And how would the Red Army treat us?

We knew very little about the Soviet Union or about its collective farms and its industries. What we had heard were horrendous tales about its politics, about purges of leaders in disfavor with Stalin, of similar treatment of the merchant class. But how were Jews treated? We could only wonder. Of course, in the feverish climate of our escape from the S.S. troops, everyone became a philosopher and everyone had a different idea about what to expect from the Communists.

Toward the end of the day, several horse-drawn carts arrived bringing women and children to the house of Baruch Metz. A thrill of warmth went through our bodies when we saw mother, Hella, and other relatives among the new arrivals. For the brevity of a hug and a kiss, we forgot our plight. Then mother, with some relief at our being together, told us what had happened that day in Dynów.

On September 28, in the late afternoon, the Nazis had ordered the entire Jewish population to assemble in the Rynek, the town square, Aunt Rachel told us. "We were going to be deported, sent across the San. We were given very little time to prepare for the departure, allowed to take just what we could carry in our hands. You should have heard what our Polish neighbors had to say, when we crowded into the square," she said, "They gloated They cursed us using vile words. You would think we had harmed them in some way. Of course the other way around is the case."

My cousin Escia's lips quivered as she spoke, "Desolate, the women and children cried and appealed to the soldiers for mercy. Alone, their menfolk scattered or murdered, their outcry was deafening. And do you know what one Nazi officer answered?"

"What a beautiful concert."

Mother put her arms around Hella, as if to shield her from some of the sad details. "We walked that long path to the river, and from there we were taken across on the barge by a Polish farmer, a good man who did not demand any payment."

In my mind I could see the picture of that barge going back and forth on the river, transporting people and horse-drawn wagons.

"How did you know to come here?" I asked.

"I knew father had friends in Ruski Javornik. I hoped to find him here. Anyway, what choices were there?" mother answered sadly. "Luckily we met good people who brought us here by horse and wagon. They too did not ask for money."

We stayed with the family of Baruch Metz, who opened their hearts, not only to us but to other townspeople from Dynów. They housed us, fed us, and made us feel as if we were members of their own family. Now we could only wait for the arrival of the Red Army. What lay ahead was uncertain.

With the arrival of more refugees, rumors and reports floated in all directions. Brucha, a woman from our town with a talent for gossip and purveying news, repeated her tales endlessly.

"There's a Soviet patrol unit in the next village," she announced. "They tell me that someone asked the officer how Jews would be treated under their rule. If you can believe what he said, it's hopeful."

"What did he say?" father asked, his finely arched eyebrows rising. His deep dark eyes demanding the truth. Father, a sincere realistic man, did not humor gossip.

"The officer answered, '*Vse ravno.*'" Brucha intoned.

"That doesn't make sense," father stated. " Maybe he said '*Vse ravneye,*' which is hard to believe, because it means 'everybody is equal.' Are you sure the Russian officer said we Jews are just as equal as everybody else?"

Brucha took offense at his doubts about her report. "I'm telling you, that is exactly what he answered. '*Vse rumno.*'"

"How is it possible that they will treat us the same as others?" My brother Shmulek smirked. "The Russians have a long history of brutalizing Jews. We've all heard the stories about Cossacks raiding villages, plundering, killing. The tsars had their troops, the Black Hundreds, who rode into Jewish villages on their big horses, demanding ransom. They sacked, they burned, they raped women. Equal? Big joke."

But Brucha was adamant. Her round body shaking as she stamped her foot. "Say what you want, I heard what I heard."

The unfortunate uprooted people, however, were eager to believe what she said. Their evening prayers offered wavering thanks for their safety. They bedded down that night with a filmy pillow for reassurance.

My own family gathered together when we were ready to go to sleep, but my mother's and father's anxious voices told us that we had much to worry about. Our only possessions were on our backs, but we were relieved when mother told us that she had sewn a bundle of dollar bills into her girdle. Mother, with her broader view of world politics and her keen foresight, had converted our Polish zlotys, hoarding the money for an emergency. She knew that American currency would be accepted everywhere.

Two days later, a Red Army cavalry unit galloped into the village. Rifles and swords slung at their waists, one hundred men approaching in battle formation looked ominous. When they halted, and we were able to see them up close, their faces were not unfriendly. Encouraged, we went forward to greet them.

One of our people, who had some familiarity with the Ukrainian language, stepped up to the commanding officer and in spite of some difficulty managed to communicate with him.

"We are Jews driven from our town," he said. "They took our homes, our belongings, everything we owned."

In turn, he translated the officer's response for the rest of us. The officer told him we had nothing to be afraid of. We would be treated the same as everybody else. I could hear the sighs of relief from the group.

Several of the soldiers dismounted and entered nearby peasant houses. Passing close to me, their bodies smelled of fetid clothes and horse sweat. They held eating utensils that had greasy, sticky remains of food clinging to the metal. Some had Asiatic features. The hair on the backs of their heads was rounded, as if bowls had been set on their heads when their hair was cut. I could not help comparing their appearance with the Polish cavalry, who, though not decked out in lavish uniforms, were neat and soldierly. We loitered, hoping to hear some news, trembling somewhat with anticipation. Than we saw the soldiers emerging from the houses, carrying hay for their horses and requisitioned food, the peasants eyeing them ruefully.

Later, the Russians addressed the villagers, announcing that they had come to liberate them from the pans—the Polish landed aristocracy.

"The land of the pans will be distributed among the landless peasants," the Russian was preaching. "Know this, the Polish workers and peasants asked us to change your system. From now on, this land will be called Western Ukraine, and new rules will apply."

They said nothing about how the German and Soviet governments had agreed to divide Poland.

The announcement pleased the peasants. Most of the Ukrainians had not fared well under the Polish regime. Few owned land. Most earned their food by tilling land owned by wealthy aristocrats. The report boded well for the peasants but badly for the landowners.

Within a few days, the intentions of the Russians were manifested when the soldiers called on a wealthy Polish landowner. "Pan," the commander said, "You want to eat meat? How about eating a raw potato from now on, for that is what you are going to do."

They ordered him off his land and distributed it to the landless peasants in the area. No compensation of any sort was offered. No consideration for the welfare of the landowner and his family was taken into account.

To me, this treatment was not much different from the confiscation of our property in Dynów by the Germans. Disturbing as it seemed, I had much more to learn about the Soviet Union and its policies.

My father felt the same uncertainties, and did not want to impose upon our hosts longer than good breeding allowed. He felt we should move on, go to the city of Przemysl or Lwów, where we had relatives. Our hosts were most congenial; they asked us to stay, offering to share their home and food, but father was restless. In October 1939 we left, starting a trek to Bircza, where we stayed with distant relatives.

They, too, were very friendly and opened their house and hearts to us. They sought out even the most distant members of the family, asking them to help us. Polish Jews stuck together as if they were family, showing warm, close feelings for one other.

Situated near the river San, the agreed-upon dividing line between the German and Soviet occupation zones, the town of Bircza became the chief Soviet bridgehead. Heavy tanks rumbled through the streets. Awestruck, I watched tank after tank go by in a long line, thundering and screeching, followed by tractors pulling heavy artillery pieces.

Impressive as this display was, I soon saw the more terrifying *tachanka* with its four heavy machine guns. A frightening weapon, capable of discharging a salvo of shells in
unison at an attacking enemy. As these powerful weapons
pulled by horses or tractors went by, the soldiers sang a
love song about the *tachanka*.

Over the past few years I had been fascinated by military history and strategy, but nothing I had read about
could compare to what I was seeing now. I felt stuck to the
ground. My eyes were fastened on this parade, as unit after
unit, six or eight soldiers abreast, marched through town.
Often, as a unit marched past, one of the soldiers would
play a balalaika, an accordion, or a *bayan* (a smaller accordion), and another soldier's rich voice would resound with
the words of a song, the entire regiment joining in on the
refrain. Each unit would play and sing a different song.
Forceful, beautiful, melodic martial songs. People came out
of their houses, housewives stopped their marketing, children were drawn to the sidelines as the town streets
became a stage for military might. And I was stagestruck.

My eyes followed the marching, heavily equipped soldiers. The female units were another surprise. The women
soldiers wore uniforms, carried arms, and sang along with
the men, their voices adding to the lyricism so enticing, so
contagious. I hummed along with them, wishing I knew
the language. I made up my mind to learn Russian, soon
committing their songs to memory. Then, as I heard them
sing, I sang along, aloud, from the civilian footpath.

If tomorrow there is war,
If tomorrow there is a march,
If a dark force should threaten me,
Better to be ready to march today.

I learned their plaintive song about Moscow:

Shiroka strana moya rodnaya
Mnogo wney polye, lesow i rek
Ya drugoy takoy strany ne znayu
Gde tak volno dyshat cheloviek

Wide is my dear country,
With its many fields, forests, and streams.
I know of no other country
Where man can live and breathe so free.

I wanted to believe this song of freedom was true. I wanted to believe these soldiers would protect us, I wanted to trust that what the commander had said about Jews being equal with everyone else was true. I did not want to believe that it was all propaganda, as the Polish villagers claimed. That these were special units sent to play and sing their stirring songs, that the soldiers in Cossack dress dancing in the middle of the street were a ploy for the seduction of civilians. I did not want to believe that this was a grand show of happiness to lure the villagers and peasants to Communism. The singers, the accordionists, the balalaika strummers looked too rapt in their songs, their arms outstretched, enfolding bystanders, urging them to join in dance and song. This could not be all just to deceive us.

Willing acceptance, searching for friendliness, hungering for gaiety, we sang "Katusya," a song about a Russian girl named Catherine, and "Na Ribalke," a song about a fisherman. These were folk songs, songs that appealed to us. Never had the Polish army displayed such camaraderie. We wanted to believe there was something good waiting for us in Russian-conquered territory. We wanted to believe because the Russian officers mingled with the Jews in Bircza, something a Polish officer would never do.

We continued to believe until the songs faded and another side of the Russians was revealed. It happened when a Soviet soldier reached out and touched the beard of a religious Jew, saying:

"Shave it off. Forget your faith in the Messiah. Communism will answer your prayers. Communism will fulfill all your wishes."

Now our trust faltered. When more orthodox Jews were approached this way, we were alarmed and skeptical. From the Jewish people living in Bircza, and there were many, we began to hear the Soviet line:

"You've been praying all your lives for the Messiah to come. We are your Messiah. Come with us and you'll be a happy person. Shed your beard and side-curls and live as an equal under the joyous life of a Communist state."

Stories filtered in from other parts of eastern Poland telling how the Russian troops has descended on the stores like a plague of locusts. They bought up everything in sight: clothing, shoes, personal items. They didn't select for color or size. They purchased everything on the shelves and racks. They did not bother to try anything on for fit. They did not bargain about prices. One soldier saw a tallis (prayer shawl), and even though he had no idea of what it was, he bought two and bound them around his bare foot as a substitute for socks. Soldiers went into restaurants and often ordered everything on the menu. Several soups, several entrees, and continuous cups of tea to be placed in front of them. They gobbled it all in one sitting. I had a teenager's appetite, but this was astounding. Did Communism foster such appetites?

My curiosity prompted me to ask some questions.

"Do you have shoes and suits in your country?" I dared to ask one soldier.

"The people have everything," he replied. "You think

you have good food? You should see what our people have."

"Really? Do you have oranges?" Citrus fruit was a rarity in Poland, a delicacy.

"Of course! We have just about everything. We have a factory in Kiev that manufactures oranges."

I had him there, but I also had the good sense not to tell him that oranges grow on trees, not in factories. I began to feel my wonder pall. The dancing and singing began to seem artificial, forced. The brash display lost luster. Like tired circus performers, the Russians began to look mechanical.

Little by little, we learned the truth from villagers who invited soldiers to their homes.

"Don't believe a single thing they tell you," they said. "It's coming out of the propaganda machine in big doses. Food is scarce in the Soviet Union. Even the basic foods—bread, vegetables, meat. Why do you think the soldiers order everything on the menu in our restaurants? The Russians live one day at a time, eating whatever comes into the market that day. If it's cabbage, everybody eats cabbage. Or lemons. What can you do with bags of lemons? Maybe somebody else has potatoes. They barter. They grab anything and everything today, because it may not be there tomorrow. Yes, this is what the soldiers tell us after a few glasses of wine. The truth."

I followed the soldiers around town. I wanted to hear for myself, find out if that was the truth. Then I overheard the restaurant owner tell his local clientele:

"There are shortages of everything in Russia, that is what they tell us."

Now I understood why they ate so voraciously.

One night, as the family gathered to eat and talk about the situation, the stories became more ominous.

"They are telling us about collective farms," my father said. "Collective, sure, for the overlords. The same story all over again, but in a different setting. The peasants don't get anything for their work, so they don't work. They steal what they can, and you have shortages."

"And you should hear about people disappearing in the middle of the night," said Brucha the gossip, forgetting her recent praise of the Russians, and instead now adding her pinch of spice to the tales.

"I hear they have their own secret police," someone said.

"Oh, yes." Brucha nodded her head. "The NKVD. The People's Commissariat for Internal Affairs."

My cousin winked at me. "Come outside, Lusiek." In the quiet of the garden, he said, "Stalin is glorified as a hero, but he is one of the most evil men who ever lived. Listen, but don't ever let a stranger hear you say such a thing. The walls have ears. A criticism like this could wipe you off the face of the earth."

"Is what they say about the NKVD true?" I asked. I could feel the air heat up from the fear these words provoked. Or was everything a lie?

"Listen," he continued, "One of the soldiers turned out to be Jewish; he spoke to us in Yiddish this morning. Not everybody is in with the NKVD. But he said to be careful what we say. And who we speak to. And don't criticize the system. Do you know what the letters USSR stand for?"

He didn't wait for an answer, whispering in my ear, "Translated into Yiddish, it means: 'It wasn't. It will not be. Don't talk yourself into it.'"

Don't talk yourself into believing the change is for the better, was what he meant.

As the days passed, we learned that the more things change, the more they remain the same. Here in Bircza we had a relative, a religious Orthodox Jew who owned a leather goods store. The Soviet soldiers went to his place of business and confiscated his entire stock.

"You're a capitalist," they told him, "an enemy of the working class."

What is even more horrifying, they took him away. He just disappeared. We never found out what happened to him.

I saw the same fears, uncertainties, and concerns become part of our daily existence. I heard it in my father's worries. How to provide for his family, how to avoid provoking Soviet officials, how to keep the family safe. My father, relying on past contacts, tried selling textiles, but ran into dry sources for procuring and peddling them. His venture did not last long. But he was a shrewd and resourceful businessman, alert to current needs and shortages. There were those who wanted to escape, willing to pay off the guards on the Rumanian border in order to get to Palestine or even to America. A good price would be paid for American dollars, and my mother had some sewn in her corset. American dollars were solid, desirable. My father secretly engaged in this monetary commerce. It was a dangerous enterprise. Black marketeering in currency was punishable by a long jail sentence, but my father was a courageous, determined man. He took the risk.

Risk was not even a choice. Risk was a daily fact of life. It was survival. Everyone knew that the new border was closely guarded by the Soviets. Some people, unearthing foreign currency and jewelry they had buried, made a dash for the border, hoping somehow to bribe the guards. A futile attempt. Others swam the river to get to the border, but Soviet guards shot them as they groped for the shore. The Soviets proclaimed any person attempting to cross the border a spy.

As 1939 ended, the naive hope prevailed that England and France would defeat Nazi Germany, and we would be able to return to our hometown. We still considered Poland our motherland.

Feeling uneasy and pursued, my father, after discussions with mother and the rest of us, decided we should leave Bircza for Lwów, the third-largest city in Poland. Mother had family living there and in Przemysl. Father packed us into a hired horse-drawn wagon. We traveled along side roads until we reached Przemysl, the next-closest city, from which the daily newspapers used to be delivered to our town of Dynów before the war. We visited the relatives who lived in Przemysl but did not stay long, anxious to reach Lwów, where mother's stepsister and cousin lived.

Continuing our flight by train we reached Lwów, where our first steps took us to mother's stepsister, Faigele Munzer. What a surprise awaited us in Aunt Faigele's house. Mother's sister Bucia Silber with her family, who had fled Dynów just as we did, had managed to reach Lwów before us and was already at Aunt Faigele's. They were all so happy to see us.

Aunt Faigele Munzer was very glad to have us. She offered us food and tried her best to make us comfortable, even providing us with warm clothing for the winter months ahead. The weather was getting pretty chilly, for it was the end of October. But we did not stay with her. Having additional family in town, we decided not to overcrowd Aunt Faigele Munzer's house and went to sleep at my mother's cousin's house. Faigele Kraut, the cousin, lived at 8 St. Anne's Street.

The Russians had been in Lwów more than a month, since the middle of September, and had changed the lives of its citizens in many ways. Cousin Faigele Kraut filled us in on what had happened in Lwów since the arrival of the Russians.

"The city, as you know, was in the path of the German conquest," she said. "The Polish forces made preparations to defend it against the advancing Germans, but when they learned that the Red Army, with tanks and heavy equipment, had reached the eastern outskirts of Lwów, they were jubilant. The Polish officers, believing the Russians had come to help them defend the city, went out to greet them as friends. How shocked they were when the Russians took them into custody as prisoners-of-war. The Polish city of Lwów, now part of the Soviet domain, has become the capital of Western Ukraine. For Poles, seeing a Polish city become part of the Ukraine is a stab in the back, and yet the Polish army and the Polish people did nothing about it."

Sitting together in cousin Faigele Kraut's house, my brothers Mundek and Shmulek, young men uneasy about the looming danger, expressed their fears. Mother's young face, now altered by fine lines, showed signs of fatigue. Father's deep lines were now dark furrows, his deep dark eyes stern with anger and disappointment. He was used to having control over things and being able to take care of his family. I perked my ears up, eager to hear more of the discussion which continued.

"The Polish people you are asking me about," Cousin Faigele answered bitterly. "The Russians told them they were here at the invitation of the workers, peasants, and Ukrainians. That they had come to free them all from the yoke of the Polish lords and capitalists." Faigele paused as if to figure out the sequence of events to share with us.

"The infamous city prison, the Brigitky, where Polish Communists were kept along with many other prisoners, was visited by the Russians upon their arrival in Lwów," she now continued. "They opened the gates of the prison, releasing all the prisoners, the Communists being the first ones out. These Communists, some of them Jewish, are now running the city government," Faigele intoned her, lips turned up in disgust. "Brigitnik scum," she called them.

"And the refugees?" my father asked. "Are they safe?"

"Like all of us," Cousin Faigele's husband, Pesach, said. "Trying to survive. There are shortages of almost everything. We get up early in the morning to stand in line for food, especially bread. That is one serious problem. The second is the fear which fills every moment."

"Yes," Faigele responded as if to stave off questions, "the NKVD wants to find out who might be spying on them, helping the Germans. We hear every day of people disappearing. Sometimes for just making a simple complaint. They have put fear in everybody. Listen," Faigele raised a finger in warning, whispering ever so softly, "Don't ever criticize the Communist system. Trust no one. People are being forced to spy on one another. Even the superintendent of this building is an informer for the NKVD, reporting who comes and goes. Even the children, my son too, are being brainwashed in school to spy on their parents. It has reached the point where we cross the street or walk away when we see Russian soldiers stop at a store or a house."

"We are caught in another hornet's nest," father stated, troubled by Faigele's account.

"Do you think, Faigele, that it would be possible to get to Rumania?" father now asked, the seriousness of the subject visible in his knitted brow. "I have to figure out how to get to the United States, to New York City, where my brother lives."

"You're dreaming," Faigele answered. "There is no way you can get through. Specially trained border police are killing people at the border every day."

My father should have known this from our experience in Bircza. But he was not the giving-up type.

"There's got to be a way," he said. "Two hundred and ninety Jews were slaughtered in our town of Dynów. The synagogues were burned down with the refugees in them. Who knows what else may happen?"

"Not only in Dynów," Faigele's husband, Pesach, groaned. "The slaughter is going on in Jewish shtetls all over southern Poland. Somehow the news seeps in; what we hear is frightening, gruesome."

A weak smile on her lips, my cousin Faigele patted her husband's hand. "As bad as it is, the Communists haven't killed any Jews yet."

Determined to avoid trouble with the Communists, Faigele turned to me, her face brightening somewhat.

"Let me tell you something else, Lusiek. In a few days, on November seventh, the Russians will be celebrating the Great October Revolution. There will be parades, flags, music everywhere, right here in Lwów also. To give you some idea of what goes on here, the building superintendent warned us that we'd better be out on Legionow Street on November seventh to show our enthusiasm for this Great October Revolution."

"Already there are better supplies of food. The stores have white bread, cake, even chocolate. Things we haven't seen for weeks," Cousin Pesach added.

"But what does it mean?" I wanted to know.

"What it means," said Pesach, "is that this is all temporary." Alarm swept over Faigele's face.

"Don't say such things. The walls have ears. You don't want the children repeating those words and getting us in trouble. I can tell you it is not easy when you're afraid to talk or to do anything that might get the NKVD after you."

I was impatient with their warnings. I wanted to hear about the big celebration.

"Will they parade with their tanks and artillery?" I wanted to know. "Will they sing their songs, play their instruments?"

We had seen them in Bircza, and my eyes must have popped with the possibility of seeing the military spectacle again.

"The Jewish Marshal," my father snickered. "Look what is in a boy's head."

I left the room, my face smarting. They just did not understand the awe I felt of military splendor and pageantry. Already, I was thinking how I could get to the center of Lwów. Having been told while still in Dynów that the German air force had bombed the Lwów railroad station, an impressive Baroque structure, I wanted to see the destruction. I might even see the military installations, I thought excitedly.

The following day, as I rode the trolley aware that I looked shabby in the cheap clothes my parents had been able to buy for me in Bircza, I avoided looking at the other passengers. I found my way to the railroad station through streets teaming with people and soldiers. I had never seen a structure so massive and imposing. Sections of the building lay in rubble.

As I walked back and forth studying the architectural details, I noticed a man with a Russian *shapka* on his head. Short, thickset, broad-shouldered, he seemed to be watching my movements. He walked over, his icy blue eyes staring out of a grim face, and said something in Russian which I did not understand. When I showed my annoyance, he grabbed my hand and pulled me past the clustered people and Red army sentries into a very large room in the station. I could see part of the glass-domed roof which had been destroyed in the bombing.

Holding my arm, he led me into a bare white-walled room. The room had a crude wooden desk, chairs, flags, and the ubiquitous pictures of Lenin and Stalin. I found myself facing two men in Soviet uniforms. A third man, in civilian clothes, seemed to be in charge. He motioned for me to come forward. The man who had brought me in said something to the others in Russian.

"What were you doing in the railroad station?" the civilian official asked me in Polish.

"I came from Dynów just a few days ago. I heard about the big Lwów station and wanted to see it," I answered haltingly.

Translating my words into Russian, he looked sternly at me and shouted, "You're a German spy! The Germans told you to come here and spy on us." He pointed a menacing finger at me and said, "You're never going to see your mother again."

Frightened by his threat, I started to cry.

"How could I, a Jew, be a German spy?" I uttered between my sobs. "The Germans shot my three uncles and took away everything we had in Dynów. They forced us on the road, like beggars."

I was sobbing and pleading with them to believe me. I wanted to confide all the unsaid reasons why I didn't want to die. I had not finished school yet, I had ambitions. I had not had my first real love affair, even though I had touched Mania Frankel's body.

I was trembling. They could see me shaking. The civilian translated what I said to the others, who conversed for a while.

"We'll let you go this time, but you are never again to come to this station," I heard the Russian say. My heart, like a bird flapping its wings against the bars of a cage, felt as if it would break through my breastbone. I gulped and ran from the station before more questions and threats could be directed at me. I took the trolley back to my cousin's apartment. Still quaking with fear, I told my parents and my cousin Pesach what had happened. Pesach was not too surprised.

"The Reds are paranoid," he said with a faint smile. "They imagine spies all around them, everyone is suspect. Obviously, the railroad station is a strategic point, and anyone hanging around there must be a spy."

My father was cross with me for having endangered the family as well as myself.

"You learned a good lesson today, Marshal Wenig," father thundered, his stern eyes upon me. "Now you will know to mind your own business and keep your nose clean."

On November 7, at the formally declared celebration of the Great October Revolution, I was able to stare and gape without fear of being bruited about by strong-arm colluding Poles. In the square, a raised platform was draped with red banners and flags bearing the symbols of the Revolution, the hammer and sickle. Wherever you looked there were pictures of the Soviet leaders: Stalin, Molotov, Voroshilov, Marshal Budenny, with his dark, drooping mustache, and others I could not identify. Martial music blared from loudspeakers. Horsemen, imposingly dressed in red, wearing Cossack fur hats, passed in parade formation, whipping the crowds into frenzied cheers.

It surpassed anything I had ever seen before. My thin clothes offered little warmth on that cold day, but I stood transfixed, watching as soldiers in columns of eight, eyes right, with bayonets affixed to their rifles, marched by. Accompanied by songs and cheers, they marched past military and civilian leaders, who cheered them on with slogans.

"Long live the Soviet Union, the party of Lenin and Stalin, Hurrah!"

"Long live the Communist Party, the party of the workers and peasants, Hurrah!"

There was a cousin of mine named Kuba, the son of another relative who was also staying in Faigele's house together with us. His wealthy parents owned an oil derrick and had been drilling for oil in Boryslaw, the town Kuba came from. Kuba had been living with his cousin Faigele Kraut while studying engineering at the Lwów Polytechnic. He understood and spoke Russian. Having joined me at the parade, he now translated the slogans and explained their meaning. On and on went the parade of military might, as banners bent in the breeze and new shouts arose.

"Long live Comrade Khrushchev."

"Comrades, long live our Leader, the World Leader. The Great Stalin."

A line of students carried flowers. As each contingent passed, a student would rush forward and present a floral tribute to the dignitaries on the platform. Some of the marchers carried pictures of factories and officials as well as slogans. Kuba translated the legends on the banners lauding the victory of the October Revolution and the resulting unity of workers and peasants. Other banners bore praises of the Soviets for liberating the western Ukraine.

Marching masses of peasants and workers followed the soldiers, not so much because they were inspired by the music and pageantry, but because they had been ordered to march. Taking up the slogans, they called out praises and hurrahs.

Was this proof of the success of the Revolution? I wondered. Were conditions better under this system? Awed as I was, I already had my fears and doubts. Should we believe the catchwords on those banners, trust the faces on those pictures? I asked Kuba what he thought. His answer was a half-smile and a quick side-shake of his head.

"Power passes from one diminishing victor to another who is ascending, but rarely changes."

In the days following, I repeated my appeal to God. I did not want to die. I had not finished school yet. We were into November and I was not attending school. We had no permanent residence, so Hella and I could not be registered to go to school. This meant long daily hours with no schooling. However, I found a way to use my time. The library had enough books to appease my hunger for knowledge. I learned Russian, and although not with full understanding, I read the Communist papers and kept up with the news in the Polish newspapers.

While the lack of schooling concerned my parents, their more immediate needs worried them more. They did not want to be a burden to their sympathetic cousins. They had to find a way to support themselves. Refugees could not get work. My father had already tried one business venture and failed. There was no way to establish a new business. True, he had hidden dollars, but they could not be used openly. My father, a very resourceful man, took chances trading on the black market, since there was no other way to provide for the family.

Father still nurtured the hope that help would come from his brother Irving in New York, and he pursued this idea like a man possessed. Irving had to know where we were, and why we were no longer in Dynów. Irving had to know our circumstances. He prodded, pressured, and coached my older brother Shmulek to write letters of entreaty to Irving, baring his heart. Shmulek knew that the letters would be censored, and probably would never reach their destination. Nothing could be said about our dire economic difficulties in such letters. That would reflect upon conditions under the Soviets and would get us in trouble. How then could we reveal our situation and beseech him to arrange our passage to the United States?

Many Jewish refugees, facing similar problems, had devised a way of writing to relatives in the United States without arousing the suspicion of a censor. Shmulek learned about this ploy and wrote the letters in Yiddish, a language with idioms that have subtle meanings.

"We have everything but we lack sugar and candles." A translator would read this as a foolish request, but the Yiddish reader would know it implied *Es ist finster und bitter* and decoded would tell our relatives that things were dark and bitter. A Soviet censor would find nothing subversive in a request for sugar and candles.

The ruse worked, or so my father and brother liked to believe. But how it worked, how two hundred dollars, a large sum for those days, became available to my father, had its own devious course. Outright sums were quickly confiscated. My father was careful not to reveal the exact details of the transfer for fear that the secret police might arrest his children and force him to talk through them.

In time, I learned how the transaction had been handled. Let's say that someone in Przemyśl or Lwów—call him the intermediary—had money he wished to hide by depositing it in an American bank, possibly under an assumed name or in the name of a relative. Naturally he couldn't do this directly. Instead, arrangements would be made for someone in America to deposit a specified sum of money in a bank—in this case it was my uncle in New York and the sum was two hundred dollars—and once confirmation of the deposit was received by the intermediary, he would pay the American's relative in Lwów the same amount.

Of course, this money had to be discreetly handled. Any party to a deal in foreign currency was criminally liable to a long prison term, or even execution. It was a risk my father willingly took. With dollars it was possible to get documents that would enable one to leave the "Workers' Paradise" for America or Palestine. While dollars could not be used openly to buy provisions, they were indispensable for bribes.

I was an adolescent, out of school, braving the streets, secluding myself at times in the library. You hang around, you learn. It was common knowledge that officials, no matter of what rank, were open to bribes. Not so much out of greed as necessity. Food and coal were scarce, and a black market flourished. Ironically, this system operated through bribes to officials who overlooked the black market traffic. Through this subsystem goods that never reached the open market filtered through to the public. But these goods were expensive. Who then but those with money in their pockets could afford the scarce items? It was a corrupt, circular system. It was awesome and yet amusing to watch this game, for it was a game with risks. Some Soviet officers got their kicks out of catching and prosecuting black marketeers.

Until such time as we could emigrate, which was the plan, my father and brothers, like most of the uprooted people, traded on the black market. They obtained food products, textiles, and even bread, always transacting purchases with foreign currency. They found a way to engage me too in this traffic. I was a pickup man. A store manager would arrange for me to pick up loaves of bread, or flour, or macaroni. Of course, he was illegally peddling products meant for his shelves, but he was easily seduced with bribes to turn these products over to me, to be delivered to a "retailer" who in turn sold the products at a bazaar.

The passage of goods from store or warehouse to the black market was a common pursuit of high-ranking officials involved in the illegal traffic. The higher the position, the bigger the thief. I began to think that everyone in the Soviet Union stole and profited.

Of course, there were laws and law officers. Periodically, the militia or the NKVD made a display of arresting *spekulyanty* (black market speculators). The *spekulyant* was brought to trial, but in most cases a payoff would set him free. The higher the position, the bigger the bribe. The judge presented no problem. Unless the victim did not know how to handle a bribe or lacked the guts to offer one to an NKVD officer. Such a poor slob would be arrested, brought to trial, and convicted.

The bizarre way of doing business, the ramifications of black marketeering, the consequences of arrest and sentencing, the whole system, while a mockery, had a formality that intrigued me. One day I decided to witness a trial in Lwów. On any given day, the defendant might be a black marketeer, a smuggler, or a thief of socialist property, but on that day a man accused of smuggling goods from Przemysl to Lwów was on trial. I have a vivid recollection of the proceedings. Streicher, a famous Jewish lawyer in prewar Poland, was the attorney for the defendant and up against a Russian judge and a Russian prosecutor. This was to be a trial by jury, but "jury" had its own connotations in the Soviet Union. Lawyers did not pick the jurors. Two representatives from a factory or a collective farm, called assessors, served for the day. They sat at the left and right side of the judge, who occasionally bent toward one or the other to apprise them of the proceedings.

The question was not one of guilt or innocence. In the Soviet Union, a lawyer had to be careful of how he presented evidence and testimony, lest he himself be judged in collusion with his accused client and end up in jail. He had to begin with the premise of guilt. The issue was the sentence.

The prosecutor's bombastic voice bounced off the stone walls. "This criminal, this vermin, is an enemy of the people who has stolen socialist property. This parasite has no place in the glorious Soviet Union. This enemy of the people should be condemned to ten years of hard labor in a corrective camp."

"The defendant does not deny his guilt," the defense attorney countered, "but consider that this man comes from a working family. He is a member of the proletariat who has erred in judgment. May the court show leniency."

As for the two assessors, laymen, they had absolutely nothing to say. With every detail of the crime, they shook their heads as if such acts could find no lodging in their heads. It was safer not to think compassionately. It was safer to condemn and convict.

I watched and listened carefully. The prosecutor made his case for a heavy sentence. He was a product of the system. His was the instructed voice of the conqueror. The defense attorney had little bargaining power. The enemy of the people was given eight years in a labor camp.

I did not witness justice. I witnessed Communist control. I witnessed vindictiveness, and it all had an impact on me. I vowed that if I survived and someday lived in a free country, I would become a lawyer, a defender of the disadvantaged.

I was to learn more about the crushing effect of Soviet law in the months ahead. One of these, the law of *progul*, was extremely harsh on workers; it said, in effect, that absence from work was tantamount to shirking. Why, I kept asking myself, is cruelty compounded? Weren't people finding it hard enough to survive? Why come down so hard on the poor workers? I wanted to know, so I listened and watched.

In the factories, confiscated and nationalized, the salaries were meager. There were no benefits. Discontented with the forced quotas, hard work, and poor pay, the workers began to slack off. What little they earned bought them scant food or comfort, as there were great shortages of food and fuel. The workers began to curse the Communists for every deprivation. They even blamed the Communists for the harsh winter weather bearing down on them from Siberia. Cold, hungry, depressed, they often failed to come to work. If they did, they came late. They found excuses for leaving their jobs.

The new government officials responded with regulations that severely punished workers who were late or failed to come to work. Taking time off was punishable unless the worker had a letter from a doctor stating that he was too ill to work. Because of the stringent work rules, doctors were reluctant to write such letters. But here too were conditions primed for corruption. The doctors earned less than the average worker. What with the small recompense for their services under the socialized medical system, and the fact that they, like everyone else, were affected by the terrible shortages, they too could be bribed.

Like the weather, conditions became more severe. Production lagged in the factories, farms did not yield as expected. To have better control over the newly occupied territory, the Soviet Union sent in administrators from Russia, the Ukraine, and the Caucasus. They arrived in frayed, shabby clothing, each of them carrying a well-worn suitcase to which was tied a night pot. That told a lot about personal habits and the state of sanitation in Russia, and was repulsive to our more discreet body care. Coming in great numbers, the Communists claimed living quarters, displacing and crowding people, and generally causing a shortage of apartments. They were indifferent to the hardships they created for others. They were callous, intent upon establishing a classless society. Former capitalists, manufacturers, landlords, and Polish landholders regularly disappeared. Poles who were known to have been members of a nationalist party were whisked away during the night to remote corners of the Soviet Union. A fear, as of a scourge, gripped the inhabitants of the cities.

The fear was palpable. The Russians thought to ameliorate it with promises, each to his own ability to receive his fair share of the common goods. Propaganda campaigns ensued to lure workers to other parts of the Soviet Union. Posters on walls and lampposts appeared reading: WORK IN THE DONBAS COAL MINES! ENJOY A BEAUTIFUL LIFE WITH BENEFITS GALORE!

Young single men who went off to the mines in the Donets coal basin, known as the Donbas, soon found that they had been duped. They sent back letters telling of the miserable working conditions. They ate in a communal dining room. As for the food, one wrote, "The Russians boast about a delicacy called the Donbas Schnitzel. This so-called cutlet is ninety percent bread and ten percent meat held together with some gook." He wrote of sharing a room with several others in communal apartments called *Obshchezhitiye.* The communal living quarters provided conditions that enabled the government to spy on them. Many returned as soon as they could.

One day a young man walked in to the Krauts' apartment, where we were being sheltered at the time. Dressed in the characteristic proletarian khaki tunic, trousers tucked into boots, a Russian fur hat on his head, he frightened us, particularly because he was wearing the *shapka* headgear of the secret police. We knew that local people had joined the security services and thought him to be one of them.

When he saw my cousin trembling, he reached over and patted him on the back.

"You don't recognize me in this uniform, huh? Don't worry, I'm not an NKVD man, look closely. See, your barber. Just back from the Donbas Garden of Eden."

With a groan of relief, my cousin said,

"Sit down, can we give you some tea? Tell us about that Garden of Eden."

"Hot tea would be good, do you have any sugar?" He laughed, letting us enjoy the joke with him. "You think things are bad in Lwów? Let me tell you, it's a thousand times worse in the Donbas. What little I earned, I used to bribe one of the managers of the coal mine for a permit to return to Lwów." He sipped the tea noisily. "Let me give you all haircuts. The truth is, I have no money left."

He took out his scissors and shaving equipment. All the men in the apartment—my father, my brothers, my cousins—took turns on the improvised barber chair. While he trimmed one, the others gathered around him and talked about the Soviet plan to increase productivity, the Stalin Five Year Plan.

"*Dognat i peregonyat Amerika,*" Wherever we went, we saw and heard the slogan "Catch up and overtake America." The barber described the new propaganda campaign. "*Sotsialisticheskoye sorevnovaniye,* socialist competition, with quotas assigned to every factory, collective farm, office, and other businesses. You wouldn't believe how they have everything figured out to reach the quotas."

"There's a story going around," my cousin added, "that they found a man—Alexey Stakhanov, they say his name is—a coal miner who mines vast amounts of coal every day, and does it with no more than a pick and shovel."

The barber, while cutting hair, told us how the Russian propaganda exaggerated stories of this kind. "Look, with a pick and shovel, you can't mine hundreds of tons of coal a day, it's absolutely impossible. But to enhance this ridiculous fable, they announce that they're giving him a nice apartment and modern conveniences. Such heroic socialist workers deserve extra benefits, they say. The truth is, it's just a ploy to trick others into imitating him." He expanded his chest in mockery, "For the socialist fatherland! So, what are you supposed do? Compete with everyone else."

As I knew from the newspapers I was reading in the library, the workers in one factory had challenged the workers in another factory to produce greater quantities for commendation.

"You see this kind of nonsense on the front page," I contributed.

"The quotas are listed on the back page of *Izvestia*. Yes," I said to their surprised faces, "I look at them. I can read some Russian. The steel workers are told how many tons they have to produce for the state. The same for the workers in the copper and aluminum plants. Even the farmers are told how many tons of wheat, cotton, corn, and sugar beets they are expected to grow. Milkmaids are told how many liters of milk they must deliver every day."

With the same cynicism I was hearing on the streets, I dared to say, "I wouldn't be surprised if the NKVD were told how many arrests to make every day or how many 'enemies of the people' to execute."

Behind the barber's back, my cousin wagged a cautionary finger to keep quiet, but I wanted them to continue talking. I knew that to them I was a curious boy who had to be controlled. Precisely because I saw things from my own vantage point, questions kept seething in my mind. In school, I had known students competing for honors and medals. For an army or navy officer, it was a matter of pride to wear a medal on his uniform as a symbol of bravery rather than to get higher pay. But what good was a Hero of Socialist Labor medal to a worker who needed decent wages to provide for his family?

As we were all uncertain how far we could go in criticizing the system, we gradually became nervous and restless, and the discussion came to an end. My cousin paid the barber for his services.

That first winter of our exodus was fiercer than any I recalled from childhood, perhaps because of the lack of no invigorating sleigh rides and ice skating on the lake, as there had been back home. Here in Lwów, when we ventured out, the winds beat icily on our faces, the cold penetrated our papery clothes. To get warmer clothing and coal to heat our dwelling, my father turned to his black market contacts.

Despite Soviet claims of productivity, food became scarce. Long lines formed for bread or vegetables or any comestible. A truck coming to a store with produce had everyone scurrying to get on line. It didn't matter what was available; if possible you bought it, and if you didn't need it, you could always barter it for something else.

In our household, we fared slightly better because Mundek, my nineteen-year-old brother, a courageous, determined young man who had mastered the tricks of the black market, regularly traveled to outlying parts of the western Ukraine to barter tobacco, soap, and candles for butter, cheese, and flour. To reach these areas, he needed a special pass from the authorities. By this time, he knew the long chain of hands held out, from intermediaries to security officers, for the fees to arrange passes for him.

Mundek brought back stories along with the supplies.

"No wonder we have shortages," he would say. "In

Przemysl, I saw trainload after trainload of food, oil, and other mineral products passing through on the way to Germany."

"I could give you more reasons for the shortages," I braved.

I was keeping up with the Finnish war news as well as gaining fluency in the Russian language. I knew that the Soviet war with Finland, which had begun at the end of November 1939, was not going well.

"The Russians are not winning the quick victory they hoped for. The Finns are putting up a strong resistance."

"Listen," my father warned us. "Talk to each other all you want, but don't talk this way to outsiders. If someone comes in and hears you, you're asking for trouble. An NKVD man could come in any time, and then you'd better pretend you're talking about a movie or a relative who is sick or even about the weather."

He stopped to make sure we understood. "Decide now, because when they break down the door and take you two away separately to ask what you were discussing, you most both tell the same story."

My mother, small and fragile, constantly worried about our safety, picked up on this.

"If they accuse us of complaining or attacking the system, off we go to a socialist corrective labor camp, you know.

"So, what movie is playing now?" mother asked, to substantiate her warning. Once this was settled, the conversation continued.

"Go on, Lusiek, tell us what you heard on the Finnish broadcast."

Before I could respond, my cousin Kuba, the Polytechnic student, broke in.

"You might say that Stalin made a major strategic error when he executed the best of his officers, thinking they were conspiring against him. This left him and his army with a bunch of poorly trained commanders."

"He's paranoid," I submitted, a new word I had gleaned from the Finnish newscasters. "He trusts no one, not even the new officers he put in to replace the old ones."

"They can parrot all the Party slogans," Kuba, the cynic, said, "but as military commanders—forget it."

"I know." The conversation was now where I could show off my knowledge of the war. "They blame it all on the impregnable Mannerheim Line. They lost a lot of men. I could tell you right now about the Russian widows in Lwów. Between them, Hitler and Stalin want to divide up Europe. Then what? Asia? Africa? I'm glad the Finns are putting up a strong fight."

"You know," Mundek, deep in thought, was frowning, "everyone is paranoid these days. Do you hear yourselves? A knock on the door no longer means a guest, no one trusts anyone."

"That's true," father interrupted, his eyes ringed with shadows. "Here in Lwów, a Jewish family struck up an acquaintance with a Jewish Red army officer, a veterinarian tending the cavalry horses. He often visited the family but never said a thing about the Soviet system, and neither did they. Caution on both sides, as was prudent. Until one day he started to criticize the Communist system. The people in the Jewish family paled with fear, because they thought they had encouraged a provocateur who might turn them in. Afraid to agree with him they asked instead why he was talking that way. They even began to praise the system, 'Communism is good for the people.'

"The veterinarian admonished them for being such conformists to Communist dogma and suddenly started to sing the Hallel, the Hebrew prayer recited on the first day of the month and on holidays. As he sang, tears ran down his cheeks. 'I was born in the Ukraine.' he told them, 'my father was a ritual slaughterer. I am a Jew like you. I know you're afraid of me just as I'm afraid of them.'

"He then went on to tell about the horrendous killings and persecutions in the Ukraine during the period of collectivization. 'Things are bad here,' he said, 'but even so, they're a lot better than in the Ukraine.'

"His hosts told him that what he said might be true, but Jews were not being persecuted and vilified and murdered as they were in Hitler's Germany.

"He answered that this might be true, but the Communist system was evil, run by evil people, bad for the Russian people, bad for the world, and very bad for the Jews."

Evil was a palpable shadow extending in front of me, stepping where I stepped, turning every corner with me, darker even than the darkest night. I felt its chilling jabs to my body. I thought a lot about evil in those days.

We had been living with our cousins Faigele and Pesach Kraut for several months now. Her stepsister, Faigele Munzer, had taken in my aunt Bucia and her husband, Lemel Silber, and their four children. We were all grateful to the relatives who had made room in their apartments for us and treated us so kindly, but when it began to seem as if we would be in Lwów indefinitely, my parents and the Silbers decided to pool their resources and get an apartment. On a cold winter day, we moved to an apartment at 38 Dwornickiego Street rented from a Polish Christian professor at Lwów University named Szyskowski. The apartment was just one room. The six Silbers and the five Wenigs were now living in one room. The parents slept in the two beds, and the children slept on the floor.

No sooner were we in our new quarters than a heavy snowfall began. Snow fell and blanketed the houses, the trees, and the shrubs. The white snow in its pristine beau-

9 June 1997

Mr. Larry Wenig
Suite 911
150 Broadway
New York, NY 10038

Dear Mr. Wenig,

I enjoyed meeting you at the luncheon hosted by the Conference of Presidents of Major Jewish Organizations. The story of how you overcame such terrible obstacles to come to America was a harrowing one.

Your story epitomizes the American Dream – building a new life and taking advantage of the many opportunities our Nation offers. You have much of which to be proud.

With best wishes for all your future endeavors.

Sincerely,

JOHN M. SHALIKASHVILI
Chairman
of the Joint Chiefs of Staff

A personal letter to Larry Wenig from General John M. Shalikashvili, Chairman of the Joint Chiefs of Staff.

1

Mr. Larry Wenig
With best wishes,

General John M. Shalikashvili, Chairman of the Joint Chiefs of Staff.

2

Left to right: Escia Silber, the author's cousin; Bucia Silber, her mother and his maternal aunt; Gonia, Buscia's eldest daughter; Hella, the author's sister; his mother; Bucia's youngest daughter, also named Hella. Photograph taken in Dynów before the war.

Left to right: Escia Silber, the author's cousin; Adka
Bieber, the daughter of Dynów's Jewish barber, Adolph
Bieber; Rivka, the sister of the author's friend Dufciu
Feingenbaum, who told him about midwives and the
stork. Photograph taken in Dynów before the war.

3. The author's mother, rear row, extreme right, and some of her relatives, photographed in Dynów
before the war. Front row, left to right: Ruzia my mother's sister; cousin Lakia Heilman; aunt Serkala
Heilman; sister Bucia Silber. Rear row, left to right: cousin Gonia Silber; cousin Ruzia Kasser; sister-
in-law Yenta Kasser.

4

The girls' class of the Tarbut school in prewar Dynów. Rear row, extreme right: Mania Frankel, the author's girlfriend.

The Wenig family in Uzbekistan during the war. Left to right: the author's mother, his father, his sister Hella, his brother Shmulek, the author. Photograph taken by Russian-Jewish neighbors of the Wenigs.

5

The home of the author's uncle Lemel Silber in Dynów before the war.

The Polish public school in Dynów before the war.

6

פ'נ

אונזער טייערער אונפֿ,ארגעסליכער
זאהן ברודער אונ קאזין

שמואל זאבודל דוייניג

דער אינ אויף לעבענם אהר
זורו אייבען אונפֿאל אין טראגישער
ווייזע אומבעקומען

געב' 26.6.1923 בעשטו 12.9.1945

NIEZAPOMNIANEMU I NAJDROZSZEMU
SYNOWI, BRATU I KUZYNOWI,
SAMUELOWI WENIGOWI
KTORY ZGINAŁ W MŁODYM WIEKU
TRAGICZNĄ SHIERCIĄ

RODZICE BRAT SIOSTRA
KUZYN Z RODZINA

The tombstone of Larry Wenig's brother Shmulek in the Vienna Jewish cemetery. Shmulek died on September 12, 1945, just a few minutes away from freedom and safety in Vienna. He either fell off the train or was pushed off by Soviet agents.

Larry Wenig and his wife, Selma, at their wedding in New York, June 13, 1954.

The American relatives who helped the Wenigs during and after the war: center: uncle Irving Wenig, left: his younger son Jerry, right: his older son Norman. Photographed at the wedding of Larry and Selma Wenig.

Aunt Ruthie, the wife of Irving Wenig.

Larry Wenig with President Haydar Aliyev of Azerbaijan at a meeting of the Conference of Presidents of Major American Jewish Organizations in New York.

Larry Wenig and other Zionist leaders with Prime Minister Menachem Begin in his office in Jerusalem, 1982. Left to right: Larry Wenig; Prime Minister Begin; Ivan Novick, president of the Zionist Organization of America; Sidney Silverman, national vice president of the ZOA; Begin's secretary.

Larry Wenig on the outskirts of Beirut, Lebanon, in 1982.

11

Larry Wenig in Jerusalem with General Ariel Sharon.

Larry Wenig at a ZOA convention in Washington, D.C., with Senator Joseph R. Biden of Delaware.

Larry Wenig in Jerusalem with Israeli Defense Minister Moshe Arens.

Larry Wenig at a ZOA convention in Washington, D.C., with Jeane J. Kirkpatrick, then U.S. representative to the United Nations.

13

Larry Wenig at a ZOA convention in Washington, D.C., with Senator Daniel K. Inouye of Hawaii.

Larry Wenig and Senator Alfonse D'Amato of New York at a ZOA breakfast on Long Island.

14

Larry Wenig and General Alexander M. Haig, Jr., at a ZOA convention in Miami, Florida.

At a ZOA convention in Israel. Senator Arlen Specter of Pennsylvania, Mrs. Specter, and Larry Wenig.

ty was an artist's joy, but for us it was an extra hardship. Snow piled on the walks and roads and made them impassable. The entire population of the city was ordered to shovel the snow from the streets. I had to help clear the street where we lived. The brutal cold wind blew through my clothes. I shivered, blew on my hands, and stomped my feet to warm them. Like the longtime residents of the city, I began to blame the Russians for bringing their frigid air with them. I too began to grumble as my stomach rumbled with hunger. Food was getting scarcer, and portions smaller, meager, yet nobody in our household complained.

But among the others, particularly the refugees, we heard complaints about shortages of food and fuel, dissatisfaction with the distribution system and the politics that governed every aspect of our lives. There was a growing sense of disappointment, particularly among the Christians who had left families and friends to run away from the advancing German army. They felt that they had fallen victim to greater dangers here and wanted to go back home. Despite the reports of persecution and executions, there were even Jews who wanted to return to their cities and villages, feeling they would fare better in familiar surroundings.

The Soviet government did not restrain them. In fact, to facilitate their departure, it opened an office in Przemysl, the border town on the eastern side of the river San. Long lines formed outside the office. Arbitrary preferences to petitioners made it apparent that there was hanky-panky going on.

Seated at the kitchen table reading my book, I overheard our landlord, Professor Szyskowski, confiding in my father that his married daughter, who had escaped the German armies advancing on Warsaw, now wanted to return and rejoin her husband. Her husband, a director of the Warsaw airport before the war erupted, had elected to remain there. Without an official permit, she would not be permitted to enter German-occupied Poland.

I pretended to turn the pages, but that did not obscure my view of the professor, whose eyes were appealing to my father but at the same time measuring the likelihood that he would consent.

"Can you take her to Przemysl?" He asked. "Get her to the front of the line or whatever way there is of getting preference?"

My father's heavy brows knitted. There was no expression of agreement or refusal on his implacable face. He said nothing. When the landlord left, I heard my mother and father whispering. I heard movement and knew my mother had relinquished some American dollars for the necessary bribe.

The next day my father left for Przemysl with the young woman. When he returned, he nodded to my mother and gave her a twenty-dollar gold coin. "Twenty Hard Ones," as we called it, was a coin that could buy your way right to Iosif Vissarionovich Stalin. You could get right to the top, to the People's Commissariat of Internal Affairs, with so valuable a coin. The woman had the necessary permit and transit papers.

It took bribery to get permits. Were the Russians so mercenary that they would use any ploy to wring money out of petitioners? Or had there been a political change because of the victorious turnabout on the Finnish battlefield? After Russia suffered a series of humiliating defeats in Finland, Stalin replaced the army's commanders with more efficient, ruthless men. The Finns suffered great losses. They faced defeat and capitulation. In March 1940, Finland agreed to cede more territory than had been demanded initially.

During that same month, Daladier, the French premier, one of the architects of the capitulation at Munich, was forced to step down. Paul Reynaud, who replaced him, was greeted with optimism. Now we hoped that the British prime minister, Neville Chamberlain, would follow suit and be replaced by Winston Churchill, who was gaining support for his more confrontational stance. Seven months had passed since England and France had declared war on Germany, yet they had done nothing to prosecute the war against Hitler.

I followed these events with vague apprehension, unsure how the war would affect my family's refugee status. Our hosts were cordial. We had our chores to do in the household, and except for days when we had civic orders, our life followed a routine. But rumors spread, rumors that soon came to be called *odnaya baba skazala* ("an old woman said"), O.B.S. for short. O.B.S had it that the government was going to register all the refugees.

This rumor, substantiated by the press and radio, became a reality by the end of April 1940. Registration agents came to our apartment. My father, answering their questions, gave the date, year, and place where he was born, as well as the names of his wife and children. They wanted to know what kind of work he did or what kind of business he was in. The most important question was where my father wanted to go.

My father opted for the truth in the hope they would arrange for us to go to the United States.

"I have been a grain merchant and a distributor of fertilizer and agricultural machinery," he declared.

Why did he have to brag to them, I thought. Didn't he see that he was presenting himself as an outsider? He was immediately classified as a capitalist and an enemy of the working class.

"But let me tell you," he continued, his manner that of an experienced negotiator, "the German army killed my relatives. I want to leave Poland. I have a brother in New York who will vouch for us."

"What does your brother do, they asked. Is he a businessman or a worker? What is his name?"

My father, my proud father who was used to giving orders in his thriving businesses, obviously wanted to impress them. "My brother is a big metal manufacturer, he employs many workers." My father could not think of his brother as an oppressor of the working class, a member of the bourgeoisie. That was Communist pap for gullible peasants.

The interrogators stopped right there and left. The silence that clung to the room was broken when my brother asked, "Why did you tell them that you were a merchant?"

"So they would know we can be self-sufficient. I could be a manager for them in a store or some other enterprise." Father had a powerful sense of himself. He could not imagine a difficulty he would be unable to overcome. Had he not gotten us out of Dynów safely?

My father grasped the seriousness of the situation when he saw how worried we were about the information on our registration. Since we were now unprotected, he made a quick decision. My mother was to sew all the foreign currency, dollars as well as two twenty-gold dollar coins, into her corset.

With the corset covering her body from breast to thigh, reinforced with enough heavy laces, metal, and rubber rods for an armored Nordic Valkyrie, she was a walking bank safe.

My father kept his own counsel, but since we did not know his plans, we paced apprehensively. My uncertainty was reinforced by the controlled news in the papers and on the radio. I was already self-taught in Russian. Although my knowledge was limited, I could read the Moscow papers, *Pravda* and *Izvestia*, and could convey information to my family. Both were propaganda papers. The former published by the Central Committee of the Communist Party, and the latter by the government. Most of both papers was devoted to production quotas to be filled by the "heroic and patriotic workers of the glorious Soviet Union." There were "Challenges" whereby milkmaids, for example, challenged each other: Who would milk more cows? How many liters of milk would be delivered to the state?

I turned eagerly to the last page for news. Half of the page was devoted to foreign news, which was disheartening. The Allies were not engaging Hitler on the western front. Bold and unchallenged, he invaded and occupied Denmark. Undaunted, that April 1940, his troops invaded Norway. Then, finally, the alarm rang. England sent troops to protect Narvik, an important western Norwegian port. Our patriotic feelings soared at the news that Polish troops harbored in England participated in the action, but were quelled when we learned of the Allied defeat.

There was nothing to cheer us, unless you could believe the trounced-up proclamation fed to the people on May Day. Celebrations of the special holiday in recognition of the workers and peasants took place everywhere. These were meant to bolster morale, spurring the workers to fulfill and overfill the quotas set by Stalin's Five Year Plan. For a second time, we saw quantities of food, cakes, and sweets available in the stores. Posters of Politburo members and army commanders were mounted on Legionow Street. Like the other Soviet informers, our superintendent told us that everyone was required to witness and march in the parade. He had his officious role and a checklist of tenants. Nonetheless, my mother and Aunt Bucia remained at home to do their housekeeping and cook the meal we would have when we returned from the parade.

Legionow Street was a sea of humanity with waving placards and banners on which were printed slogans of love and allegiance to the Communist Party. Directed by workers and militiamen, my father, brothers Mundek and Shmulek, little sister Hella, and I moved into line behind the Red Army units with their red flags, tanks, and artillery.

Over a loudspeaker came the voice of a Party leader calling for the parade to begin. Then came the blaring sounds of "The Internationale," the Soviet anthem. We were ordered to sing but stood mute, not knowing the words, nor feeling included in the system.

Each of the military units, including the cavalry, was followed by a civilian contingent waving huge red banners and shouting out the messages imprinted on them: LONG LIVE OUR GREAT LEADER STALIN! GLORY TO THE COMMUNIST PARTY! WE PLEDGE FULFILLMENT OF OUR PRODUCTION QUOTA ON THE OCCASION OF THE MAY FIRST HOLIDAY! With each shouted slogan, a chorus from the spectators exploded with shouts of "Hurrah!"

Impressed as I was by the pageantry and the military display, I was amused by the Polish bystanders, who like us did not identify with the parade. They just joined the shouting with nonsensical shouts of their own. The Jewish marchers, with their own brand of humor, yelled loudly in Yiddish, *"Zol leben lokshen mit yoych, hurrah!"* ("Long live Chicken Noodle Soup, Hurrah!" *"Zol leben gefilte fish mit retech, hurrah!"* ("Long live gefilte fish and horseradish, hurrah!"). How bizarre a farce. Poles and Jews together, screaming all kinds of ridiculous slogans.

There were frenzied movements, carnival gyrations, skipping and hopping like pagans adoring Dionysus. It was madness to engage in, parody. Unreal euphoria with treacherous responses. If the authorities had been able to translate the mottled voices, there would have been arrests, but they did not expect the populace to participate so enthusiastically and took it for sincerity. Such enthusiasm was convincing.

Our faces, as we returned to our building, must have looked rapturous. Our superintendent smiled, "Your first May Day holiday. Did you enjoy it!" I was learning fast. Deception, graft, flattery were the coin of the realm.

May 10, 1940 brought increasingly bad news. Using paratroops and tanks, the Germans broke through Holland's defenses and with spectacular success ripped that country to shreds. Unimpeded, Hitler's army marched into Belgium and launched another attack through the Ardennes forest into France.

There was only one radio station in Lwów, providing news directly from Moscow. We listened to every newscast, becoming more and more depressed. I kept my map of Western Europe spread open on the table and followed the German army's movements with pain in my heart. What we gleaned from the official broadcasts was supplemented by news passed on by people who had illegal shortwave sets. From them we learned that within several days of the German attack, Churchill, the new prime minister of England, had flown to Paris to assess the situation and to bolster the spirit of the French government.

If there were any glad tidings in this chain of events, it was that Neville Chamberlain was no longer at the helm of the British government. According to the reports we heard, the Allied generals were performing poorly. With a shake-up in the high command, General Gamelin, commander of the French forces, was dismissed and replaced by General

Maxime Weygand. He too was unable to impede the German advance. Speedily, in pincer formations, the Germans pushed forward, entrapping the Allied forces.

In my immature enthusiasm I pounded the table and stamped around the room, wanting to knock heads off. Since September, when they had declared war, there had been plenty of time for the Allied commanders to prepare their troops, yet they were still acting like the tin soldiers in the *Nutcracker Suite*. By the end of May, the British Expeditionary Force was encircled in the port of Dunkirk. By June, the British had abandoned their weapons and their aspirations on the shores of France and Belgium. A flotilla of all kinds of vessels—steamers, small craft, fishing boat, anything that could float—was commandeered to transport the British army, as well as more than a hundred thousand French soldiers, back to Britain.

I could not sleep those nights, my stomach was churning. I followed every military maneuver, suffered every reverse as if indeed I were planning strategy and prodding the poorly led, disorganized, dispirited Allied forces.

After the fall of the Netherlands and Belgium, it did not take Hitler's armies very long to crush France. They circumvented the Maginot Line, on which the French had pinned their hopes. The French seemed to have lost their will to fight; as a result chaos followed. On June 14, 1940, the German army marched into Paris. France capitulated. A puppet government, soon known as the Vichy government, was installed under Marshal Henri Pétain.

Why did the United States, the most powerful democracy in the world, not see the threat from this relentless conqueror? America apparently had no intention of sending its great armies and navies to halt the invasion of one peaceful country after another. The Americans were silent, and so were the Soviets. Looking at my map, I imagined a line of Nazi troops stretching to the Soviet border. Didn't the Russians see the shadow of the invader behind the trees on their snow-laden steppes?

In fact, the question was put to the officers of the Red Army, who clustered with the civilians around every radio. They shrugged and looked at us as if we were stupid children. "The war in the West involves the capitalist nations," they declared, "it's not our concern; let them kill each other off."

Not their concern? I thought. Then why were they hovering over the radio like the rest of us? Every setback for the Allies was like the shockwave of an earthquake, throwing us into a panic. The turbulence was too real, the reverberations too close. We lived in constant fear of the brewing trouble. As it turned out, we did not have to wait very long.

The Expulsion

On June 28, 1940, after midnight, we heard a loud knock on the door of our apartment. Even as my father called out "Who's there?" the door was smashed in.

Backed up by two soldiers with rifles and fixed bayonets stood a short khaki-clad official.

"*Sobirai s veshchami!*" he ranted ("Get your baggage together!").

My father, responding in the dignified military manner he had learned while a soldier in World War I, faced the official. Taller, broader-chested, my father was not intimidated.

"What's all this about?" he asked in an assured tone of voice. I almost expected him to threaten the official or to blurt out his record of honorable service in Kaiser Franz Joseph's Austro-Hungarian army. But father made no impression on the official. Instead, he found himself held back by bayonets. My mother's delicate body cringed, her small face pale.

The answer from the official, more like the bark of a hound than the words of a human being, was:

"You wanted to go to America to join your brother. That's where we are going to send you."

With those bayonets pointed at my father's body, we knew we were going somewhere else. My mother and my little sister Hella, sobbing pathetically, clung to each other. My seventeen-year-old brother Shmulek and I stood lamely by, unable to comfort them. My brother Mundek was on one of his business trips to a village near Przemysl. That meant that one member of our family would not be going with us.

"Hurry! Quick! Move!" the official roared as he shoved us. I had no doubt now that he was an NKVD man.

"Don't play the hero with me," my father shot back, his dark eyes flashing angrily. "I'm an old soldier myself. The last thing I would do would be to torment women and children."

Mother, totally distraught now, cried out. "You'll get yourself killed. Do what they say."

The shouting, weeping, rushing about awakened our Polish landlord. A gentle professor, he came in to see what was going on and paled at the sight. Trying to comfort and help us, he was suddenly grabbed by the soldiers. Appalled, he pulled out his documents. Seeing his impressive credentials, the soldiers apologized. Realizing that he could do nothing more for us, he wished us a safe journey and left.

The two soldiers kept prodding us to pack faster, but father, ever proud and officious, argued with them, and cursed them for mistreating the women. My proud, stubborn father, deceiving himself that they meant to expedite his emigration. My mother saw the futility of reasoning with them and pleaded with him to stop.

After we had thrown together some bundles of clothing, cooking utensils, and blankets, we were led down the stairway. Passing through the lobby, we saw our superintendent, who we were convinced was an informer for the NKVD. We shuddered when he told us that we had nothing to fear and everything would be fine.

A soldier stationed outside read off our names from a list. "One is missing," he said, "the boy, why isn't he here?"

"He's with friends in Przemysl," my father answered.

The soldier consulted with the others, then folded the

papers in his hand and ordered us along. We carried our bundles to the waiting wagon. A husky Polish peasant, patting his horse with a subdued expression on his face, mumbled something about not having any choice but to take us, while complaining that he probably would not even get paid. When he saw the soldiers eyeing him, he shut up and pretended to be loading our bundles. That done, we piled into the wagon. Five Wenigs and the soldiers. In the eerie half-light of the dawn, there were few people in the streets. No one said a word as we began moving. In the total silence, I looked at the faces of my family members, sitting woefully resigned to fate.

We soon found out that we were not the only victims of the midnight mandate. Our driver drove his wagon into a long line of vehicles carrying expelled, unwanted refugees, Jews and Christians. The horse slogged along, each hoof beating a hammer to our fears, until we reached the Lwów railroad yard. There, thickly packed horse-drawn wagons with their human cargo jostled for space. Our wagon stopped alongside a waiting train, where we saw a mass of people being herded into freight cars by swarming security policemen. Treated like worthless insects we stood there devoid of courage or initiative. Feeling like prey in the presence of the voracious soldiers, mute and indifferent to the roar of human weeping. Their grins, their scowls oblivious to the cries of infants and children, the moans of the elderly as they struggled to obey orders, scoured of hope.

As soon as we stopped, NKVD officers surrounded us, yelling orders to start unloading our baggage. We were goaded into a boxcar refitted for human cargo by the expedient of a small hole drilled in the middle of the floor, about ten inches in diameter, under which hung a small metal pipe, readily identified as a toilet, open to view. On either side, partitioned in upper and lower sections, were spaces into which people were abusively shoved. About forty people were packed into each car.

My father, a strong muscular man, kept us close and pushed through to the upper level, having quickly assessing it as more advantageous because there were two small openings on each side, windows to the outside. Throughout our ordeals, I continually found reasons to marvel at his resourcefulness. Despite all the adversity we suffered, his cool logic and strong body always managed to protect us; he took charge in every situation.

Not so my mother. The woman who had been brought up securely, in extreme comfort and care, was frightened, confused, her eyes vacant. She was mumbling to herself.

Here again, my father held the helm. He must have been shaken by our predicament. He must have felt the insult to his own dignity but he managed to comfort mother. He put his arm about her, talking gently, calming her.

As I lay squeezed between Shmulek and my father, I longed for such solace. My up-ended life now confined to a wooden cattle car was as dark and unpromising as our destination. Long lines of displaced persons, crude bundles, and cramped freight cars superimposed by my former fascination with war maps, tactics, and strategy. The pageantry of marching bands replaced by bullets and bayonets aimed at innocents. For the first time in my fifteen years, I found myself questioning the meaning of life. Is so much suffering and humiliation a necessary test of living? Does life have a purpose? Is it worth the effort to struggle to live?

Glancing over at my younger sister, Hella, not quite eight years old, toward whom I had grown protective and affectionate, I wondered what she was thinking. Did she understand what was happening? I wanted to spare her the pain of dislocation, travail. What does an older brother do in a crowded freight train to help his little sister? Try to give her a little more space? Hardly noticeable, hardly helpful, still, instinctively, I inched away to give Hella some more room.

"Our help is in the Lord." In that cramped car, the words were like a tallis wrapped around my shoulders. I yearned to believe that God would not permit my life to end now under these conditions. My destiny was not in this moment, my destiny was beyond this time. I took heart in that belief, and told myself that I had to go on living.

Fumbling my way to the door and looking out, I saw an endless stream of horse-drawn carts loaded with human cargo. Along the tracks as far as I could see, people were lifting and loading bundles, boarding the freight cars. A long line of trains stretched beyond my line of vision. An incalculable mass of human beings was waiting to board the trains. Who had made this plan to evacuate what seemed to be the entire population of the city? How many horses, carts, drivers, trains were needed? Did the peasant drivers understand what they had been asked to do? What promises, what payment could they get from a Communist government to agree to this job? How long had this vast operation been planned? Where were they going to take us?

In our car, I could hear people complaining, revolted by the crude toilet. "I can't take this," I heard them say. "Relieve ourselves openly, in front of each other. They want us to be like animals." Amidst these outcries, someone pulled out a blanket and a cardboard carton, creating a crude enclosure around the hole in the floor.

As the hours slowly passed, the train still loading, the people in the car began to speak to one other and share their histories. Except for two Polish Christian families, all the rest were Jews, refugees from the German-occupied part of Poland. One man was an engineer, another a university teacher, one a lawyer, one a banker. But most were small merchants and landlords, assuredly classified as capitalists. No one had the vaguest notion where we were heading, but from the way we were being treated, we speculated that it would be to a slave labor camp in Siberia.

The Russian guards came along and closed the doors, glowering at us, ignoring the pleas to keep them open, since it was the only way for air to come into the car. But all such requests were futile; the soldiers would not talk to us, they shouted as if we were dogs.

At dusk, we heard movement on the roof of our car. Scurrying feet, sounds of tools being used. As night fell, the train began to move out of the station. We were hungry, but there was no indication that they meant to give us food. If we had been cattle in that cattle car, assuredly they would have given us food.

Worms couldn't have tasted worse than the chalky coating on my tongue. Dread like the weight of a horse pressed on my head. Hunger made my stomach churn. Nobody in the world seemed to care that we were cargo, which is what we seemed to be. To the occasional wayfarer who watched the train go by, the sight of people piled and pressed into freight cars should have been met by more than just a vacant stare. To allow this grotesque picture to register in their minds without any reaction was to call the very idea of reason into question. Reason was a casualty of the war.

In this choking atmosphere where confusion and fear added to the foul air, a young man began to sing. A sweet melody I did not recognize, but I understood the words and realized it was a song of the political prisoners in Siberia.

Sibir, Sibiru nie boyus,
Sibir ze tozhe russka yest zemlya.

Siberia, Siberia, I do not fear you.
Siberia, too, is part of Russia.

Surprisingly, some people, though sorely tired and abused, were still able to sing, but not I. Tired, sad, humiliated, I fell asleep with the melody humming in my mind.

In the middle of the night we were awakened by banging on the door. We could feel that the train had stopped. A guard announced that we were getting food. One person from each car was to go and bring the food for all the others.

As the delegated man went out, he groaned, "We're in a small town somewhere in the western Ukraine." All eyes followed the man, anxiously awaiting his return and the food he might bring. Soon he came back with two big pails of soup. Thin watery gruel, but no one questioned the ingredients; hungry people will eat anything as long as it fills the stomach. I too ate, sharing a plate with another rider. We had to, for there were not enough plates to go around. They also gave us bread, and some hot water, which they called *kipyatok*. The water came from a tank kept hot in the station house. Mother, ever the practical person, had thought to pack some tea. Her eyes downcast, she fixed only enough for her family. She could not afford to be generous to the others. Our travel and our travail had just begun. Soup and hot water were our food on this journey.

Fed, I fell into an uneasy sleep again. The heavy rattle and thump of the train brought back memories of the crunching sound of cartwheels rolling over the stony roads in my hometown of Dynów. Startled, I would wake up to hissing noises that sounded like horses and wagon wheels sloshing through Dynów's muddy streets. Confined, my body felt cramped, with no space to turn to a more comfortable position. My hands crawled along my legs to keep them away from other bodies, all the while feeling revulsion over someone else's bad breath in my face, strange arms were flung in the dark across my chest. I was revolted by having to expose my most primal needs. My body rebelled at the thought that I would no longer know the joy of exercise on a volleyball field, my sexual organs ever reminding me of my maturing body.

Around me were the night sounds of humans, like sour chords on a piano, a cacophony of grunts and groans, or a cry of anguish, as a knee jerked and hit a belly. The air turned foul, smelling of putrid soup, while a person wakened by nature's call could not help but wake up those next to him, and befoul the air even more.

The dawn presented its own awful hygienic problems. Throats and noses cleared with unavoidable indelicacy. The small hole in the middle of the floor had to suffice for everyone's evacuation. A line of uncomfortable people formed, waiting impatiently, courtesy to women and children totally forgotten. Abusive shouting insults, pleas to hurry, were hurled at those who seemed overlong. The stench that emanated from behind the improvised, blanketed area was foul and overpowering. Self-respect was hard to maintain in this barnyard climate. How shameful these elemental needs had become for us.

Every jolt and joggle of the train frightened us. A knock on the door was a summons to face the executioner. When the train stopped at a small station somewhere in the Ukraine proper, a knock on the door sent shivers down our spines. Again, a barking command to delegate someone to come get food for those in the car. This time, my brother Shmulek volunteered to go, and brought back the same Russian black bread and hot water. The water supply was only enough for drinking. There was none for washing or brushing of teeth. Shmulek also brought back a newspaper and distributed it to be used as toilet paper. From Shmulek we learned that the noise we had heard overhead was from the installation of machine guns on the roofs of the cars. The routines of our journey were set.

Our journey continued, the train now chugging and thumping in a monotonous clatter. We passed forests, fields where rabbits scampered freely, where snakes shed their skins without shame, where grasshoppers chewed on sugar-rich tubers. On summer days like this, I remembered poking my toes through the grass, looking for strawberries clinging to stones, running through meadows and orchards ripening with fruit. My head hurt from the sounds and smells of our confined quarters. The only air came from the apertures in the sides of the car, which the guards made us close when we passed peasants working in the fields of collective farms. When we passed through more populated areas, the guards on the roof were at the ready with their machine guns. They stood on guard to hide the shame of their human cargo. How they could hide the human feces leaking from the openings in that line of trains I will never know.

My father, a fearless broad-shouldered man not used to being stepped on, resisted their commands. He yelled back at them in the broken Ukrainian he had learned from his Ukrainian customers.

"There are women and children in here suffocating and suffering from the heat." He found a stick and used it to force the shutters open. The guards kicked the stick away and shoved it back, but he obstinately kept trying. He

fought with them throughout the journey, while we pleaded with him to give up. We were afraid they would haul
him off to some other place and separate him from us. The
fact that we were not cargo to boast about was no gratifi-
cation to us.

As we traversed the countryside, we discovered sights
the Russians were surely not proud of. Sun-drenched field
workers licking salty sweat from their parched lips,
women bent over with heavy loads on their backs. When
our train stopped at a village, men and women rushed over
from their work in the fields, telling us they were hungry,
pleading for food. How ludicrous a scene, the free begging
from the prisoners. Supervisors, overseers, whatever they
might have been called, chased them away, but the imprint
was there. Anyway, since they were plowing and seeding
and reaping for their country, why were the field workers
so poorly fed as to come begging from us? Was this a joke
or the coarse reality of Russia's problems? I was reminded
of what Mundek, my older brother, had told us about the
trains loaded with grain, oil, and raw materials being sent
from the Soviet Union to Hitler's Germany. Russia was
more concerned about appeasing its supposed ally than its
own people.

The same routine, the same food, the same arguments
with the guards to let us keep the windows open for a
breath of air. From the moment we boarded the train in
Lwów, we were not permitted off to stretch our limbs.
Only one person, a volunteer, was allowed out, to bring in
our soup, bread, and hot water. I was too depressed, too
numbed in mind and body, to volunteer. Crated in boxcars
in transit, as we were, I ceased believing that daylight followed the darkness or that hope would dispel the gloom.

The man who gave us our first geographical sighting
turned out to be an engineer who had an atlas. As he read

the signs on the stations we passed, he informed us of our whereabouts. When we passed the city of Ufa, he announced that we were east of the Ural Mountains, definitely going to Siberia. After a long stop, our train was rerouted.

"According to this map," he yelled out, "we are now heading for Kazakhstan. They'll probably dump us in the Semipalitinska desert, one of the worst places in the world. We'll be eaten up by scorpions."

A shudder went through my bones as he described the desolate area. One pessimistic report after another made me more listless. As the train continued on and on toward this bleak prospect, I no longer kept a mental record of the day of the week. I knew it to be July with one stifling day after another in this train stuffed with people and stagnant air. Others in the car told us that two weeks had passed since the beginning of the trip. That it was morning when the train came to a stop was discernible from the faint light filtering through the shutters. No placard marked this stop.

Trucks rumbled toward the train. We were told to take our bundles and disembark. The bright sunlight was blinding. As our vision cleared, we could see the inky outlines of a forest. Ours was one of ten cars uncoupled from the long train and shunted onto a siding. The rest of the train continued on to some other destination.

The command was given to get aboard the trucks with our belongings, upon which the trucks took off, destination unknown to us. Next to the driver of each truck was a large tank filled to the top with wood chips. A strange gassy smell came from the tanks. We soon learned that the vehicles did not run on gasoline but on gas produced from the burning wood chips in the tanks. My mind restless as usual, I was wondering about the Soviets' huge gasoline reserves. Were these, too, going to Hitler?

On the rock-strewn dirt-road through the forest, our truck shook and rocked and then stalled on a rise in the road. We were told to get off and start pushing it up the hill. After pushing and heaving, the engine began to roar again, only to break down after every little gain. And so it was: down from the truck, push, press our weight onto the truck again, when the motor started up. We became adept at the process, which was a diversion after two weeks of confinement. And, small things to give thanks for, our family was together.

Arrival in Gulag 149

Our truck came to a stop in front of a wooden structure. Several such barracks stood in a clearing in this vast forest. On one of the roofs, painted on the wooden planks, was the number 149, Gulag 149, located in Ozero. An ominous indicator for the far reaches of this territory, even though translated it meant "lake." We were told that we were in the county seat of Morki, in the Mari Autonomous Soviet Socialist Republic.

We unloaded our belongings and were assigned to a barracks. In the middle was a large oven meant only to provide heat. The section of the room assigned to the Wenigs had three wooden double bunks. My father, mother, and sister took the three lower bunks. Shmulek and I had two of the uppers. We used the remaining bunk to store some of our belongings, and put the rest under the lower bunks. In total, fifty people were housed in this barracks.

Fifty people looked at each other stunned, silent, distraught. For the moment, I thought we had lost the physical ability to speak. What could we say to one other that would not echo our despair? Even interest in eating disappeared. Not that we were not hungry, we just did not feel like eating. We retired to our individual bunks after being told to assemble the next day in front of the barracks.

Shipped here like cargo on a shelf in the freight train, my bones ached, my head pounded. I wanted to sleep, to yield my body and mind to oblivion, but my past was sobbing for its loss. The comfort of my mother's hand taking me to cheder at the age of three. The Jewish holidays cele-

brated in the company of uncles and cousins with abun-
dance and joy. The cantor's voice resonating in the synagogue. The stirring Zionist gatherings with Mania's friends
came back in mind, mated with music. Mania's sweet
breath on my face when we kissed. Would I find her again?
Was she safe?

Pictures of people living as free men in a country
known as America came to mind, adolescents my age in
school, at play, at parties. Here was I lying on an upper
bunk in a barracks in a camp that went by the number 149.
At fifteen and a half, I thought my life was coming to an
end.

In the bunk below me, I heard my mother sobbing and
my father trying to console her, telling her that he would
protect her, would somehow get us out of here. I wanted to
press my body against theirs, to breathe in the words of
hope, the hope that dissipated as it drifted upward. Facing
us was imprisonment and slavery, at best. Death was more
likely. Sleep was useless.

In the early dawn, the inhabitants of the barracks
already stirring, I rose to go to the toilet, the only one, at the
entrance to the barracks. I had to wait in line for my turn to
enter. We had to bring water in from a well outside.

After bread and tea that morning, we assembled in
front of the barracks, as instructed the previous day.
Addressing us was a slim man of average height, dressed
in shabby black pants and knitted red shirt, hatless. The
early light cast shadows on his pockmarked face; his thin
lips parted in a straight, expressionless line as he spoke.

"I am Commandant Zakharov. My deputies," he pointed to left and right, "are Ivanov and Moiseiev." The latter
were evidently much younger. "In this camp you are classified as *spec pereselentsy*, meaning 'special settlers.' You are
here because you are capitalists or members of political

parties that are enemies of the Soviet state. However, with good work and reeducation, you can be rehabilitated and become good citizens of the Soviet Union.

"You will be put to work, both men and women, to cut down the trees in this big forest." The girth of those trees looked to be about a meter and a half, surely as wide as the chest of a well-built man. "You will be paid for the work. Production norms will be set for cutting and logging the trees."

His lips never lost their cutting edge when he announced, "A special bonus will be awarded for exceeding the expected norm! You will be organized in brigades, each with its own leader."

He walked toward the edge of the forest. "There are trees here of special importance, *avio* trees, marked as you see by Soviet specialists. They are used in the aviation industry for military airplanes."

Having outlined the order of work, he went on to explain the regulations governing life in the camp. Pointing to the various sheds, he said, "There is the bread bakery where you will be getting your bread, there the *stolonaya* [dining hall] where you will eat, and there the store for other things."

The *stolnica* looked more like a canteen than a restaurant. We saw no cooking facilities, but he told us we could do some of our cooking outside the barracks. "Make a fire and pile up some bricks to put your pots on.

"You are in the Mari Republic. The capital city is Yoshkar Ola, meaning 'Red City,' in *zon smeshannykh lesov*, the mixed-forest zone south of the tundra and the taiga. You won't find a single road even if you go through the whole forest all the way to Siberia and reach the Pacific Ocean."

I do not know how many of us thought about getting away from this place. A wild useless thought quickly dissipated by his next comment.

"Don't try to escape; the forests are full of wolves. Many nights, especially during the winter, the wolves come into the camp. Snow can start falling here by the end of August. The winters are terribly cold because we are on the edge of Siberia. If it gets really cold, you'll be excused from work to stay in the barracks. Wear *valonki*." This was a heavy knee-length felt boot. "You can buy *valonki* if they are available in our store. Also, because of the heavy snows and bitter cold, make sure you wear rubber boots over the *valonki*, very necessary." Later in our stay here, I heard a song about the *valonki*.

"A foreman will teach you how to cut down and log the trees. In the stable there are draft horses to be used in the logging. You'll see peasants from the nearby villages working in the camp and forest, especially in the winter months between August and May. Expect no favors from them."

Just when we thought he had finished, his voice became harsher as he reminded us of the law against shirking we had first learned in Lwów.

"*Progul* is strictly enforced. You'll be punished even if you're only a few minutes late. You can't stay home from work because of illness unless the feldsher [orderly] at the clinic decides you are sick enough and issues a certificate to that effect. Only then can a person be excused from work. There will be school for the young; everyone else will work.

"If you want to go to one of the villages to buy produce from the peasants, you have to get a permit. The nearest village is about five kilometers away." He shifted his body, directing his fierce eyes at us. "Any questions?"

If the others had questions, they kept their mouths shut out of fear, but one brave man dared.

"Why do women have to do such dangerous physical work as chopping trees?"

Zakharov looked at the people assembled before him. By Russian standards, they were well dressed, even had an air of elegance in their bearing. These were not peasants, nor Russian muzhiks. Most were well educated.

"Comrades," he responded with no comradely tone, "the great democratic Soviet constitution states that work is a duty and an honor. Women should be proud that they have the right to work."

Seeing that the first man had asked a question without getting in trouble, someone else spoke up. "Can we visit the capital, Yoshkar Ola?"

"Certainly not! You are prisoners. You can go to the city only if you have a permit from the kommandatura."

Then followed some more warnings, then Zakharov dismissed us with a glare, stating, "You will start working in a day or two."

As we dispersed, languidly returning to the barracks, I thought of the prospects for us in the middle of this dense, far reaching forest, where we were now condemned to perform hard labor. None of us had experience in cutting down trees or sustaining ourselves in frigid weather. How long would we last in this God-forsaken place?

Back in the barracks, we soon became acquainted with the other residents. I still recall the people who shared our barracks in the gulag. There was Yankel Abend, one of the two sons of an elderly Jewish man who had owned a substantial cattle farm back home. There was Marian Kozik and his father, a widowed university professor. Also in our barracks was a Jewish physician named Tepper with his family, and a Jewish merchant family by the name of Nachman. A young Polish Christian couple named Wieczorek and their five-year-old son Andrzej occupied the bunks next to ours. At bedtime, they offered prayers to Mother Mary.

We all took turns in the *banya*, the baths in a steam-room. Stones were heated red-hot, then cold water was poured on them to create hot steam. A crude arrangement, but it enabled us to cleanse ourselves. We had not had a bath or shower for more than two weeks while traveling in the infamous cattle cars.

What time was left that first day was spent organizing our belongings. Shmulek and I, climbing into our bunks that night, were grateful that Mundek, our older brother, had not been home when the police rounded us up.

Climbing down the next morning, I saw my mother sitting on her bunk, her eyes swollen from crying. Despite her despair, she still looked beyond our imprisonment. "Lusiek," she whispered, "your father and I have decided to register you as twelve and a half years old rather than fifteen. That way, you'll be eligible for school and not have to work in the forest. It will keep your mind occupied; you've always been a good student." During our five years in the camp, they changed my age to fit the situation whenever it seemed advantageous.

Shmulek knew there was no way to avoid the forest work, so he took a brighter view. He was strong and knew how to handle horses. We did not know what mother's assignment would be. Father sought out the commandant, pleading with him to spare his aging wife. Mother was forty years old.

On the second day of our life in Gulag 149, we explored the camp and stopped in at the *stolnica*, or dining hall. We saw fellow countrymen working in the kitchen under the supervision of the chief cook, a local Russian woman. The dining hall had no menu, nor was there need for one, for two soups and kasha were the sole fare offered. *Sup shchi,* cabbage soup with no discernible cabbage except a few leafy particles, and *sup lapsha,* noodle soup in which one had to slosh around to locate a noodle. The kasha was a buckwheat glob. The eating utensil was a wooden spoon, all right for kasha but a challenging implement for soup.

The *stolnica* served better as a kind of town hall. We met some of the other detained people with whom we shared our concerns about being completely cut off from the outside world. No newspapers, no radio. No way of finding out what was happening in England after France's defeat and surrender to Hitler. No way of knowing where Hitler's conquests would end.

The following day, all the able-bodied men and women went off to the forest, led there by Pierogov, the forest manager. I went to the camp office, where I was able to get a brochure describing the geography of the region. By this time, I knew enough Russian to glean some information about Mari, an administrative subdivision of the much larger Russian Soviet Federated Socialist Republic. I learned that in the north it bordered on the Volga River and the Tatar Autonomous Republic, whereas southward lay the Chuvash Autonomous Republic, populated by Turks who had settled in eastern Russia. Most of Mari was forest land — pine, fir, and spruce. Hundreds of small rivers and streams flowed from the Volga into this vast territory. Resources and geography combined to make lumber and timber processing the main industries, with interspersed farming given over to growing potatoes, cereals, and flax.

My innate curiosity about history, spurred by being so close to them, led me to find out what I could about the Mari, a Finno-Ugrian people living west of the Ural Mountains. A mix of Estonian, Finnish, Lapp, Magyar, and Chuvash, which tells a little about the migrations and conquests of the people who criss-crossed the land in past cen-

turies. The confluence of different languages had ultimately combined into Uralic, called Mari, the most widely spoken language in the region. The other language used was
Russian. On the map in the brochure, I located Yoshkar
Ola, the capital of Mari, situated on the Malaya Kokshaga
River, a small tributary of the Volga. At least I now knew
where we were, but I still could not fathom why we were
here. What I did come to understand was the scope of
human slaughter and displacement in the course of territorial conquests. My life meant little in the vast struggle of
combat and the domination of new dominions.

At the end of the third day, the day the men and
women went into the forest, my father and Shmulek
returned dead-tired. They described how dangerous cutting down trees was for the inexperienced. They told us
that the foremen had demonstrated the process only once
and then gone on to another group to do the same.

Local Mari villagers brought our people back in their
horse-drawn carts from the first day's work in the forest.
Seeing these carts harnessed differently from those in
Poland was like a lesson in languages and cultural differences. In Poland, the horse was tethered by leather straps
and chains to one pole linked to the cart. In Mari, carts
were much lower to the ground and had two poles held
together on top by a high wooden bow. The returning men
told us they had been assigned to the heavy, dangerous
work of cutting down the huge trees. The women did the
lighter work, such as cutting the branches from the
downed trees.

When everyone alighted from the carts, I saw further
differences between the Mari and ourselves. They were
shorter, leaner, with paler complexions and blond hair.
What surprised me was the way they were dressed. They
wore the Russian *rubashka*, a typical collarless shirt, and

thick brown pants tucked into strange footwear. Their feet and lower legs were wrapped with strips of thick linen, somewhat like bandages, tucked into sandals made of twigs with two strings laced around the banded legs. This may have been the traditional footwear of the region, but I could not resist feeling that the Great October Revolution, if it had really been so great, should have been able to provide sturdier boots for the citizens of the Workers' Paradise. But then, in Bircza I had seen a Russian soldier buying a tallis and wrapping it around his legs. I could see now how primitive needs were answered in a wilderness.

The Mari were a kind, solicitous people, friendly and sympathetic to our sorry state, but afraid, as we were, to criticize the political system. When someone complained about the harsh conditions and the hard labor exacted from our people, the response was, *"Privyknesh, a jesli ne privik-nesh to zdechnesh"* ("You'll get used to it, and if you don't, you'll drop dead"). Very encouraging and reassuring. Obviously, they had learned to endure. Some had a discharge from their eyes that, as we later learned, was symptomatic of glaucoma, for which they had no medication or medical services.

Although the Mari had small plots of land of their own where they grew some of their food, and were allowed one cow for each farm patch, they worked along with our countrymen in the forest. From their farms, they brought potatoes, three-liter bottles of milk or honey, and occasionally butter to our settlement. My father bartered soap for the food and paid the balance with rubles. These foods were welcome additions to the poor fare we had in the *stolnica,* and mother managed to transform them into palatable soup.

We had another problem those first nights in the barracks. We found ourselves scratching our arms, legs, and bodies. At first, we were inclined to believe it was due to body dirt, but the itching persisted and became unbearable even after we used the steambath. We lit a candle and discovered that the bunks were full of bedbugs.

In the dimly spreading light of the candle, we could see the others in the barracks sitting up and scratching themselves too. Soon everyone was awake, clawing their skin. What could we do? We had no chemical sprays or powders with which to exterminate these pests. I doubt that the Soviets concerned themselves with ridding captive laborers of these creatures.

A common remedy was to pour boiling water on the planks of the bunks. My sister Hella and I found bricks, piled them three high in two rows, gathered dry wood, and put the larger wood chips between the rows. We found scraps of paper to add to the improvised stove. Soviet matches were not very effective, so we had to use several before one finally lit the paper. Blowing hard, with smoke in our eyes and lungs, the fire would finally take hold. We put a bucket of water on the fire and kept feeding wood to it until the water boiled. Meanwhile, mother took the straw mattresses off the bunks. When Hella and I poured the boiling water into and around the exposed planks, swarms of bugs crawled out and we took our revenge.

The war on the bug population was continuous, with never a victory. If killing bugs had been considered an important economic activity, then our barracks would have been decorated for its bountiful contribution to the fulfillment of Stalin's Five Year Plan. An occasional side-benefit of the campaign was the sputtering flame over which mother was able to cook a potato soup for our evening meal. Potatoes were our basic food. We considered ourselves lucky whenever we could get them.

In Gulag 149, concealed from the world in a clearing in the forest primeval, I learned how man survived in the most hostile climate able to provide food and shelter. One day I went with my father and Shmulek to the forest to watch them cutting down trees. First, a wedge was chopped out close to the base of the tree. A corresponding wedge was made on the opposite side of the trunk. Then two men at opposite ends of a rudimentary long saw commenced sawing through the trunk, alert to any change in the sound. At the slightest sound of splitting, each man moved to the side before the tree thundered to the ground. Groups of men and women immediately started to saw off the branches. Limbs removed, the trunk was sawed into specified lengths. The remaining upper sections were used for poles and firewood.

A crude roadway of logs laid side by side on the ground extended from the operating zone to a clearing. Using long poles, the men lifted the trunk, one section at a time, onto the logs, rolled it to the clearing, and there added it to the ever-growing pile of trunks. *Trylovka,* the piling of the long trunks, was the first step in transporting and converting the trunk sections into lumber. A long, tedious process requiring the physically hard labor of many people.

The work was done by brigades. Each brigade was named for its best worker. My father belonged to the Chupka Brigade, so named for Mr. Chupka, a professional engineer heading the team, which consisted of my father, my brother Shmulek, and one other person.

Mr. Chupka had the requisites of a leader. He was a good Christian man, a gentleman. He inspired intelligent, cooperative work, and when he and his team came up with the suggestion to have a horse haul the heavy trunks, the Russian forest foreman gave permission to try the method for a few days. They bound heavy chains around the tree trunk and hitched the load to the horse. The animal pulled it to the pile. This eliminated the backbreaking lifting of

enormously heavy tree trunks. With time and strength con-
served, the results were impressive. The four men of the
Chupka Brigade surpassed the designated quota several
times over. The local camp authorities notified the county
forest authorities about this new process.

It is hard to believe that in a country with vast lumber
resources, simple horsepower was not used to increase
production. I eventually concluded that brainpower was
suppressed, and intelligent suggestions often ignored,
from fear that the incompetence of minor officials would be
revealed, along with Soviet inefficiency.

What the Chupka Brigade grasped quickly was how to
use the system. In the Soviet Union, if you surpassed your
designated production quota, the norm, you were entitled
to many benefits. First, you received a bonus for overpro-
duction. The greater the production, the larger the bonus.
With it went public acknowledgment of your accomplishments, your names posted on the bulletin board, better and
more food, better medical care, clothing, and cooking utensils, and possibly a break, a vacation from work.

The first bonus for the Chupka Brigade was, by Soviet
standards, a hearty meal. The monetary bonus was substantial. The Russians made a dramatic show over this
bonus. The paymaster came monthly from the county and
paid the workers in rubles on the basis of production
achievements. He counted and distributed the rubles in
front of everybody. The Chupka Brigade was paid first, its
special bonus for the month announced. Of course, this was
to impress and encourage other workers to produce more.

The Chupka Brigade's production was so impressive
that leaders from the county and republic forestry departments came to visit our camp and meet the new socialist
working heroes to whom they accorded the honored title of
Stakhanovites, a title named for a renowned coal miner in

the Donbas coal region of the Ukraine who had mined many tons of coal using only a pick and a shovel.

My father became a Hero of Socialist Labor, and I, who had many reasons to admire, respect, and love him, knew he was a man who always seized opportunity and pushed beyond duty if it would benefit his family. My heart embraced him for his devotion to us, for never showing lesser concern for his stepson.

My father also had an inherent magnetism toward higher-ranking officials and the ability to draw interest to himself. I had noticed this in earlier negotiations. I saw it now with the appearance of the two officials from the country forestry department, Comrade Anuchin and Comrade Roller, who made the awards. Oddly, the higher-ranking one was the Frenchman, Comrade Roller. How and why he was in the Soviet Union, in the remote Mari Republic, and how he had superseded the Russian Anuchin was puzzling, but we could only speculate. High-born, fine-mannered scions of the wealthy were sometimes drawn to social causes. Did not Lord Byron, the English poet, when he was thirty-six years old, die in the cause of Greek independence? Perhaps Comrade Roller, very much Byron's age, envisioned himself a leader in the Workers' Paradise. Were the Russians testing his allegiance by sending him to the Mari Socialist Autonomous Republic? Or had he misjudged and misstepped by finding fault with the Communist system? Was he spared execution and exiled, as we were, in this isolated corner of Paradise? An aimless adolescent has little control over his reckless imagination! He weaves fiction in his mind that substitutes for the books he aches to read. The heroes he needs to frame his future are of his own making.

Comrades Roller and Anuchin both took a liking to my father. Comrade Anuchin gave him preferential treatment.

When my father and the other members of the brigade asked for private housing for their families, they were told they would get it when they achieved even higher production norms. The thought of getting out of the barracks, the possibility of obtaining more food, more potatoes, milk, butter, eggs, possibly honey and fresh vegetables, better clothing for their families spurred them on. My father and Shmulek were able to get *valonki*, warm felt boots.

Of course, the Chupka Brigade's awards caused dismay in the camp. One of the men pleaded with my mother to stop father, fearful that the authorities would institute *sotsialisticheskoye sorevnovaniye*, a form of socialist competition under the Five Year Plan that pitted work brigades and individuals against one another to produce more.

"They will impose higher norms of production for everyone else," the man said, groaning about his aching back and legs. "Tell Wenig not to push so hard."

But the opportunity for privileges was uppermost in my father's mind. And before long the Chupka Brigade was exceeding its norms. With the money reward, the men were able to purchase food from the peasants in the surrounding villages. They had no trouble obtaining permits from the camp kommandatura to go outside the camp to buy things from the peasants, for they were Stakhanovites. Father and Shmulek brought back basic foods that supplemented our diet of soup, as well as some *samogon*, homebrewed vodka made from potatoes. The vodka was not so much for father's own use as it was a social bridge for contacts with those in power.

The worst part of our isolation was the powerlessness. There seemed no end, no solution to our predicament. When my father decided to write to his brother Irving again, we took it for an idle whim to give us hope. Anything we wrote would be scrutinized and censored. So the letter was simple: "We are in good health and would like to hear from you." We hoped that our return address would prompt Irving to look at a map to locate Yoshkar Ola in the Mari Republic. Then, if Americans were aware that the Soviets were relocating Polish Jews to work camps, he would be able to draw the proper conclusions. All in all, however, we had little faith in a reply.

Meanwhile, we concentrated on enduring the daily ordeal of barracks life: the public sleeping, the fifty-odd people lining up to use one toilet, the prison food made somewhat better thanks to father's buying permits. As we moved into the middle of August 1940, the authorities told us to start cutting and chopping wood for the coming winter. All the youngsters, both boys and girls, as well as the older women, were pressed into this task. Bracing the logs on a wooden horse, we sawed them into sections. The logs were then chopped into smaller pieces that would fit into the oven.

Then, another of my father's requests was answered. Comrades Roller and Anuchin arrived to inform the men of the Chupka Brigade that they would get their own private living quarters. Each member was permitted to build an *izba*, a one-room hut. The authorities would provide the wood, nails, windows, and bricks for a stove. Hallelujah! Our own room! Our own outhouse! The five Wenigs would have privacy at last! Father had made this possible! He shyly dismissed our show of joy. Perhaps he understood the gesture and its impact on the others, for whom this was a showpiece, an impetus to produce more and be rewarded for it—the Stakhanovite strategy.

However, my father moved quickly to complete the *izba* before winter set in. He received beams for structural frames, tools, and other supplies, but no boards for siding. Logs would have to be sawed into usable boards. In the camp there were two native Russians who were skilled in this type of work. With the offer of pay, they were glad to help with the work, as well as to show us how to do it.

A long, unfinished log would be extended across two wooden horses somewhat taller than a man's height and set several meters apart. Taking a ruler to the log, the two Russians measured and pencil-marked the widths they wanted to cut. One of them climbed atop the log, and the other stood directly underneath. Starting at one end, with a two-handled saw, they worked their way along the length of the log, sawing it into planks. A backbreaking tedious process, one that Noah must have used when he built his ark thousands of years ago. How else but with crude tools could this have been accomplished? In Gulag 149, we were not in the electric-powered age.

The *izba* was finished about the first week of September 1940. We moved out of the barracks and into our one-room castle. Inside was a stove for warmth and cooking. Hella and I no longer had to blow like bellows to start a fire under a brick contraption. Best of all, we had our own out-house. Forget plumbing. We continued to lug buckets of drinking water from the communal well. Our beds were still bunks, and we still slept on mattresses made from burlap sacks and straw, but we no longer had the nightly combat with bedbugs, what a luxury! The Chupka Brigade became the envy of the camp.

The one added chore for me, which I did not mind doing, was chopping logs for firewood. It was for our own needs. The first day, in the glow and warmth of our new stove, we appreciated the primitive comfort of our own shelter. From the new iron pot which my father had been given by the Soviet state as a Stakhanovite, wafted the aroma of the potato soup my mother was stirring for our first meal in the *izba*. This time the soup was enriched with onions and parsley. What with the strange Russian bread, pirogi (potato dumplings), and tea with milk, we celebrated our first meal in our new room.

Practically all of our meals, every day of the week, were one form or another of potatoes. That was our mainstay. We had no meat and would not have eaten it anyway because it would not have been kosher. We would never eat non-kosher food. We were classed lower than peasants; we had less and ate less.

A few days later, like manna from heaven, news arrived. Uncle Irving had received our letter and had understood that we were not in the foothills of Siberia for a luxury vacation. He sent us two parcels with astounding contents: cans of meat and fish, chocolate bars, jars of jam, cubes of dried vegetable soup. Each item was as carefully handled as fine blown glass. We turned the cans and jars to get the full effect of the packaging, colors, and designs. We wanted to taste the American delicacies, but we had been prisoners too long to think of gorging ourselves.

My parents decided that we would eat these foods when there was a dire emergency. Better still, my father knew the value of these articles. He held up a can of coffee and with a glint in his fiercely dark eyes said, "Do you know what a *nachalnik* [government official] would do for this?" His eyelids lowered over the dreams he did not want escaping. "Maybe farfetched, but it's possible. A permit to leave for America or Palestine."

Maybe. But his first negotiation was for medical care. Father was beginning to suffer bad arthritic pain in his thighs. He worried about the consequences of falling behind the work quotas. He worried about the effects upon the family.

With these concerns, he invited Comrade Anuchin to our *izba*. Father's faculty for winning the confidence of others was exceptional. He had Comrade Anuchin telling us about his life in Russia before the Revolution. He was not from a proletarian family and had obviously studied forestry. He did not forthrightly come out with it, but he gave the impression that he had offended officialdom and in consequence been sent to the Mari Republic, where he became the head of the county department of forests. To my young mind, his life story was interesting, nothing more. My father, more astute, saw him as vulnerable and as a potential agent to help us.

My father brought out two cans of the meat we had received from my uncle. Comrade Anuchin, of course, was amazed. He examined the English lettering, commented on the fancy wrapping, showed his appreciation of the product.

"I am happy to share our gift from America, Comrade Anuchin," father said, smiling while he closed the man's hands around the cans. "A man has to do for another man, in this far-removed country."

The parrying started. "To survive, yes."

"To give our best efforts. Always. For the country."

"You are an example, Comrade Wenig."

"As long as I am able."

As if by instinct, we all rose from the table and moved to another part of the room, leaving father and Comrade Anuchin alone. Father took out the *samogon* and two glasses. He poured a hearty drink for his guest, took small sips himself.

"When a man finds he is not as able," my father continued, "and has trouble with his legs, can he come to you?"

Comrade Anuchin gestured toward the bottle. My father handed it to him, but he wanted a promise of assistance before the man got drunk. In Russia, people do not drink socially, they drink until they get drunk.

"I have this bad pain in my leg," father was saying now. "The local health clinic can't do anything for it. They have no medication, and you know, the feldsher doesn't know that much. The doctors are under strict orders to grant excuses from work only if a person is very seriously ill."

Comrade Anuchin nodded in agreement and poured another glass for himself. He gestured to father to go on.

Having established a comradely feeling, father went further. "I wonder if you could arrange for me to be sent to the hospital in Morki."

"I'll look into it." At this point, Comrade Anuchin's eyes began to glaze. He filled his glass. He was filled with sympathy, and what spilled over was his own complaints.

"Communism is a disaster, there is no hope, no prayer for its success. Stalin, the bastard, should rot in hell."

Comrade Anuchin's flow of invective and hatred for the system frightened father. The man could face the firing squad for this traitorous babbling. Father stood up and, seeing that Anuchin was unsteady on his feet, carried him out to his wagon, where his driver was waiting to take him back to Morki. Father was visibly shaken by the experience and hoped no ill would befall us because of the man's loose tongue.

The next morning, a sober Comrade Anuchin came to our house before father and Shmulek went to work.

"What did I tell you last night?"

Father shrugged and said nothing.

"You must forget anything I said about Communism. You're a good man, Don't say anything to anyone. I promise I'll try to help you, but don't utter a word."

"There's no reason to worry," father assured him, "I never heard a word against the government. You are a loyal Russian." Father repeatedly assured him that he had nothing to fear from Comrade Wenig.

For whatever reason, to buy father's trust or exhibit his influence, Comrade Anuchin arranged for father to be taken to the hospital in Morki, where he spent more than a week, during which time he received injections for his condition. They seemed to help.

There was great distress in Gulag 149 on the day we experienced our first tragedy. Young Landau, an architect, was killed instantly when a tree he was cutting down in the forest cracked and crushed him. In one moment, his heartbeat stalled, his voice stilled. The heart and voice of a young man who, like myself, had not yet explored the mysteries of life and love. A youngster whose strong legs might have led him out of the deep dark wilderness, whose mute struggle against indignity will never be known. When his body was brought back in a horse-drawn flat cart, the prisoners of Gulag 149 milled about, troubled and distressed, in mourning. It was as if the death of one were a death knell for all. If we screamed out of pain and loss, who would hear us? If we had the poison stings of the bee when the hive is disturbed, we would have swarmed and raised welts on the oppressor. In a thousand ways, our minds devised restitution for putting humans in peril.

Before young Landau could be buried, the feldsher had to examine the body. With a grave expression and soft words of condolence to Landau's family in the camp, the feldsher wrote out the death certificate. Inherently a decent man, he decried the employment of untrained and inexperienced people in the dangerous work of the forest. An error on his part. He was overheard by cohorts of the system and disappeared shortly after this incident. We could not help but wonder what transgression had brought him to this outpost. Where would they send him now? What would they do to him?

Numbed and sullen, the men and women went back to felling the trees, to the ordinary chores and routines. The silence of the forest closed around the camp, and a new feldsher for the clinic arrived. A young attractive Russian woman who came with a younger sister. Speculation became rampant again; surely no one came here willingly. Had they been separated from their parents? Had they been sent here as a form of punishment? Had they voiced grievances against the Communist system? Later, during the winter months, after the new feldsher had been with us awhile, one of the fellows in the barrack, Yankel Abend, fell in love with her and married her.

When the new feldsher arrived, in late summer, we were hustling along in preparation for the winter. The commandant announced that a shipment of *kufaikas* (jackets) and *bryuki* (pants) had arrived, and were to be distributed by the store manager, Mielnikov, to everyone in the camp. The clothing was made of thickly quilted gray cotton and made us look like clumsy, roly-poly, mechanized bundles wobbling about in the clearing. The clothing was practical, we were told, and would protect us against the brutal winter. My father and Shmulek already had *valonki*, (leg and foot coverings), and galoshes to put over them. Kierbaczok, the stable manager, we found out, wished he had more coverings for the camp's horses.

Along with the winter clothing came notice of registration for schoolchildren. There were to be two grades: one for those below twelve, and the other for those who were older. Although I was close to sixteen, my parents designated my age as twelve and a half years old. I qualified for the upper grade. We had two female teachers. My teacher, Zoya Ivanovna, was blonde, had a full round face and blue eyes, and although chubby was somewhat attractive. Ate too many potatoes, I surmised. The same could be said of the round and tubby teacher of the younger children. She was very short, tied her black hair back in a pony tail.

The dull brooding summer over at last, I was going back to school. The order of books on the shelves, the very smell of books teased my appetite for learning. I wanted very much to continue my education. Very few of the pupils in my class had any knowledge of Russian. I was already able to read and speak the language, and liked the sound of it. I liked the images conjured up by its nouns and verbs, was eager to read Russian literature and poetry, learn Russian history, sing Russian songs, and in general probe the complexities of math and science.

Our first day in school was devoted to introductory procedures and a liberal exposure to Communist propaganda. There was a native Russian girl in my class by the name of Valia; her father, the camp carpenter, had been banished to the Mari Republic. Again, I wondered why. Had he complained about the system, run into political difficulty, was he listed with "enemies of the working class"? Rhetorical questions. Who was going to give me an answer? Answers to questions were sealed in caskets. It was wiser to think about school.

Zbyszek Chupka, a Polish Christian boy, the son of the leader of my father's brigade, was in my class, as was Ludwig Poremba, a wild, uninhibited spokesman against the system. When the teacher, Zoya Ivanovna, championed the great achievements of the Russian people under the Communist system, its free education, free medical care, the right of every citizen to have a job, Ludwig squirmed and muttered under his breath. When she told us of the great accomplishments of the Five Year Plan and how Comrade Stalin labored long hours for *blaga narodow* (the good of all the people of the Soviet Union), Ludwig asked:

"Does he saw lumber in Siberia?"

Ludwig was lucky she disregarded his interruptions and continued the line of propaganda she was instructed to teach.

"The output of tractors and machinery being built by the Communist workers is for the people on the collective farms, who are now the owners of the land, and not for the big landowners of the tsarist regime."

Unconvinced, too intelligent to accept statements without proofs, Ludwig blurted out, "Great machinery, Soviet trucks that run on wood chips, engines that have to be fed continuously, more efficient than gasoline? Have you ever been in one of those Soviet trucks?" he dared ask, like us having been brought to the camp in a ramshackle Soviet truck. "What a big joke, talking about what the Communists are producing."

He showed no fear, no dread of punishment for his unpatriotic slanders. At a time when the crime of one reflected on all, I worried about his unbridled criticism because he was Jewish.

We sat in numbed silence, Zoya turned pale. She changed the topic, becoming more academic. She discussed literature, told us about the Russian poet Pushkin, introduced us to Lermontov, another great writer, and Maxim Gorky, the writer of the people. She read from Gorky's *Sketches and Stories*. Stories about the vigor and valor of the peasants and workers.

"Gorky was a true revolutionary," she said; "he was the father of Soviet literature."

She was glorious when she read the poetry of Mayakovsky.

For those brief hours in the shack we called school, I was in a world transformed. The maps of the Soviet Union became real fields, rivers, and mountains, and I wandered through the constituent republics, visiting their capital cities. Geography and history had always been my favorite subjects. I hoped the class would learn current events, so we could hear how the war was progressing.

"What happened to the eastern part of Poland which the Russians now occupy?" one student asked.

"It is now called Western Ukraine and is a part of the Ukrainian Socialist Republic," Zoya responded.

As if on cue, she had her opening to talk about the October Revolution, organized and inspired by the great Lenin, the great leader Stalin, and their comrade-in-arms, Marshal Kliment Voroshilov.

"Does anyone know any Soviet songs?" she now asked.

When no one responded, she called on the only Russian girl in the class, Valia, to sing to us. Valia was a cute blonde girl with an upturned nose and pursed lips. She was pretty enough to hold our attention and surprised us with her sweet-sounding voice. She sang "Raskinolos Morie Shiroko," a beautiful song about a sailor at sea. She then sang another song, a Communist song, about Stalin and the dynamic activities in Moscow.

After a recess, Zoya Ivanovna wrote some arithmetic examples on the blackboard. Next, as a first step in teaching us Russian, she wrote out the Cyrillic alphabet, truly a foreign language to students new to the country. We knew only the Latin alphabet. She was patient and pronounced the names of the letters as if she were offering us compliments. She taught all the subjects and knew them well.

I walked home with my sister Hella and two of her classmates, Lola and Leszek Kohane. When I asked them what they had learned, they answered, as if in chorus, "How great the Soviet Union is, how heroic its leaders are, how much better off Russia has become since the overthrow of the tsar."

When my father and Shmulek, weary and humorless, returned from the forest, we sat down to our daily potato soup, kasha, and tough black bread. Than we told them what we had been taught our first day in school.

"I want you to listen, you Hella especially," my mother declared, her sad eyes beseeching us.

"The Communists want to influence children with their propaganda. Do you remember what you were told in Lwów when the teacher stood in the front of the class and ridiculed the grace we say, 'God gives us bread.' How she sneered when she asked, 'Did God give you bread? Stalin gives you bread!' Then some teachers came into the class-room with trays of white rolls and distributed them."

"They don't want you to believe in God. They want you to follow in their footsteps," my father cautioned. "Remember, keep your faith and hold your tongue."

We promised him we would. We would take advan-tage of the education offered and learn what was useful, but would reject everything else.

The following day, we clustered around Ludwig Poremba. We thought he was very brave to challenge the teacher. But Ludwig, his dark flashing eyes blinking, his rosy cheeks pale, told us that during the night he had been awakened from his sleep, hauled to the kommandatura, and severely scolded by the camp commander, Zakharov.

"They threatened to take me away from my parents and said I would never see them again if I made any more disparaging remarks about the system."

Obviously, our teacher had reported him to the author-ities. I suppose she had no alternative. But Ludwig, whom I liked because he had a keen, inquiring mind, was quite chastened after that. Actually, he was lucky, for any other NKVD commander would have severely punished his boldness. Zakharov had been rather lenient. We were soon to learn what this would cost him. In a system built on force and oppression, minor officials gain favors from the powers that be by spying on their superior officers and reporting lapses to higher authority. Such a system is like an acrobatic circus act that needs a wide base of brute power to support it. To watchful eyes, although we did not know it at the time, Zakharov's light reprimands and threats were a sign of weakness. The whole act could crumble and we would all be caught in the crush.

The threat to one was felt by all. On that second day of school, we took our seats noiselessly, submissively. There were no further outbursts. We had the same subjects and schedule as on the first day and were assigned quite a bit of homework. Each of us received textbooks, notebooks, pencils, an eraser, a pen, and a small jar of ink. We listened to more tales of the heroes of the October Revolution. There was Comrade Chapayev, a hero, Marusha Vandalenko, a heroine. Zoya Ivanovna dramatically described the storming of the Winter Palace in St. Petersburg, the bombardment by the guns of the cruiser *Aurora* anchored offshore in the Neva River, the surrender of the forces of Kerensky's counter-revolutionary Provisional Government.

"The starving, oppressed peasants rose up against their rulers," echoed our small teacher, her voice infused with patriotism. Her eyes scanned the room, while her outstretched arms moved as if to encompass us. "Today every child is educated. Under the tsar, children had no schooling, no opportunity to improve themselves. The landowning aristocracy was not going to surrender its power. There was civil war. The counter-revolutionary White armies under General Denikin and Admiral Kolchak fought to preserve their property and status but were defeated. Those not killed went into exile."

Zoya Ivanovna was feeding knowledge to a starving Jewish boy. In the absence of food, knowledge was as strong a need. The desire to live and learn waged constant battle with despondency. I listened to her history lesson with rapt attention until she said, "Those not killed went into exile."

Our exile had no such history. I ached to tell her this, tell anyone, tell God. We still had faith in Him, so why our misery? Every time my mind took this track, I suffered the numbing effect of depression. I drifted away until her persuasive voice sang with poetry. I looked to see whether my classmates were responding the way I did. I saw disciplined students paying attention, but here and there a tear or a trembling lip revealed their struggle to understand. Only two or three, like me, knew enough Russian to follow her. Most were struggling to learn the roots and grasp the vocabulary. It was possible by appending or affixing the roots to the simple words needed to converse.

I found comfort in the stories and poetry we read, particularly the pre-Revolutionary writers, the masters of Russian literature. I willingly memorized the assigned poems because their messages were consoling. One by Pushkin stays in my mind, a poem dedicated to the political exiles of the Decembrist uprising in 1825 when a group of progressive noblemen rose against the autocratic tsarist regime. Although they were arrested and executed or sent into exile in Siberia, Pushkin thought of them as heroes because they had defied the despots of his time.

Fifty years have since passed, but I learned his poem because the words were so meaningful then and now, so promising of freedom for me. I can still recite them in Russian:

Sibir,
Vglubino Sibirskikh rud
Khranitye gordoye terpeniye
Ne propadyet vash skorbny trud
I dum vysokoye stremlenye
Okovy tyazhkiye padut
Temnitsa rukhnut i cvobodu
Ras primyat u vkhoda radostno
I bratya mech vam otdadut

In the well-known translation by Max Eastman it reads
as follows:

Message to Siberia
Deep in the Siberian mine,
Keep your patience proud;
The bitter toil shall not be lost,
The rebel thought unbowed.
. . . .
The heavy-hanging chains will fall,
The walls will crumble at a word;
And Freedom greet you in the light,
And brothers give you back the sword.[1]

We also had to memorize a poem by Lermontov about
Napoleon's invasion of Russia in 1812. The most important
battle of that war was waged near the town of Borodino,
the approach to Moscow, where Napoleon's army was victorious but grievously weakened. Here is a portion, in my
own translation:

Skazhika dyadya,
Viet nie darom Moskva spalonaya pozharom
Frantsuzom otdana
Viet zhe byli svatki doragye
Da govaryat yeshcho takiye
Nye darom pomnit vsya Rossiya pro dyen Borodina.

Tell me, uncle,
Not for no reason was Moscow given up to the French.
After all, there were heavy battles there.

[1]"Message to Siberia," translated by Max Eastman, in *The Poems, Prose and Plays of Alexander Pushkin*, edited by Avrahm Yarmolinsky (New York: Modern Library, 1936), pp. 62–63.

It is for that reason
That Russia remembers the day at Borodino.

Oddly, these poems dispelled my gloom and gave me hope. Even the songs, patriotic and martial, separated me from the conditions outside the classroom. When Zoya Ivanovna told me, as she did everyone in the class, to stand up and sing one of the songs, I sang with fervor, as I had with our cantor back in Dynów when he had trained me for my Bar Mitzvah. I did not realize it, but she was testing our voices. My classmates liked my voice, and so did the teacher. She told me that one day I would sing solo. I had no idea what her prediction meant.

The rustic school was, in its own way, a sanctuary. I was in a juvenile world where banishment and hardship were suspended. While in the classroom, and until I once again stepped out into the chilling scenes of the settlement, I was wrapped in the euphoria of learning. Then, when I looked at what was now home, a mantle of gloom shrouded my body. I remembered how in former days I would come home to my mother's gentle kiss, a sweet snack she had prepared for Hella and me, eager and curious questions about our lessons. Now her tearful eyes, her hopelessness, her deep despair about our possibilities for survival in this remote clearing was what would greet us. When we pointed out the improvement in our housing, it did little to cheer her.

She cried constantly. "We are going to die here in this wilderness, and nobody will know where we are or what happened to us."

It was this statement, more than anything else, that revealed to me the fragility of our life, how absolutely necessary it is for humans to document their struggles and survival, how inconsequential human life is if no record is kept. Without a record of human experience, life becomes purposeless, as if lived in a void. With nothing to set it apart from the life of an insect that crawls about sniffing and snipping at its patch of sustenance. I did not know then what an imprint was being made on my mind by historical events. How the impact of the displacement of people had conquered my young mind. What an impression man imbued by human resources makes on his children. I was in awe of the ways my parents and other adults constantly found to help them survive the hardships and sorrows of life in our century.

All this while, as the brief autumn season grew colder, my father and Shmulek went to the forest, bracing their backs for the hewing of trees, and returned long hours later, dead-tired, with barely enough strength to finish the day with the bowl of potato soup and kasha which they ate by the dim light of the kerosene lamp on the table. After our meal, Hella and I did our homework on the same table. Something reassuring came from the evening time together. Shmulek or I would feed the oven with wood to keep the fire going. We would talk about family, friends, and old times in Poland, so as to feel united and keep our courage going. We were starved for news. The outside world was just that, out there somewhere where wars were being fought, battles won or lost, destinies decided by despots. It is for these reasons that I remember the settlement of Ozero.

In this bleak outpost, any change was tantamount to news and caused a flurry of activity. One day, a new NKVD officer arrived in the camp. We trembled at the sight of him. Was this good or bad for us? We kept our distance, but the Russian stableman, frightened just as we were, watched him carefully and passed news as fast as a wireless.

We learned that the officer, a lieutenant, was a Tatar. That was enough to terrify us. Every European schoolboy had learned about the Tatar hordes who had ridden with Genghis Khan on his march of conquest through Turkistan, Persia, and Siberia. Aleiev, the Tatar, was tall, with penetrating brown eyes. In his impressive military coat, he had a slim but powerful build. His headgear had a very sharp point on top, with flaps that could be rolled down for protection against the cold. The lieutenant strode about the camp, stopping talk to some workers who were on their way to work in the forest. He bawled them out for being late. He accused them of violating the law of *Progul*. They slunk away fearfully, carrying their axes and saws.

Fierce-looking in his military attire, Aleiev turned to Zakharov, the camp commandant, and railed against him in a booming voice. One of the women stepped to the commandant's side and asked what he was doing in the camp.

He snapped back with the cryptic declaration, "*My vas zastavim robotyat. U nas yest zakonov*" ("We'll make you work. We have laws to that effect"). He was evidently there to observe conditions in the camp, and, as we suspected, to report on Zakharov. When he left after a few days, Zakharov was nowhere to be seen. Many of the camp inmates shrugged "What do you expect? A commandant who allows workers to slack off or who stops to say *zdravstvuyte* [hello] can't be much of an enforcer. He doesn't enforce Soviet obedience. His usefulness is questionable."

Zakharov was put on trial, a blow to us, for having failed to report the first feldsher's disparaging statements against the system. He was charged, further, with failing to enforce the law of *Progul*, allowing workers to come late or not report for work, and for permitting some of the women to do no work at all. He was accused of making advances to my teacher, Zoya Ivanovna.

The main witness who testified against him was one of his deputies, Moiseyev. Zakharov acted in his own defense. To our surprise, he was feisty and fought the accusations.

"We have people here who come from a bourgeois society. They are bewildered by the scope and goals that socialism offers. I have been going slowly and have been making good progress. Look at our school, it is working well, the children will eventually embrace the Communist system."

Moiseyev scoffed at Zakharov's "progress."

"And what about your affair with Zoya Ivanovna? Are you making progress there, too?" His accuser made a scandal of their collaborative efforts and prodded him on every concession to young and old in the camp, building up a case of dereliction of supervision.

There was a limit to what we were allowed to see as spectators. Obviously anything that scored for the controlling officers was done to impress us with their power over us. Zakharov did not accept their harsh protocol; an intelligent man, he had never abused us or used foul language. Whenever we encountered a officer like Zakharov, we concluded that he was of a better class or had run into trouble with the system. Why else would he have been assigned to this miserable place? We spoke of his predicament with pity.

Serious concerns surfaced for us after the trial and Zakharov's disappearance. How had the higher-ups found out about his violations? Who was telling them about people not reporting to work on time? How had they learned about Zakharov's simple but honest criticisms of the system? Who was the "bird" among us who was spying for the Soviet authorities? Whom do you trust? We were not permitted to attend the full court hearings. These perplexities remained with us.

I had my own suspicions. Andzia was a tall Polish Christian girl who worked in the *zaklad* (store) where we received our *payok* (rations of bread, marmalade, kasha, and other provisions). She was brusque and tough, her long blonde hair doing little to soften her masculine movements. Why did this strong young woman, not more than thirty years old, have an easy job in the store when she was more physically fit to hew logs? To me, it suggested preferential treatment, and I have to admit I was wary of her.

A few days later, the new commandant, Zolotov, arrived. Short, stocky, dour, tough, and humorless, he was a typical apparatchik. Under his supervision, people reported on time. No one was excused from work because of illness. Appealing to the new feldsher, Anna, for a exemption certificate was pointless. Now married to Yankel, one of the prisoners, she was under constant scrutiny herself.

Tight supervision constrained our movements, but father and Shmulek found favor and were given a permit to go to one of the nearby villages, where they were able to buy beets, cabbage, and dried mushrooms. This was like finding a treasure trove. When mother added these vegetables to our potato soup, we felt we were dining sumptuously.

The carved furniture, draperies, silver, of our Polish home were dimming in our memory. Values changed with our changed circumstances. We were in a cold, heartless environment slurping potato soup, grateful for anything to add to the pot.

I was continually amazed by my father's ability to find resources and befriend people who could be of use to him. He soon had a collective farmer bringing him butter and honey, occasionally some eggs. In the months of our exile, I had forgotten the velvety sweetness of a soft-boiled egg.

Food was constantly on my mind. Food was also uppermost in the mind of the government. Winter was coming and produce would be scarce.

Zoya Ivanovna informed the class one day in October that it was our duty to help the collective farmers in the area harvest the potatoes before the snows fell.

"Students and factory workers are needed to harvest the crops of the large collective farms. The farmers need extra hands," she preached.

Everyone in the class was taken by horse and wagon to the potato farm. The farmhouse we stopped at, owned or reserved for supervisors, had one large room, the *izba*, where the family slept, ate, and gathered for social purposes. There was a big stove in the middle of the room, and a very large wooden table. On the table was a tall samovar surrounded by tea cups. Several students were housed together in the attic. We burrowed into the hay intended as our beds and covered ourselves with thin blankets, but did not sleep very well because we were cold.

The following morning, we were called to breakfast. Sitting in the *izba* with the farmer and his wife was another person, probably someone important, whom they addressed with a patronymic name, a prefix added to indicate lineage. This man did not say much. He sipped his tea and kept watching us. We talked little, being afraid and not knowing what to say. The host seemed cautious too, but he urged us to eat as much bread as we wanted. The home-baked black bread tasted better than the bread in the camp. We also had homemade marmalade which they scooped out of a large stone crock. We took tea from the samovar. The owner himself drank many cups of tea, but his mouth was clamped shut most of the time. Nobody ventured to talk about politics or conditions in the country.

After breakfast, we were driven out to a huge field where a foreman showed us how to harvest the potatoes.

We dug up potatoes until the noon break. Then we saw that they had made a fire and put on the tea kettle to boil. The same plain black bread and tea were our lunch. We spent the long afternoon working diligently again.

Before the day ended, I had a picture of how things were. There were several collective farmers working in the field, mostly women, but neither they nor the men over-worked themselves. It became clear why the schoolchildren and city factory workers had been mobilized to gather the harvest. The collective farmers had little to gain from their labor. They told us they were not paid in rubles, and instead received what they called *trudo dnei*, an amount based on how many days they worked. With little compensation came little effort. From time to time, I saw collective farmers walking off the field with sacks of potatoes. It did not take much to deduce that they were stealing whatever they could. They ignored the rules about socialist property. They did not fear authorities the way we schoolchildren did. We worked hard and took our work seriously. The resonance of authority within us threatened our lives. We were prisoners, and the farm work earned our right to live.

In all probability, the farmers knew we were Polish Jews and did not think we could understand what they were saying. They resented us because we seemed better dressed. How could they know that this was the last vestige of self-esteem in our barren lives.

They were a coarse, rough bunch, sitting on their haunches in the middle of the field, pouring themselves cups of samogon vodka, and speaking freely to one another in Russian. I soon recognized the vulgarities they used so frequently—words boys learn long before they hear Pushkin's poetry. Every sentence ended with the words *"yob tvoyu mat"* ("fuck your mother").

"I had a fight with my wife this morning. Fuck your mother," a man would say. "This is one cold morning. Fuck your mother," another would answer. "We're going to get snow soon. Fuck your mother."

Not much more would comprise a conversation. They relished the chance to vent their anger with foul language. And anger was there against the degrading treatment by the officials.

The women looked worn and weary, stooped and shabby. By this time I had seen enough to know that Russian women worked in the fields as well as in their homes. They had little self-respect.

When it was time to return to the farmhouse, our foreman told us to come back to the fields after dinner for a bonfire and entertainment. We had soup—cabbage soup, of course—bread and marmalade, and tea, and talked about going to the bonfire. Some of the students were too tired and retired to the attic. The host again urged us to eat as much as we wanted.

I joined the group that was to meet at the entrance to the field. Walking toward the field, I saw two women stop, squat, and urinate in the middle of the street. Startled, shocked, and sorry for them, I compared them with Polish women, who would never act so shamelessly. In my hometown in Poland, a man would greet a woman by saying, *"Caluje roczki"* ("I kiss your hand") and would actually do so. It was a show of respect. I learned to bow and kiss the hands of women and girls. We were a romantic people. I was a romantic person and early on knew the flattery of a kiss and a poem. Repulsed by the scene and the vulgar talk in the field, I wondered what their entertainment would be like.

As we approached the bonfire, I saw a young man playing an accordion. The peasants sang and clapped to the fast and lively *krestyanskaya,* as the peasant songs were called. My body responded to the merry melodies. Russian lyrics and melodies are robust, a vigorous contrast to the squalor of peasant life, so full of inner energy and hope, so full of echoes of our conditions. I yearned to raise my voice with theirs. I and my companions felt the same longings that were expressed in their songs. Would it be treason to sing with them?

I didn't dare confide my feelings. Listening ears might betray me. The rhythms, the lusty reedy sounds of the accordion, the voices doled out lightness to a shackled body. Shy and restrained, I listened and watched until young and old gathered around the bonfire to rake out the roasted potatoes. They gave one to each of the students. The smoky taste was good.

Then, to my surprise, a few older men started to open up about the work on the collective farms. One whiskered old man with thick eyebrows that shaded his eyes scoffed at the whole scene. *"My rabot ni boitsa, na chui robotat budyem."* A vulgar encapsulation of the situation: "We aren't afraid of work, but we're not going to work for a prick!" These were rough, tough, coarse field workers whose existence depended upon their toil, and who accepted their hard life, but that did not make them submissive to brutalizing conquerors, whether tsars or Communist bureaucrats. They expressed their resented subservience by sloth, curses, and disregard for their supervisors. They were impervious to shouts and whips. They gave little thought to schoolchildren and city laborers drafted to harvest their crops. We were ears to hear their gripes. We were faces that were a bit friendlier than their overseer.

In a gesture of goodwill, they offered their horses to the students to ride to the fields. I, who had watched them ride their horses wildly through the countryside, their hair whipping in the wind, their legs butted to the horses' sides, impulsively thought of this as pleasure. But mounting a horse without stirrups, controlling the horse without the security of the leather foot supports, riding without a saddle, I quickly found it terrifying. I held tightly to the reins. My legs didn't seem long enough to grip the girth of the horse. I rode slowly and carefully through the potato fields, not raising my eyes, which were fastened on every forward hoof stride. I could feel the life of the horse pounding within him, matching the heavy pounding of my own heart. Every time my body came down on the horse's backbone, pain shot through my groin. I had to admire the rugged peasants, but wondered if they had padding in their pants or callouses on their bottoms. They were showmen atop their horses, galloping wildly down the roads. I hoped my future would offer saddled horses to ride through meadow lanes.

The peasants were indifferent to the demands of the system. They were often late for work, and what they harvested was a poor showing of produce. The students brought in most of the crop. When we finished a large field, a driver came through on his tractor with multiple hoes. Our foreman explained that the driver and tractor came from the Machine Tractor Station, which owned all the farm equipment. The workers at the station were responsible for the plowing and any harvesting that could be done by machine. They were compensated with money rather than produce like the collective farmers. Taken all together, it was not hard to understand the grumpiness and laxity of the farmers. They received no incentives. They stole what they could from the fields and put their time and effort into their own small private plots.

With the harvesting over, we returned to the camp, where our parents embraced us as if we had returned from another, more awful gulag. They were grateful that we had not been sent away to "children's houses" by the ever-present secret police. "Comrades" could easily banish and erase the life of any person they thought disloyal.

Our teacher, Zoya Ivanovna, thanked us on behalf of the Soviet government and specifically the Soviet people for doing a good job. With a serious face, she praised our performance, announcing: "You have touched Russian soil and fulfilled your socialist obligation."

How naive of her to think that the earthy smell and heavy bushels of potatoes made us converts to Communism. She was full of patriotic pride in all matters of state and glowed when she announced that there was to be a celebration in camp of the twenty-third anniversary of the great October Revolution. Our school was to participate by performing on the evening of November 6 for the local Russian workers. Everyone in camp would attend. There would be speeches, and we students were to read poems extolling the heroic deeds of the Soviet leaders and participate in the choral singing; the good singers would be soloists.

Soon auditions were held. Valia, the Russian girl in my class, was one of the selected soloists, and I, too, was chosen for that honor. I dreaded having to sing a Communist propaganda song, but fortunately, the song was "Orlonok," which tells of an eagle who flies above the sun to sing a song. A beautiful melody that I can still remember, one that Jewish survivors of the Nazi concentration camps adapted to express their caged existence.

Rumors also circulated about special foods, particularly white bread, bound for the camp in honor of the Great October Revolution. To our amazement, we did get white bread, biscuits, canned meat, honey, candies, and other sweets for the children. With undisguised cynicism, we whooped: "Hooray for the Great October Revolution!" To comment privately on the grand display without arousing suspicion, we could only whisper among ourselves: "Was it really necessary to have the October Revolution in order to get white bread?" We were becoming adept at disguise, learning the strategy of survival, jokes and ironic gibes.

The foods, of course, were welcome, since we had not eaten white bread since leaving Poland. Biscuits, honey, and candy were real treats, a pleasant relief from the monotonous poor food we ate every day. The problem was what to do with the big cans of meat, surely not kosher. They were filled with mutton in sauce, a product disdained back in Poland. Here, where a blanket of snow already covered isolated Gulag 149 in the village of Ozero, canned meat was a delicacy. My parents deliberated long and hard on this question. They could refuse to eat it, or could give their emaciated children some palatable, nourishing food. Again calculations about survival prevailed. My mother, Miriam Kasser Wenig, the daughter of the wealthy Leib Kasser of the town of Dynów, now living in the infamous Gulag 149 in the village of Ozero, Siberia, Russia, had to weigh her options very carefully. With her intelligent mind and worldly outlook, still ever the practical one, she said: "God will understand and forgive us."

The celebration on November 6 had all the pomp and circumstance that an exiled community could rig up. From a dais for the local potentates of the Soviet system, the county leader delivered the opening address on the significance of the event. He introduced the other occupants of the dais, then called on NKVD officer Zolotov, our new commandant, to speak of the great accomplishments of the Soviet people, inspired by the great leader Stalin.

Zolotov, hypnotic in his stern martial stance, reeled off production figures. Enumerating how many tractors had been built, how many tons of steel had been poured, how many tons of wheat, barley, and cotton had been raised, how many cows had calved, how many liters of milk had been delivered, how many eggs collected, how many tons of oil pressed, and how many trees cut down. His voice droned on, reading from lists of farm stocks and quotations from local sources. Although the reports, undoubtedly being rendered all over the Soviet Union, bored us, we had no choice but to listen and applaud. He ended his speech with: "Long live the Communist Party. Long live the wise and great inspirer of the Soviet people, Comrade Stalin."

Not applauding vigorously would throw one open to a late-night interrogation. We were aware that police informers were watching us and reporting everything. Any of the Russians, or any camp inmate looking for favors, could be spying on us. Like programmed puppets, we responded even as we wrestled with sarcastic questions about the scruples of the Soviet leaders. The production figures were incomplete: how many people had the NKVD shot this year? Surely that too had surpassed the "norm." How many people had died in the gulags? Not enough to brag about?

Heavy-hearted, I now had to join my fellow pupils in the recitation of poems and compositions about the heroic accomplishments of the Soviet leaders and workers. The choral group had to sing martial revolutionary songs along with innocuous folk ballads. Then Valia rendered her song about a Soviet flier who soars into the wild blue yonder, sending sky-writing greetings to Comrade Stalin.

My solo performance was next on the program. My voice resonated with the opening strains of "Orlonok," and I could see the pride in my teacher's eyes. Perhaps it was that, perhaps faulty adolescent vocal chords, perhaps my conscience was scrapping with me for participating in a tribute to Soviet ideals, but suddenly my voice cracked. I felt the blood rush to my head, struggling with the words, the melody lost. I wanted to run off the stage, but Zoya Ivanovna urged me on, directing me to keep singing. My voice was scratchy, but I finished the song. All I wanted to do now was hide. It was as if God Himself had intervened with an admonition not to sing at a Communist celebration.

The choral group, next on the program, sang a few more songs, ending with the "Internationale," the Soviet national anthem. Than the crowd dispersed, walking home on the snow-covered ground of Gulag 149. My older and wiser brother Shmulek tried to console me.

"Don't be upset, forget it, none of our people care or give a damn whether you sang or what you sang."

Shmulek had a way of setting things in proper perspective. He made me think of my performance as a minor victory for the exiles.

November 7, the day after the public ceremony, was a holiday. Everybody had the day off. Although it was very cold, I walked over to the barracks to visit my friend Marian. I went, not only to see him, but to sit with Marian's father, who was the only person in our camp who subscribed to *Pravda* and *Izvestia*, the Russian newspapers. A professor back in Poland, he was fluent in Russian.

The papers were often delivered a few days late, but that did not diminish the importance of the news. As soon as his newspapers arrived, he notified some select people and they came together to discuss the latest world events. Both papers were but four pages. With propaganda the main thrust, little space was given to foreign news. The section called "Za Rubezhom" ("Beyond Our Shores") was found on the lower portion of the fourth page.

That day, Marian's father read about the air and sea battles between England and Nazi Germany. The news reports were not good. Large German air fleets were bombarding Great Britain. The British were putting up a brave resistance against the tremendous pounding by the Luftwaffe. Since our hope of salvation rested with England, the only European country still free and fighting the Nazi menace, this news was crushing. Moreover, England was encountering great difficulty in getting supplies from overseas because the German U-boats were sinking so many vessels.

We hoped, with some pride, that the Polish government-in-exile in England, headed by General Sikorski, was helping the beleaguered Britons. There had been news of Polish troops fighting heroically at the side of the British soldiers in Norway.

Now the talk in the barracks turned to the attitude of the Soviet government toward the war. Nothing in the newspapers indicated that the Russians were concerned about what Hitler might do if his forces defeated England. The group in the room were educated, professional people grappling with serious questions.

"Are the Soviet leaders naive enough to trust Hitler?" one asked. The news reports aroused a deep sense of apprehension.

"Does Russia really think she'll be able to stay out of this war? Why is the Soviet government feeding Hitler's war machine by sending oil and other raw materials to Germany?"

There was a feeling that the Soviet Union would be drawn into the war. Some wondered how a workers' state could have permitted the Nazis to defeat and subjugate the workers of France. The same lack of consideration for workers was apparent in the Western European countries. That would be antithetical to the Soviet ideology. A former historian tried to fathom the dilemma.

"After all," he said, "France has a substantial Communist Party. Don't the Soviets care what happens to it? They offer no protest and no explanation. There isn't a clue to their views in the newspapers."

I voiced my surprise at the United States' neutrality. What bothered me, as it did the rest of the group, was that Soviet raw materials were going to Germany, including our output of lumber. The talk eventually centered on local concerns and on uncertainties about relatives left behind in Poland. One man was worried about his daughter in Lwów. Had she been able to make her way to Palestine, as planned, to meet her betrothed? I sadly thought about my older brother Mundek, who had not been with us on that fateful June 28. We did not dare write to our relatives in Lwów. If they were in hiding somewhere, our inquiries might betray them to the Soviet authorities.

With personal fears being shared, young Goldman, an ardent Zionist, spoke up.

"The war will end with the defeat of the fascist countries, you'll see," he said with fervor, "and then there will be a reawakening of world Jewry, who will declare a Jewish state in Palestine."

His convictions, based on what he had learned from Dr. Nachum Goldmann, one of the foremost Zionist leaders of the era, whom he knew personally, were so strong that he lifted our hopes.

The group felt that something would happen to draw the Soviet Union into the war. They were still analyzing the news when I left to trudge back to our *izba* through the thick snow. It was early November and already very cold.

When I entered the *izba*, I heard my parents and Shmulek talking about the shortage of food. Given the fact that it was already so cold, the winter ahead would probably be fierce. Fuel and food we received, but the *payok* from the camp store would not sustain us. Father and Shmulek decided to ask the kommandatura for a permit to go to the surrounding villages before the expected heavy snow storms made the only dirt road impassable. Up to this point, father had never had a problem getting a permit because he was considered a key worker and fine example in the Chupka Brigade.

Father not only was able to obtain the travel pass but somehow garnered a horse and flat wagon. He always amazed me with his small triumphs. It is quite possible that he had to pay someone, but he knew who and how to approach without setting off alarms. And from this foray, he and Shmulek brought back a stockpile of provisions: sacks of potatoes, beets, cabbage, onions, garlic, three-liter bottles of honey and butter. I was puzzled by the fact that butter came in bottles, not tubs. Obviously the butter had to be soft enough to pour it into the bottles, then put out in the cold to solidify.

How father paid for these provisions I never knew. I do not believe he would have offered dollars to the Mari, but the details of bartering was not shared with children because it was known that the authorities sometimes inter- rogated them. A frightened child might say something incriminating and endanger his or her parents.

More horrible, the children were being taught to spy on their parents. We were told about a young boy named Pavlik Morozov, who was considered a hero because he had reported his parents' disloyal criticisms to the author- ities. The parents had then been executed, and the boy's relatives had killed him in revenge. The government had made a martyr of this "patriot" and dedicated a monument to him in Moscow.

My parents knew that Hella and I would never have knowingly endangered them. What they probably feared was that children break down and divulge secrets under threats and physical pressure. Under the Stalin regime, this was common practice.

The snows were coming down with a vengeance. Intruders in the deep, densely canopied forest, we would gladly have relinquished our camp for safer, more hospitable climes if we'd that option. But the snows were relentlessly covering everything around our moving bodies and rough-hewn hovels. The paths through the camp were completely covered, while the forest laborers had to stamp the snow down with their boots to make footpaths for themselves. My father and Shmulek, wrapped in layers of clothing under their *kufaika* and *bruki,* wrapped their feet with wide strips of linen before putting on their knee-high felt *valonki,* and venturing into the forest. Practically every day, I had to shovel snow from the entry to our *izba.* I wore outer clothing and boots like theirs, but the cold whipped through it anyhow. Cold days brought hungry wolves looking for food to the clearing near our place.

The cry of the wolves during the late-night hours was haunting, ominous, eerie. We heard their scraping paws on the frozen windows and could see the marks their claws etched in the glass. During the bitter-cold winter days, they were bold enough to come into the camp. I never saw one during the day, but others did. When my classmate Lester Kahane, whose Polish name, Leszek, was almost the same as mine, Lusiek, described the crystal gray eyes peering over the mounds of snow, their furry bodies sneaking around the barracks, it was as if I were seeing them myself.

There were days with snow so high and so brutally cold that the workers were excused from work. These were days that the men described as cold enough to turn spit to ice. The Mari consoling us would say: "If you don't get used to it, you'll just drop dead."

Our one-room hut was a veritable warehouse of food and firewood. Although we had piled up a high stack of firewood outside, father was not satisfied that we had enough to carry us through the entire winter. My task was to add to the stock, sawing and chopping the wood. Mother and Hella helped me to stack it up against the outside walls and to haul an extra supply inside. On the approach of winter, there were logs everywhere; we breathed the smell of the wood, brushed against piles of it as we navigated to table, bunks, stools, and around the stove. That stove served as an oven and was our source of warmth and sustenance, whereas the woodpile was the lifeline.

The stove was our dryer as well. When mother did the laundry, she poured boiling water into a wooden tub, scrubbed the clothes on a ribbed washboard, then hung them near the oven to dry. When the weather was warm, she hung them outside, but with the advent of cold weather, we had to duck beneath hanging clothes and skirt heaps of fire-wood in our one-room dwelling. The stove was a useful utility for many aspects of our life, but also the reason for our old problem, the bedbugs.

The battle recommenced, the reddish-brown bugs, parasites that live on warm-blooded animals, struck during the night, crawling over our bodies, sucking our blood, disturbing us, making us daffy. They attacked; we retaliated by spilling pails of boiling water into their dark hiding places in the cracks of our wooden bunks. Hot boiling water brought out them out in swarms. A further douse of boiling water killed our tormentors. Periodically, they returned, and we took our revenge.

But revenge did not come easily. With the heavy snows, access to the well was difficult. Raising the two needed pails of water in the biting cold was my task. I went

after those bedbugs with a vengeance. They sent for rein-
forcements. Every victory was temporary. Their survival
depended upon finding red-blooded hosts. We were
unwilling to house night-nipping visitors. Unwilling and
unobliging. Their marauding could drive you insane. Cold
as it was outdoors, I went to the well for my ammunition.

On one particularly glacial day, mother sent me out to
fetch water. I had several layers of clothing on my body
and at least three pairs of socks under the bandages covering my feet. At the well, I found the links of the metal chain
caked with ice. The links around the rotating bar were
frozen together. I could not crank the handle that would let
the long chain down into the well. Everything was a solid
mass of ice.

A few other people who came to the well tried but had
the same difficulty. We took turns using an axe to chop the
ice from the chain to free it so that we could lower the
bucket. Although I was wearing two pairs of gloves, my
hands soon felt numb and frozen. I beat them against my
chest to get some circulation as I lent my strength to our
communal task. Ultimately, we had the bucket in the well,
and I took my turn at filling up two buckets of water.

When I returned to our *izba* with the water, I felt
absolutely frozen. Icicles hung from my eyebrows and my
nose. I could hardly talk. My mother immediately took off
my gloves and heavy clothing and immersed my hands in
a pail of cold water, alternating it with warm water until I
began to regain sensation in my hands. The incident affected my body and mental state, I was totally disoriented.

Slowly, under my mother's care, I regained my bear-
ings and saw my father and Shmulek hovering over me,
assuring me that I would be well again. The day was so
brutally cold that work had been canceled, and school was
closed too. We recalled the Mari predictions of severe cold

in the region and remembered the warnings about frostbite and hypothermia.

I told my parents about the Polish Christian lady who had frozen to death. Apparently, she had walked out into the open night and was found the next morning, her body curled up, her arms as if hugging a warm lover to her body, lying in the snow, frozen. The poor woman had either lost her mind or had simply found a way to end her torment. I told my mother what the other people at the well had been saying. "They claimed they felt like howling like wolves into the cold, bleak wintry sky, or like following the example of the frozen woman."

My mother looked at me queerly and busily prepared soup and hot tea. We sat around the oven to keep warm and began to talk about our situation. The more we talked, the more we were aware of our despondency. We could see nothing through the windows, they were so covered with ice. But we knew there was endless whiteness out there. White sky that kept shaking flakes onto a white grave for humans out of their normal habitat. Branches that shook under the weight of white snow. Barracks so covered with snow, they looked like caves with dark peepholes where the doors and window openings were.

Inside our *izba*, everything was rough-hewn and brown. Three wooden bunks, one shared by my mother and father, one that Shmulek and I shared, one small one for Hella. At one end of the room was a ceiling-high stack of logs. A large crude table and stools occupied most of the room, a kerosene lamp our only light. A few shelves holding our food supply and our meager belongings. That was all we possessed.

We saw no future in our lives. None of us, even Hella, who was eight years old at the time, could foresee a way out. We were in this God-forsaken place in the middle of a huge forest. No one of consequence knew where we were. The authorities told us nothing, gave us no indication of how long we would be here.

The world outside was in chaos. Western Europe was occupied by Hitler's armies. England was fighting for her life, her people bombed constantly by the Nazi air force. The United States, in which we placed our hopes, was staying out of the conflict. The Soviet Union was not only not involved in the fight against Hitler, but was supplying raw materials for his war machine. There was no escape from here. Even if we wanted to try, there was only one narrow dirt road, now deep in snow, leading to the forest. The forest was full of wolves. We were approximately sixty miles from a railroad station.

How long could we survive in this brutal climate? My mother became so despondent, we were afraid something would snap. Even my father, always the optimist, always the resourceful one, the man with the proud bearing and calculating eyes, bowed his head.

"We'll find a way to see this through," he would say, but his voice was flat, his eyes moist, and we sensed that he too had lost hope.

I did not sleep well that night, the conversation gnawing at my guts. Even though I wore my clothes to bed and the stove was still burning, I could not get warm. In fact that night the kerosene lamp was not extinguished because we had to get up several times to stoke the oven with logs to keep the fire going. No one in our family slept that night.

The next morning, the windows were solid sheets of ice. Shmulek opened the door to heavy snow falling on the camp, snow drifts so high they obliterated buildings. Not a soul was outside; the cold so bitter again that there was no work and no school.

In the morning my father woke, took out his tallis and his phylacteries, and recited his morning prayers. When he finished, my mother took the prayer book from him and gave it to me. "Pray to God, Lusiek, ask Him to help us," she said desperately.

I had not prayed for a long while. I saw my mother trembling, and all I could think of was that her mind might snap. She looked so forlorn, so utterly full of despair. Her voice not more than a whisper. She needed my voice, my heart, to wrench salvation from a remote God. Her hands, as I reached for the prayer book, were so chilled, so fragile, I felt as if she were slipping away from me. If I held her, it would not give her solace. Solace could come only from God. I prayed more fervently than ever in my life, rapt with grief for her, for all of us. I called out to the silent God in the silence that went through walls, through the frozen regions, through the cold sky where not even a bird could deflect my prayers, and I beseeched Him for help. I beat my breast as I told Him I could think of no sins I had committed. I had lived up to all of His commandments. My small transgressions, my thoughts about touching a girl's body, were they so sinful that I and my family deserved to be punished so severely? Should I be condemned to this hellhole for such minor transgressions?

After two days of savage weather, the cold slightly abated and the people went back to work in the forest. Trudging through the deep snow, they made a path only for human passage. Hella and I went back to school. It was almost Christmas time, which was not observed in the Soviet Union, where Santa Claus was replaced by *Ded Moroz*, "Uncle Winter" or "Uncle Frost." Our holiday of Hanukkah was not mentioned at all. Opposed to religious observances of any kind, the Communists prohibited religious displays and church attendance, and, in fact, tried vigorously to eradicate belief in God. Our teacher distributed textbooks about the *yunnye bezbozhniki*, bold young atheists who searched out Bibles, both Old and New

Testaments, and destroyed them. And in an attempt to turn us away from religious parents, we were encouraged to report parents or relatives who prayed or observed religious rituals.

Zoya Ivanovna followed the Party line by reading us stories that were intended to wipe out religious ties.

One story concerned a Moslem girl in one of the Moslem republics who ridiculed her mother for covering her face with a veil. The point of the story was that the young girl felt free of religious injunctions under the Soviet system. I didn't think that many Moslems succumbed to such propaganda. Nor did it impress Jews.

Isolated as we were, our faith helped us to hold on to hope, for we were not blinded by political shifts and pressures. The problem was that we had little information. There was a radio in the camp office, but all the news broadcasts were from the government station, which mainly beamed music and propaganda about the great achievements of Soviet workers. At certain hours, there would be a report from Moscow on international news, but we were not allowed to listen.

All our news came from Marian's father, who subscribed to *Pravda* and *Izvestia*, but the deliveries were delayed by the heavy snows, and when the papers finally arrived, the news would be several days old and principally propaganda. Hella, I, and others were drawn to the barracks to cluster around Marian's father, who had a remarkable faculty for reading Russian, then translating and relaying the news in Polish. He read about the heavy German bombing of England. London and other cities had been hard hit, evidently the preamble to a planned invasion. He shook his head in dismay.

"Don't these stupid *chaverim*"—the Hebrew word for "comrades"—"see the handwriting on the wall? Don't the Communists see they will be next?"

In the ensuing days, I listened closely to the news, but most everybody else in the camp was focused on the approaching civic holiday of New Year. Our teacher wished us a *c novym godom* (good year). Each family received extra rations from the store, nothing that could enhance our plain diet, except for the vodka. Work in the forest was suspended for a celebration, but we had little reason to rejoice. The Russians had their own way of celebrating. They relished their vodka, drank heavily, and lost themselves in euphoric fantasies as they swayed in the snow.

The holiday made little difference in my life. I had my chores around the house. I was the official drawer of water from the well. I had difficulty with my left hand, a weakness resulting from a poorly set fracture years before in Dynów, but I learned to balance the two pails of water. In fact, a school holiday was a bore. I preferred school, where I could concentrate on improving my Russian, which would give me access to other books. Over my own diligently done homework, I watched Hella, to see that she was doing hers. I felt especially protective of my tender eight-year-old sister. I wanted to spare her sorrow and pain, particularly since it looked as if Hitler was doing so well.

One would think the Russians would also have been worried, but this was not the case at all. When questioned, they would sneer.

"Nothing to worry about. Comrade Stalin knows what Hitler is doing. If Germany ever dared to attack the great Soviet Union, they'd get their comeuppance. But they won't; they know how strong and powerful we are."

The Russians believed in their country's strength and power. They believed the Kremlin-inspired press releases, which never contained a hint of apprehension.

The Jews in the camp lived in fear, contemplating what would happen if Hitler attacked the Soviet Union. The most recent Moscow reports were of the bombing of English cities, of the war at sea between the British and German navies. There were no commentaries. Then, in March 1941, Germany sent troops to Finland and Rumania. (In 1939, Finland had lost border territories to Russia. In 1941, when Germany attacked Russia, Finland vindictively joined the Germans, hoping to reclaim its territory. They were allies of convenience, as was Rumania, which also joined Germany in the war against Russia.) Shortly thereafter, we read that the Germans had defeated and occupied Greece and Yugoslavia. Couldn't anyone see that the Soviet Union would be next? Still, there was no sign of apprehension.

Then, in early May 1941, for the first time, we noted a change, in a news item in *Pravda* gleaned from Stalin's speech to the graduates of a military academy. It hinted that they must be prepared to deal with surprises. Nothing specific, but to us it did not have to be spelled out. Stalin had finally seen the long shadow cast by Germany's war machine.

Now that it was May, we looked to better weather. The snow was gone, the ice melted. My father once again got a permit to go to one of the villages to replenish our dwindled food supply. He and Shmulek brought back potatoes, cabbage, beets, onions. Some milk and cheese as well. There was not much else. We ate what we could get.

May meant added activity in the camp. During the winter months, the Chupka Brigade had carted felled trees to the banks of a river where a dam had been built to form a lake. When the ice melted in May, the dam was opened to float the logs down to the lumber mills. Peasants from nearby collective farms specialized in preparing the huge tree trunks for transport. They roped several together to be carried down the fast-moving water into the Volga River. The large lumber mills, on the banks of the Volga, sawed, distributed, or exported the final product. Then the process continued all over again.

May and even June weather did not bring a complete thaw. The upper layer of the ground thawed, but the substratum remained solidly frozen. A permafrost condition, which required extended sunshine, remained. The thawing upper layer became a breeding ground for mosquitoes that become fierce during the summer months. Now there was something more to look forward to. Blood-sucking insects during the day as well as the night.

As appalling as that was, so was the news. An official communique from the Tass news agency confirmed the rumors. Tass issued the formal statement: "Russia has peaceful intentions." No elaboration. Of course, this set off a flurry of excitement. What was the source of the rumors? To whom is the Soviet Union declaring its peaceful intentions? What had stirred and awakened the huge Russian bear from its hibernation? Was it sufficiently awake to the realities of sharing *tchai* (tea) with an enemy? Which would declare war first, Germany or the Soviets with their peaceful intentions?

Sunday, June 22, 1941, dawned with the sun on a normal bright path and temperate climate, obliterating memories of the harsh ruthless winter. At noon, when the sun was in its most hospitable arc, we opened our doors to let in the natural warmth. We raised our heads to welcome its rays, felt the warmth and renewal of life that only the sun can assure, grateful that we had endured and survived. It was then that a very agitated Russian from the camp administration ran by, screaming, repeating an announcement he had heard on the radio.

"Nazi Germany has invaded the Soviet Union!"

That was all he said, there were no further details. He kept running around shouting, "*Sukin syn* [Whore]! Hitler is a whore!" He had the wrong sexual connotation. But he was correct when he shouted, "The cur, the son-of-a-bitch! He double-crossed us."

"Why are you so surprised?" the camp internees asked. "We always said this would happen. You didn't want to believe that the dog who hid his fangs from you would snap at a friendly hand."

We hated the Russkis for what they had done to us, but we wanted them to defeat Hitler. If the Russians had sided with the Allies at the beginning, Hitler might have been stopped before he was able to conquer so many countries. But that was hindsight. At this point, we wanted to know how strong the Red Army really was. We had been exposed to its martial songs, its bragging and its pompous parades of tanks, artillery, and air power, but we did not know how its military might compared with Germany's. The Russians had done poorly when they attacked Finland, yet Finland was a flea compared to the German cur.

Aside from the Russian Paul Revere who ran through the camp shouting "The Germans are attacking," we heard nothing from Stalin. We were now permitted to listen to the radio in the camp office, but there was nothing but broadcasts about collective farmers and various workers' brigades fulfilling their production norms. Business as usual. Absurdities in the face of startling developments. Absurdities such as trucks fueled with wood chips rather than gas, vehicles that ran out of power or broke down. When we were transported to the camp, we had to get off and push and pull the truck in order to get it started again. The Polish cavalry with its horses and sabers had more of a chance against the Nazi army than the Russians would with the equipment we had seen.

Suddenly the radio went dead and there was total silence. In other circumstances, this would not have been surprising. Sometimes Party and government officials would broadcast messages and orders to local officials over the radio, but why do so when there was a national emergency?

After some silence, an announcer came back on, stating: "Stand by for an announcement from Comrade Molotov."

Then Molotov came on to inform the people that in the early hours of the morning, the Nazi hordes had invaded the motherland. Again, the hurling of invectives, after which he reported the bombing of civilian population centers.

"The mighty Red Army, the fleet, and the air force are ready to rebuff the Hitler bandits. Comrades, unite under the leadership of the Communist Party and go forward to victory."

Molotov's voice was neither strong nor convincing. He gave no specifics. He did not say where and how far the Germans were inside the Soviet Union. The mere fact that the invasion had started early in the morning and the Soviet people had not been addressed until several hours later indicated a surprise invasion. And why had Stalin not spoken to the people?

The atmosphere in the camp pulsated with the uncertain beat of war. Every political event of the past year had been a subject of discussion in the barracks, every event a prelude to the confrontation with vast Nazi power aggrandized by successive conquests. Their blitzkrieg tactics, massive tank attacks supported by Stuka divebombers, were infamous, but most of all the element of surprise assault at night was awesome.

Up against this power was a disorganized two-headed country. One head was the Communist Party, the other a government apparatus that took its orders from the Party. The army ran on the same principle: Every decision of the professional officers had to be approved by the *politruk*, or political commissar. The political commissar was a party hack who knew nothing about military science, but was adroit at echoing Lenin's or Stalin's words. He was there because the ruling Communist Party feared the army. What was already history was the Stalin purge, during 1936–37, of the professional officer corps, which had eliminated most of the best commanders. Fearing a coup, the great and wise leader had executed ninety percent of Russia's generals, leaving strategic decisions to those who worried more about their personal advancement than about positioning their battalions for battle.

When they prepared for war, did they expect loyalty from populations whose possessions they had confiscated, subjugated, brutalized, especially the Ukrainians?

In the aftermath of the announcement, we gathered in groups and talked about the prospects for ourselves. We drew up scenarios with the worst outcomes from the invasion. What would happen to us if, God forbid, Hitler's forces quickly defeated and occupied the Soviet Union as they had Poland? Where would we run, where would we go? Facts were facts. Ninety percent of the people in the camp were Jews. We knew how the Nazis would treat us if they won, but should the Red Army stem the Nazi invasion, a conclusion conceivable only if they put up a stiff resistance, how would the Soviet government treat us? As friends or enemies?

I was an active participant in the discussions. My avid interest in world politics and matters military was aroused. What with the Soviet Union now in the lurch, would England help? Would the United States remain neutral or throw its strength against the Nazi threat? I kept hoping the world would unite to bring down the ruthless Nazi beast.

When class met the next day, our teacher told us about the German assault on the Soviet Union.

"I know," I said, "I heard Molotov's speech." I felt the provocative itch of self-satisfaction, but I knew I had to phrase my next question tactfully. If I was to make her squirm, as I wanted to do because she had boasted about Communist achievements and spewed so much propaganda, I had to give her a way to save face.

"Did you doubt that Hitler was going to invade the Soviet Union?" I asked. If I asked whether the Soviet leaders ever had such doubts, I would be criticizing them.

She was evasive. Her answer was still on the Communist track.

"But now, we all have to unite as one people and fight back and destroy the enemy."

She led us in patriotic martial songs. For the rest of the day, attention was focused on the war.

On the way home from school, I stopped to listen to the radio. The news was not good. The announcer was talking about the heroic resistance being put up by the great Red Army. But when he said that the army was moving back to better defensive positions, what it actually meant was that the Germans were advancing deep into Soviet territory. Blaring martial music followed this brief news summary. One thing can be said about Russian songs. They are really stirring and inspiring to patriotic Russians. With a summons to work harder, to produce more, to give the army all it needed, the announcer ended by saying;

"*Vso dla fronta*" ("Everything for the front"). And while listening to the radio, I overheard a similar message delivered by telephone to the camp commandant.

"Production must be increased."

There were already many trees in the forest marked *avio*, for the aviation industry. These new directives were sure to put added pressure on the Chupka team.

In our remote village, war activity had begun. Some of the Russians on the camp staff were mobilized. Peasants from the surrounding collective farms were also being called to the colors. When school ended in June, we students were assigned to pulling nails out of discarded wooden boards piled up in the camp. As raw material for the war effort, even rusty nails might be useful. I was more adept at pulling out solutions to algebra problems than at pulling out those nails. In the process, I fell on one of the boards and tore the skin on my thigh. Ironically, I bled for Russia. The clinic feldsher applied some iodine and sent me back to the wood pile.

On the tenth day after Hitler's army invaded the Soviet Union, Stalin addressed his people. Known not to have a good speaking voice, he appealed to the Russians as "Sisters and Brothers," something he had never done before. The gist of his speech was that all the peoples of the Soviet Union must join in the war effort. Not only the soldiers on the battlefront and the soldiers defending the nation in the farthest corners of the country, but the people in the factories and on the collective farms, who supplied everything for the front, must do their utmost to defeat Germany.

He called for the evacuation of factories from their present locations to remote areas of the Soviet Union safe from Nazi attack. Resources must not fall into the hands of the enemy, he stated. He asked that farmers drive their cattle to the hinterland to keep them safe. He called for a scorched-earth policy, implying that what could not be evacuated was to be destroyed. The enemy must find no quarters for their troops, he stressed. He called for the formation of partisan units behind the German lines. He reminded the Russian people of their heroic defense against previous invaders. He ended his speech with three slogans that were to be his battle cry throughout the war: *Nashe delo pravoye. Vrag budet razbit. Pobeda budet za nami* ("Our cause is just. The enemy will be smashed. Victory will be ours").

As the Nazi panzers penetrated deep into Russia, occupying vast and valuable territories, gloom spread among the people of the Soviet Union. The Ukraine, the Soviet breadbasket, was overrun. From the tenor of the radio reports, we could deduce that the government was panicking. They did not have to tell us that army units were surrendering en masse. We could tell from the special order that was issued: "A soldier who surrenders will have his family incarcerated."

When it seemed as if the situation could not get worse, we heard very good news. Great Britain, under Churchill's leadership, had decided to help the Soviet Union with war materials. They were gearing up to engage Germany on the western front. The United States was involved in talks with the Soviet Union. There were speculations that it was about to declare war on Germany. This gave us hope that the democratic nations might alleviate our plight.

The possibility of an end to our detention and the resumption of life as we had known it was dim. There was never any reference in the newspapers to labor camps or to trials that would establish our innocence and procure our freedom. We had little hope of anyone knowing or caring what happened to us. Soon we would just die here, if not from the backbreaking work and scant food, then from the brutally cold winters that had all but frozen our bodies and hopes. We would die before the free nations were able to subdue the Nazi monster, we thought.

Then came electrifying news: The Polish government-in-exile in London had entered into an agreement of mutual recognition with the Russians. Under the leadership of General Sikorski, Poland would help the Soviet Union in the war effort against the common enemy. Under the terms of the agreement, all Polish citizens incarcerated as political prisoners in Soviet slave labor camps would be set free and resettled in specified areas of the Soviet Union. In the communities where Polish citizens settled, they would be represented by a Polish official designated by the London government. A Polish army would be formed on Soviet soil. Its commander would be General Wlasislav Anders, who at present was a prisoner in a Soviet slave labor camp. The Polish army so formed would fight side by side with the Red Army against the common enemy, Nazi Germany.

Shouts of disbelief were heard in the gulag.

"We're going to be set free! We have a new lease on life!"

We would be led out from slavery, just as our ancient ancestors had been led out of Egypt. My mother, always the pessimist, managed to smile, but wanly asked. "But is it true?"

She believed it when Commandant Zolotov called us together and said: "*Soyuzniki* [Allies], continue to work until the details are formalized. You are working for our victory." Most agreed to do so.

Energized, overwhelmed with this change in our fate, we talked late into the spring night. So pleasant, yet disturbed by the mass of insects summoned from the surrounding swamps favorable to their breeding. They bit and we slapped, as if it were vengeance against the Nazi tormentors. Our exhilaration was pervasive. We had endured, we were alive.

In a few days, officials from the capital, Yoshkar Ola, visited the camp, among them NKVD Captain Sokolov. He looked less brutal than Lieutenant Aleiev. Several men in civilian clothes came with them. All were polite and solicitous. They informed us that we would soon receive special documents enabling us to leave the camp as free people. We were to select a place where we wanted to settle. They would make our travel arrangements.

I had studied quite a few maps in the past few years for two reasons, because geography interested me, and because of political and military strategy, which were my forte. This was one time when a map was perused to decide my family's destiny.

Father, Shmulek, and I made an immediate decision. We would go to Vladivostok, the farthest and largest port on the Pacific Ocean. My father wanted to go there because he hoped we would be able to board an American ship that would take us to the United States, where we could join his brother Irving in New York. It seemed to be a great plan.

We were not the only ones with this idea. So, in the event of this plan failing, we had a second plan, to go to Uzbekistan. A decision quite understandably based on the warmer climate there. We wanted to be as far away from the frozen forest region as possible. Another reason was that the Uzbek Republic was close to India and Iran. Perhaps our dollars would buy off the border guards so we could get to either of these countries. From there, we would be able to make our way to Palestine or America.

Again, my fascination with maps came in good stead. We had a geography course in the camp school where we had studied the Uzbek Republic. I spread the map for my family and showed them one of the republic's fertile regions, the Fergana Valley, famous for its fruit, cotton, and silk.

"Let's try to get to Fergana. It's supposed to be a lovely city," I urged.

When the officials from Yoshkar Ola came again, we were among the first to be interviewed in the office.

"What is your choice, Comrade Wenig?" The commander asked my father.

"We want to go to Vladivostok," my father responded.

Without hesitation, the interviewer answered.

"Get that out of your mind. You're not going to America."

They were not stupid, they had been well trained at NKVD headquarters.

"You can't go there because it is an important military base. Your second choice?"

The city of Fergana in the Uzbek Soviet Socialist Republic was an acceptable choice. They registered our request. Many people did likewise. Others decided to go to Samarkand or Bukhara. All were requesting warm places, far from the Mari Republic and its terrible winters. Now it was a question of formal documents to be issued by the authorities.

The men working in the forest, feeling liberated, became less punctual and conscientious. They felt their supervisors were not going to threaten them when higher officials were arranging their departure. Many, like us, started to pack the things they wanted to take with them. Meanwhile, we followed the war news avidly.

Apprehension was high. The Germans seemingly could not be stopped. They were advancing and seizing Soviet territory up and down the front. Their campaign took them in different directions. They were close to Leningrad on one thrust, and past Byelorussia on another. They were approaching Kiev in yet another. Heavy panzer units were moving toward the city of Smolensk. It was ironic, but we hoped the government we so despised was not going to collapse.

I remember reading an item in the newspaper about a special defense supercommittee being formed, consisting of five members: Stalin, Lavrenty Beria, the head of the NKVD, Marshal Timoshenko, the defense minister, Zhdanov, a member of the Politburo entrusted with the defense of Leningrad, and Marshal Kliment Voroshilov, a revolutionary hero who by trade had once been a plumber, but was now a member of the Politburo assisting Zhdanov. I marked every movement, every advance, every retreat, every report on my large map. It was scary, precarious, but we hoped a turnabout could come with the opening of a second front by England. When was that going to happen, we wondered.

The big day of our release finally arrived. The officials brought us three *udostvereniye* (documents) as precious as holy parchment, stating;

"Pursuant to a decree issued by the presidium of the highest council of the Soviet Union, this person is a Polish citizen and can reside as such in the Soviet Union."

There was further verification, but delirium was already watering our eyes. The documents were made out for father, mother, and Shmulek. Hella and I were listed as minors, under sixteen, on father's certificate. At the time, I was supposedly thirteen and a half years old.

We packed our miserable belongings in makeshift suitcases. The authorities arranged for us to go by truck to Kazan, the capital of the Tatar Autonomous Republic. I wondered if this truck, like the one that had brought us to our gulag in the Mari Republic, would need wood chips for fuel and periodic human shoulders to keep it going. Impediments that would not stop us. If we had to, we would push, pull, pound on the road to freedom.

On the Road to Freedom

Our exodus from fourteen months of slavery began with a free ride to Kazan, the capital of the Tatar Republic. With few belongings, we boarded a truck at the camp, and off we went on the bumpy road to the city conquered by Ivan the Terrible in the seventeenth century. The Tatars were still renowned for ferocity.

At the Kazan railroad station there was chaos. Trains loaded with soldiers and equipment were moving westward to the battlefield. Dismantled equipment and machinery from factories in the Ukraine, following Stalin's orders, were being shipped eastward to factories beyond the Ural Mountains, where they were setting up new factory sites. Other trains, filled to capacity, were coming in with refugees escaping the German invasion. Scurrying in all directions, people clamored for access to the eastbound trains. We tried making our way through the swelling, shouting sea of people, to the railroad ticket office to get our tickets to Fergana. It was futile. We were blocked by a human barrier more impenetrable than a stone wall.

Looking for some way to gain access to the ticket window, I saw a large poster which listed the order in which tickets were provided, ranking according to importance in the Soviet Union: Heroes of the Soviet Union, members of the Supreme Soviet, NKVD officials, members of the Communist Party, officers of the Red Army, wives and children of soldiers of the Red Army, and many more categories in decreasing preference. Perhaps because we were of least importance, I scoffed at the maxim of a classless society.

Judging from the vast crowd pushing its way to the ticket window, we knew it would be quite a while before we could approach with our request. We could do nothing but wait, and while waiting, we heard people lamenting the virtual collapse of the military front. They talked of chaos and disorganization in the army. They told about the German air force dominating the sky. Entire army units surrendered or were cut off and encircled by the Germans.

People exchanged stories of their personal plight. They came from western territories where they themselves had almost been encircled by the fast-advancing German armies. The Russian soldiers fought valiantly, but the Red Army was no match for the iron monsters in the German armored divisions. I was surprised at how freely people spoke about the faltering defense and deteriorating national situation.

In the crowd, we saw and commiserated with Mr. Lipshitz, who had been interned in our camp and was heading for the same destination. We lamented our status at the bottom of the list. Mr. Lipshitz, whom we knew to be an engineer, peered over the heads in front of us, biting his lip as he scanned the list.

"The question is, will they give consideration to a Jew who was a major in the prewar Polish army?" he intoned.

My father's hand brushed his mustache.

"The question is, will they believe your story?" my father replied.

Out of his packet, Mr. Lipshitz pulled a photograph of himself in uniform as a Polish army major, predating the present war.

"I think," he said to my father, "that we should see the military commandant of the station. You too served in the army, didn't you?" Mr. Lipshitz said encouragingly.

"But that was another era," Shmulek dampened their hopes. "The commandant is supposed to make sure that soldiers and supplies are expedited to the battlefield."

"It doesn't hurt to try. I have no papers or photographs to prove it, since they were lost in the shuffle from Dynów, but maybe there's a way to check." My father had not lost his nerve in the Siberian hinterland. To him, meeting Mr. Lipshitz was a fortuitous development. This chance meeting offered a solution.

We were admitted to the commandant's office, where Mr. Lipshitz showed him his military photograph and my father proffered our impressive documents, *udostvereniye* signed by the president of the Soviet Union, Kalinin. The commandant, an elderly Russian, was very polite. He knew about our status and examined the documents.

"They use fine paper, don't they; artistic script too," he said, impressed.

"We intend to join the new Polish army being organized in the Soviet Union, to fight alongside the heroic Red Army in the battle against our common enemy," Mr. Lipshitz told the commandant. "We would like to get there quickly, get our training, show our support."

The commandant held up Mr. Lipshitz's photograph, looked at him and back at the photograph. "Now we are allies," he said, smiling.

I had a strange intuition that father would have tried a bribe to get us out of Kazan, but thanks to Mr. Lipshitz's photograph and the fate that watched over us, we were given preferred status. The commandant escorted us to the rear entrance of the ticket office. He explained our celebrity status to the staff. They issued our tickets to Fergana immediately. When Mr. Lipshitz and father paid for the tickets, we received the *kompasirovka* (stamp) validating our seats on a train. Not to Fergana, however, but to the city of Kuybyshev. From there, we would have to find another train.

Not that there was a train to board. We spent two more days of waiting, sleeping on the floor of the railroad station. During that time, we could see that Kazan was an important and strategic railroad junction through which manpower and military supplies were moved to the front. Train after train passed through the station, all westbound. Sadly, from the opposite direction came trains carrying wounded soldiers from the front.

At last, an announcement came over the speaker that the train to Kuybyshev was in the station. Again there was the crunch of humans desperate to get out of Kazan, pushing and shoving, jeopardizing our chance of getting on the train. Tired and weary, we acted with the same desperation and finally managed to board the Kuybyshev train. What should have been a short trip, since the actual distance between the two cities was not great, took hours longer. There were many delays when our train was shunted onto a siding to make way for military trains.

Arriving at Kuybyshev tired and hungry, we found the same scene as in Kazan: multitudes of refugees escaping from advancing German armies. We were able to get a little food at the station and then had our tickets validated for our next destination, Saratov.

Saratov, an important city on the Volga River, strangely had an enclave of Germans, descendants of the coterie that had followed Catherine the Great to Russia in the eighteenth century. The area was actually called Nemtsov Povolzhya ("Germans by the Volga"). Several hundred thousand Germans lived in the area. Now, with the German invasion, Stalin had ordered them arrested. They were trying to escape. Where would they be safe? Human alliances have awesome aftermaths. Loyal to one king, they are beheaded by another. Loyal to one tribe, they are pursued by another. Loyal to one God, they are persecuted by followers of another. Man did not develop and progress without the community of others. What is the lesson in all this? I had too much identity as a Jew and as a refugee. Not yet sixteen years old, my actual age, I saw the political situation as the human condition. Like my mother, I saw that survival was everything. There were no grounds for optimism.

Survival now meant facing chaos again. Travel throughout the Soviet Union was disorganized by the imperatives of war. Saratov lay on the banks of the Volga River, and as such was an important transit center. Large barges laden with ammunition came through this center. Trains filled with soldiers and supplies.

We had validated tickets to Tashkent, the capital of Uzbekistan, but we had to wait another two days for the arrival of our train. Again, we had no choice but to sleep on the floor, exposed to the foul smells of unwashed, slovenly humans and stuffed toilets. I should have been used to the smells of urine and excrement after two years of terrible toilet conditions, but I still found the odors offensive.

Our train finally arrived and the frenzy began all over again. People pushed others aside, jumped over one other, exchanged curses, and all but beat one other up in the mad rush to board. No courtesies, no regard for women. They seemed to be guided by Lenin's teaching: *Kto kavo* ("He whom . . ."): He who wants something fights for it. He knocks off whoever is in his way.

Again, a comparatively short run took four days because our train stopped often to let other trains go through in the other direction. They had to change the locomotive at least twice. Then, at last, late in the afternoon of the fourth day, we arrived in Tashkent.

At the station, for the first time, I saw people who looked different. The Uzbeks, mostly Sunni Moslems, wore long, multicolored quilted coats and *kibiteika,* a square embroidered skullcap. Some wore sashes around their coats.

The women wore ankle-length baggy pants and a long dress over the pants. Some had their faces covered with the long black veil traditionally worn by Moslem women. I heard very little Russian spoken.

Having arrived in the late afternoon, we had a long wait for the train to Fergana. It was late at night by the time our tickets were validated for this part of the trip. We were hungry and found *lepioshka,* a large round doughy bread peculiar to this region. We liked them and bought several. We quenched our thirst with *kvas,* a fermented beverage favored by Russians. Its base was rye bread or barley, or both, and a few other ingredients, nothing you would think of as contributing to a good-tasting drink. In fact, it was not. It had no bubbles, no zip, and tasted sour.

When Shmulek and I roamed around the station, we saw a vendor selling grapes. I had not seen or tasted grapes since we left Dynów. We bought quite a few bunches for the family to enjoy. They were delicious. After fourteen months of potatoes and cabbage, the grapes were a delicacy, symbolic of our return to the real world.

We soon experienced more of the real world, when finally, very late at night, we boarded the train to Fergana. After several more hours, concluding a journey that had taken ten days, we disembarked, tired, bedraggled, and exhausted, in Fergana. With no inkling of how hospitable the Uzbeks would be, nor where to find housing, we decided to lie down on a grassy area near the station. We spread our blankets and put our suitcases under our heads. Falling into a deep sleep, we did not hear the approach of a marauder who yanked the suitcase from under my father's head. Father awoke and yelled, and we leaped up to join him in pursuit of the thief but could not catch him. Our shouts brought a Russian militiaman, who listened to our sorry story. He sympathized but could offer no help, warning us to be careful. He confirmed what we already knew, that there were thieves in these parts. We had left Yoshkar Ola with few belongings, now we had even less. A fine way to start our new life in this totally alien place.

At dawn we saw clusters of people like ourselves getting up from their sleep. Cautiously approaching, our tongues always guarded against provoking suspicion in Communist Russia, we asked simple questions. In ordinary times, there would have been formal but cordial greetings between travelers, but these were not ordinary times. When asked "What are you doing here?" a nod would be a form of recognition. We were all in this place for the same reason.

From one person, we learned his family were Russians fleeing the advancing German army. Another's eyes searched ours, and in the intuitive appraisal that Jews have for one another, we would answer in Yiddish.

"We are Jews from the Ukraine," the man said pointing to several other small groups.

"We can't find a decent place to live," they would complain.

"Have you looked?" my father asked. "Where do you look? How do you go about finding a place?"

"A young Bukharan Jewess is trying to find homes for us," the man answered, his voice as dejected as the sorry appearance of his family. "A young woman who was born here is trying to help us. She will be here again this morning."

"Let me tell you," a woman standing nearby offered, "these Uzbeks do not like us. They're Moslems; they're not anxious to help Jews or Christians."

About mid-morning, the young Bukharan Jewess arrived.

"No," she answered my father's query, "I do not speak Yiddish, I am Sephardic."

The Jews of Bukhara were descended from the Jews expelled from Spain in the fifteen century. They spoke their own dialect, Ladino, a mixture of Spanish, Hebrew, and Arabic. This Bukharan woman, however, also spoke Russian and Uzbek, so we were able to communicate in Russian.

My father told her that we could not afford to pay much but needed a place to live. She wanted us to know that the Uzbeks had very different customs and adaptations to life.

"The climate is very warm here," she said. "The Uzbeks live most of the year outdoors in their gardens."

As we arranged ourselves in the horse-drawn wagon she provided for us, we pictured cascading vines around summer cottages built on hillsides, overlooking lakes with views of the sunrise and sunset.

At the address 171 First Yangi-Chek was a house in a garden enclosed by a mud wall, owned by an Uzbek family. We walked through an opening in the wall to enter the garden. Not a garden with flowers, a vegetable patch with a mud house at the end of it. The house looked as if it had been slapped together over a wooden frame in one day. Inside, it was partitioned into three parts. The Uzbek couple and their three sons occupied one large room. The room had an alcove with a fireplace used for cooking and heating, a definite indication of colder weather possibilities. In fact the landlord confirmed that the weather often dropped to forty degrees in the winter, warm compared to Yoshkar Ola.

Adjacent to the landlord's room was a small room occupied by a cow. Next to the cow's room was another room similar to the cow's quarters, with a beaten earth floor. At one end was a primitive iron stove with a metal flue reaching into the roof. There were no furnishings, since none would have fit inside anyway. A quick calculation told us that if we put in a small table and chairs, and stacked our few pieces of luggage, little space would be left to move about. As for toilet facilities, the landlord said that he would dig a hole for us in the back of the garden, closer to our side, and would provide a wooden plank to partially cover the hole. We could stand on the plank for our bodily evacuations. When the hole filled to the top, he would cover it up and next to it dig another.

I saw mother sway on her feet. I rushed to her side, fearing she would faint. I knew her sense of decency, and knew she was suffering from the affront she foresaw to her dignity and privacy. I knew her mind was flashing back to the genteel opulence of her parents' home, and later of her own house, where she had been able to wander at leisure through the parlor and bedrooms, lay her head on fluffy feather pillows, and cover herself with fine linens. Here, she would have to sleep on an earthen floor next door to a cow. The camp *izba* became a luxury compared to this.

"We are entering the stone age," she murmured unhappily.

"At least we're no longer slaves in a gulag," my father reminded her, "and we won't have to suffer another brutal winter."

He turned to the Bukharan Jewess. "Is there anything better?"

"This is how people live here," she answered bluntly.

Father, avoiding mother's grieving eyes, decided to take it. He and the owner agreed on a rental price. The owner seemed to be a decent man, sympathetic when told who we were and where we came from. He brought in some burlap bags, which, when stuffed with the straw he also provided, would be our mattresses. He spoke to us in his broken Russian, and we noticed that he had less knowledge of the language than we did, while his wife spoke only Uzbek.

When mother asked where to get water, he took her outside and showed her the irrigation ditch from which we could draw water. He then began to dig the hole in the garden for our toilet.

Over on his side, he had a vegetable garden. Under a tree, in his part of the garden, close to his room, he had a raised wooden platform piled with blankets for his family. That is where they slept most of the time. The platform was bedroom as well as dining area. The tree offered shade, cooling them during the summer and autumn months. In the ground was a clay oven where they baked their bread, the soft, spongy *lepioshkus* we had sampled at the station.

To bake their bread, they started a fire in the oven with twigs, then fed it with a mixture of straw and cow dung. Once the oven was hot enough, the woman slapped round disks of dough onto its inner sides. When they were baked, they would slowly begin to peel off and she would take them out. When she needed more fuel, she would pick up a hardened dung ball and add it to the fire. The boys shaped the dung and straw balls and set them out to harden, to be ready when needed for cooking.

Fergana was a culture shock for us. The Uzbeks lived instinctively, obeying their bodily needs, providing for themselves as their ancestors did in earliest ages with whatever was available, unaware that man had devised and invented more comfortable accessories. They did not shape nature or abuse it, other than adjust it to their agricultural needs. Still, we felt as if we had come from another world and were appalled at having to regress to their habits and customs. Even eating was done in a primitive way. The Uzbeks cooked their rice pilaf, mutton, and vegetables, such as peppers and onions, in a wok over the fire. They sat on the ground around the stove and used their fingers and hands to bring the food to their mouths.

The cow was their special treasure. The Soviet government allowed the Uzbeks to have only one cow per family. This one cow gave milk which they used in a number of ways, fermenting it for yogurt, skimming the cream to make butter, and of course, the valuable cow dung that was used to stoke the fire. At a short distance from his house, the landlord was allotted a piece of land on which he grew vegetables and potatoes and had some fruit trees. Every square inch of soil was used for the sustenance of the family. Not a patch was devoted to flowers. His family may have had all they needed, but their lives were drab and controlled by the Communists, who required them to work on a collective farm, for which they were paid only in produce.

Father, sensing that mother was unnerved by the primitive Uzbek way of life, asked if he could buy some coal. He did not offend the landlord by disdaining the cow dung, but explained as well as he could that we were accustomed to using coal. He also asked about a kerosene lamp for the evenings.

The landlord gave us a kerosene lamp and a container of kerosene. He was kind enough to give us *lepioshkas* and homemade yogurt. We did not have to worry about food that first day, and mother was able to calm herself before adapting to the differently cooked foods. She had already noticed that the Uzbeks made their pilaf in a wok by mixing rice, mutton, peppers, and onions.

That first day, after eating the *lepioshkas* and yogurt, I took a walk to familiarize myself with the neighborhood and found that there were four streets called Yangi-Chek. Later I learned that our street was First Yangi Chek and our landlords, the Uzbeks, appeared to be the only residents. It wasn't until later on that we saw a Russian family living next door and learned they were kulaks, wealthy Russian farmers who had been denounced as oppressors of less-fortunate farmers, and subjected to penalties and confiscation of property. Now they were in the same fix we were in.

When we were ready to sleep, my mother used the burlap bags and straw to make mattresses that we set out on the earthen floor. Hella slept next to mother, and I next to Shmulek, on the other side of mother and father.

The next morning, my father, Shmulek, and I took the long walk into town. There were stores along Lenin Street, the town's main thoroughfare, but there was nothing to buy. We turned in at an intersection of Lenin Street and came to the office of the People's Commissariat of Propaganda, the Agitpoint, a very powerful branch of the government which had administrative functions. Its purpose was to inculcate Communist ideology to the young, to proselytize, to persuade, to praise the system. It used every possible argument or trick to convince, lure, and enlist the average citizen to the Party. It was evasive where truth and facts were concerned, slanting and mangling both to suit its purposes.

My father and Shmulek went their way to get the lay of the land. Curious about the people, I lingered. I noticed that they had a yellowish complexion but, aside from the folds over their slightly slanted upper eyelids, did not look totally Asian. They had round heads, coarse straight black hair, and broad flat faces with prominent cheekbones. They were not heavily bearded like Europeans. Their huskier stature showed an intermingling of tribal characteristics, so much a part of the incursions and history here.

I became conscious that I was staring at the passersby and turned to look in another direction, where I noticed the Agitpoint office. I walked in. An army officer was giving a lecture about the war and I was hungry for news. There was a large map on the wall, and he was pointing out where the latest battles were taking place. Although he said that the situation was very serious and acknowledged great losses in lives and territory, he maintained that the Red Army would destroy the enemy in the end. He aimed his pointer at an area behind the Ural Mountains.

"This is where we are beginning to produce the newest weapons," he announced.

His audience was attending to every word. They were Russians, and to judge by their worried faces, refugees. I saw no Uzbeks there.

"Partisan units are being organized behind the enemy lines," the officer said. "Comrade Stalin, our great leader, is planning and organizing a strategy that will lead to victory. For security, he has evacuated most of the government offices from Moscow and moved them to Kuybyshev."

I was getting uneasy and left to seek my father and Shmulek on Lenin Street. In my absence, they had met some Polish Jews who had arrived a few days before from other slave labor camps in the Soviet Union. The fellow countrymen embraced one other, their thin bodies telling more than words about how starved they were for food and compassion, their hearts shivering with recognition of mutual suffering, their hands warily offered, unsure of trust. Having survived the internment, they were concerned about finding jobs and housing. They could not help one other, so the only consequence of the meeting was the opportunity to share the sense of freedom. To enjoy the freedom to walk the streets, to see the semblance of a normal world, where there was a hotel, a drugstore, a shop where one could make a purchase rather than wait for a *payok* (ration) to be issued.

Father learned about the open-air farmers' market, a bazaar which they called a *tolkuchka*, where new and old clothing, cooking utensils, soap, cooking oil, vegetables, and home-baked goods were sold. A black market operating with a pretense of legitimacy. When we found our way there, we were surprised to see wooden stalls with bountiful displays of fruit, vegetables, dairy products, meat, and *lepioshkas*. These products were brought in by peasants who had small private plots they were allowed to cultivate. We knew that the Fergana Valley was famous for its fruits and vegetables, but to our eyes, starved for the sight of color and something other than potatoes, this array was like straying into the Garden of Eden.

Eager to taste the blushing fruits, we bought *uriug*, sun-dried peaches and apricots, and let unforgotten sweetness ripen on our tongues. We knew that mother and Hella would savor these, too. We bought a few pomegranates, a fruit I had never seen before, and enjoyed a bright moment of guessing what taste lay beneath the leathery rind. We bought potatoes and vegetables to take home. Long captive, we felt a capillary of renewal inching its way upward within us, but it was stalled by the uncertainty and heavy dread with which we had become so familiar. I shared my own delight that I had found a library in the town.

I learned something about the Uzbeks. They are a Mongoloid people, a mix of Asian, Malaysian, Eskimo, Turk, and even American Indian.

I rather expected my father to think well of my discovery, but his deep-set eyes quickly flared. His eyebrows, when he was cautious and protective, met in a line across his eyes. I sensed his apprehension and stopped talking.

"Have no delusions," he added, "they live in Soviet territory and this is still a police state." He was pensive as we walked in the hot August sun.

"They have a library for their literature but no public transportation system," father intoned in an irritated voice.

We had a long walk back. After the Mari Republic, the heat was quite a change for us. We were breathing heavily by the time we returned to our mud house on First Yangi-Chek.

When we turned into our street, we saw a knot of our neighbors in conversation. We felt their dislike when they would not look at us. We wished they would be cordial but understood their behavior. After all, we were outsiders, intruders, we might be a threat to their very existence. They had their own history of invasions and battles, even before Russia had conquered their country and taken their land.

They had lived in Uzbekistan for centuries, had been conquered by Alexander the Great in the fourth century B.C.E., by the Arabs in the eighth century, incorporated in the Mongol empire of Genghis Khan in the thirteenth century, and had a series of other rulers, including recent memories of Russian tsars who wanted them to replace their traditional crops with cotton.

In 1916, the Uzbeks rose in revolt against the tsarist government, and thousands of them died. After the Russian Revolution in 1917, the Uzbeks resisted Soviet power, organizing a nationalist guerrilla movement that continued to fight the Soviet forces into the 1920s. They were given a separate designation in the Soviet Union but never gained independence. They continued to bristle under Russian domination. We had been sent by the Soviet Union. How could they trust us or befriend us?

I made up my mind to learn more about the geography and history of this area and kept my silence when we carried our food purchases into the house. My father, who had noticed an older Uzbek neighbor washing his hands and face in the irrigation canal where we got our drinking water, told mother that it would be a good idea to boil the water we drank.

"That's fine," she answered, "but we have no pots. They were stolen the night we arrived here."

Father and Shmulek had to go back to the flea market and returned with some second-hand cooking utensils. Shmulek also brought back a sack of coal. With primitive tools and primitive methods, my mother was able to cook our first meal in Fergana.

That night, after dinner, the family sat down to have a serious discussion. Even Hella, not yet nine years old, participated.

"Now," my father said, "we have to face the realities of life. Shmulek and I will have to look for jobs. You, Lusiek, and Hella too, should go to school. I don't know what kind of jobs we can find here. The Polish Jews we met in town knew as much as I do."

"Maybe the landlord can tell you what is available," mother suggested.

"He's a peasant on a collective farm. What will he be able to tell us?" Shmulek offered; but he had no faith in his own suggestion. "We'll go into town tomorrow, to the center, to Lenin Street. Maybe we can pick up some information there and decide what to do next."

The next morning, I asked to go along with father and Shmulek. I wanted to go back to the library on Lenin Street, but we took a turn to Pioneer Street, named for the Communist Young Pioneer organization. There we saw a large prison with armed guards posted in turrets high atop the massive surrounding walls. There were also guards marching around the prison walls, their rifles at the ready. Tall smokestacks rose above the walls, indicating that there was a factory inside the prison. Imprisoned, the inmates were actually cheap slave laborers.

When we went back to Lenin Street, we saw a large crowd of people standing near an outdoor radio speaker system hooked up high on a pole. They were listening to news coming directly from Moscow. We, too, stopped to listen. The announcer on the Moscow radio reported that despite the heroic resistance of the Red Army, Hitler's forces were advancing on all fronts.

From the weary expressions on the faces of the people, I thought them to be Russians who had escaped from territory now in German hands. There were no Uzbeks among the listeners. The people were careful not to criticize their leaders, but from their gloomy comments it was not difficult to deduce that they, as did I, deplored the stupidity of the government for entering into a pact with Hitler that had now brought calamity to the country. I refrained from responding to any comment, for silence was armor. A Soviet "bird," the colloquial term for an informer, could be there to swoop up a crumb of cynicism.

With a nudge, my father signaled for us to leave. He and Shmulek were anxious to find out what they could do to survive in Fergana, while I chose to go to the library again. Although several people were there reading periodicals and journals, they seemed to be Russians; strangely, no Uzbeks were there either. I knew the young Uzbeks were literate, they could read and speak Russian, but they shied away from the propaganda. This added to my curiosity about them and their country. I located a book that answered some of my questions.

The republics of the Soviet Union were divided into smaller units called oblasts. Fergana was the capital of the Fergana oblast and its most important city. Situated in the Fergana valley, 240 kilometers from Tashkent, the capital of the Uzbek Republic, it was the center of a rich agricultural and industrial region.

Fergana was known for its *maslo zavod*, literally meaning "butter factory," which in truth was a plant producing edible oil derived from cottonseed. By-products of the process were soap and nitroglycerine. The remaining substance was pressed into *zmicha*, a light brown paste used to feed cattle and for processing fuel.

Once the seeds were removed from the bolls so as to be pressed for oil, the cotton was sent to a very large factory for conversion into fibers and fabrics. The Fergana Valley was situated on the Syr-Dar'ya River, which provided irrigation for its extensive cotton fields, orchards, vineyards, and mulberry fields. Curious about the mulberry fields, I learned that silkworms feed on the eggs and seeds of the mulberry trees, and the fibers of the silkworm cocoons are unwound to make silk textiles. There was also a *shyolko matalka* (silk factory) in Fergana. The valley was famous for its silk and was once part of an ancient Persian silk route.

When we opted to go to Uzbekistan from our camp in Siberia, it was for no other reason than a better climate. What we did not know was that we might have made a propitious choice, settling in a republic with rich resources. I was eager to share my information with my family but kept reading, wanting to know even more about this fertile valley and its products. Unfolding for me was geography and history, subjects as nourishing as food. Engrossed in study, I did not think of the perpetual hunger or the debasement of sleeping on the raw earth. I did not have to think of the uncleanliness of body and clothes, the humiliation of urinating in full view of family and neighbors. The books in front of me were distractions from the squalid lifestyle we found ourselves in. I was still glad to be alive. At least now I had a general idea of where I was. To know more about Uzbekistan, I buried my thoughts in facts.

In the nineteenth century, the territory was conquered by the Russian tsars. Tajiks, Kazakhs, Tatars, Turks, and other tribal followers had settled there through the centuries after Genghis Khan and, later, Tamerlane, another Mongol conqueror, raided the area. They made up the populations around the cities of Bukhara and Samarkand. The Uzbeks were a Turkic-speaking people with an Islamic heritage. Russians were a minority.

When I looked at a map of the region, I saw two rivers, the Syr-Dar'ya and the Amu-Dar'ya, both of which flowed into the Aral Sea. A large desert, called Kyzyl Kum, lay beyond and was the cause of the fluctuating temperatures. There was little rain, which explained the dependence upon the rivers for irrigation. One discovery led me into another until I noticed they had newspapers. A chance to catch up on the current situation.

The Uzbekistan newspaper, *Pravda Vostoka*, seemed mainly to reprint whatever appeared in the Moscow *Pravda*, except that praise for fulfilling work quotas went to Uzbeks. That day the praise was for some cotton-picking Uzbek girls. I knew that the Moscow paper was a better source of information, but I was distracted for a while by two other newspapers: *Trud*, oddly a labor union paper, in spite of the fact that there were no labor unions in the Soviet Union, and *Krasnaya Zvezda* ("Red Star") the voice of the Red Army. One of my teachers back in Poland once said that you could judge a country by its newspapers. Here were the newspapers by which to judge this country.

In *Pravda*, I turned to the Jewish columnist, Ilya Ehrenburg, and read his appeal to the Red Army to perform heroic deeds and destroy Hitler's army. Sitting at the library until late in the afternoon, I continued reading, ignoring the signs of hunger that now began bothering me in earnest. I had not eaten since my breakfast of tea and bread.

When father and Shmulek came by to take me home, they told me they had learned a great deal that day, but did not want to discuss it on the street. I in turn told them that I had read about three big factories in Fergana that might have opportunities for work. I wanted to tell them more, but their silence suppressed my enthusiasm.

When we reached the mud house, we found mother and Hella sulking. They felt isolated in the tiny room. There was no one to talk to, and when they took a walk, the people up and down the streets were Uzbeks who turned from them like from a plague. Mother was too embarrassed to use the open hole in the ground and was uncomfortable holding back. We sympathized but had no solution to our current situation.

"Things are not promising here," father confided. "There are three factories here in Fergana, but you could not buy borscht with what they pay. People from other camps came here a few days before us and also are living in mud huts." He looked at Shmulek as if my brother should add to the sad observations.

"They told us how bad the malaria is here," Shmulek added. "There isn't much you can do to protect yourself against it. The warm weather, mosquitoes, and terrible sanitation conditions are all here." Shmulek looked at his hands and made a sorry attempt to hide them in his pants.

"We are dirty, we are hungry, and what do you plan to do to earn some food for us?" mother said in a sobbing voice, looking at father.

"The only way we can survive is by trading," father answered decisively. It was his way of telling us that he would have to deal in the black market again.

Mother, Hella, and I were worried about this decision, but my father and Shmulek assured us they would be very careful.

"You have to understand," father tried to explain, "everybody is dealing, dealing and stealing. They steal in the factories, in the stores, and in the offices. They wouldn't be able to survive if they didn't steal."

The penalties for theft were very severe, especially in wartime. From the highest officers at the NKVD down to the lowest strata, everyone seemed willing to deal on the black market for American dollars, worth a fortune in these unstable times.

"There are Russians here," my brother whispered, "who are trading in tsarist gold coins known as 'piggies.'"

My father rubbed the stubble on his face. "Some Russian Jewish refugees I spoke to are afraid the government may collapse and the Germans will defeat the Soviet Union. Should that happen, we would have to make a run for the border. Go to India, Afghanistan, or Iran. We would have to face the prospect of bribing border guards. That's what makes the demand for the American dollar so great."

"There is even talk that rationing may start soon," Shmulek said. We listened quietly. The food we were eating, meager as it was, might then become even scarcer, and available only at exorbitant prices. How much less could we eat and still survive?

At the end of August 1941, my father and Shmulek went to Lenin Street, the center of town. Father permitted me to go with them. He had already described the scene to me, but nonetheless I was amazed. Wherever you looked, men trading gold coins and American dollars. Russians griping openly about the military situation. Newscasts

blaring from the loudspeakers about the seemingly unstop-
pable German advance. Leningrad was practically cut off
and might soon fall into German hands. The Red Army
seemed to be surrounded, which meant the imminent loss
of Kiev, the capital of the Ukraine.

It was frightening to hear that the German army was
getting so close to Moscow. Russia seemed on the verge of
total defeat. If it were to lose the war, my father felt, dollars
and diamonds would buy us protection and escape. He
and Shmulek began wheeling and dealing. I kept my mind
on the war news.

In September, it was still bad; Russia suffering even
more losses, and England encountering hardships of its
own. A hint of good news came when England and the
Soviet Union invaded and occupied Persia. We wondered
why the news about the two-week campaign had been
withheld, and only the bleaker news of the fighting against
the Germans reported.

The occupation of Persia meant that England had
secured the Persian oil fields. Moreover, the British would
now be able to move much-needed supplies to the Soviet
Union through Persia. This was only a slight gain at the
moment, but did much to lift spirits.

There was another important development. A military
base was to be established in the Uzbek Republic where
soldiers would be trained for the new Polish army led by
General Anders. The base would be in Margelan, a city
very close to Fergana.

There was another piece of good news for us Polish citizens in the Soviet Union. The Polish government in
London was sending representatives to address our problems. The man they sent to Fergana was a Jew, a former
inmate of a slave labor camp, and his title was *mozh zaufany*
("trusted person"). His office had a sign with the Polish

eagle and the inscription, "This Trusted Person represents the Polish people before the Soviet authorities." Russia was putting on a decent face for the world.

Still another bit of good news: The Soviet government would permit the Polish government in London to send us food and clothing. This help was arranged through the Joint Distribution Committee, and the shipments would be routed via Persia. Meanwhile, the rumor of rationing had become a reality. The rationing of bread was most serious. The amount you received with a ration card would barely fill the palm of your hand. The bread was made of poor flour with other strange ingredients that added bulk but not taste. One never received a gram more than the official ration. Since the daily deliveries to the bread stores could not be depended upon to provide sufficient quantities, people sometimes lined up in the middle of the night for their daily allotment of bread or *lepioshka*.

There was a big oil and soap factory in Fergana, but you couldn't find a bar of soap or the smallest bottle of oil. The total output, we were told, was going to the front for the soldiers. In reality, large quantities ended up on the black market. The route from source to dealers was deftly managed. Even I, considered a child, could see the complicity between source and dealers.

The entrances and exits of every Soviet factory were well guarded, and the workers were searched as they left at the end of each shift. Ostensibly, the guards made sure that no one walked out of the factory with a piece of soap or a bottle of oil. In actuality, the guards were quite willing to take bribes in exchange for ignoring the thefts, although they put on quite a performance just in case anyone was watching. When a departing worker had several bars of soap tied to his legs under a pair of extra-large pants, the guard would make a special show of searching the upper part of his body. Or if the thief had a rubber tube filled with oil wrapped around his waist under his coat, the guard would pat down his legs.

The stolen soap and oil were sold to a distributor, who in turn had operatives to sell the merchandise at the *tolkuchka*. Everyone in this chain, from factory foreman to worker and guard, received a share of the proceeds. Still, this was petty thievery. There were bigger crooks operating inside the factories.

For example, several times a day a man would come by to haul away the waste from the factory's cesspools in a horse-drawn tank. Most of the time he really left with a tank full of oil or soap. This operation could only be effected in collusion with the factory's managers and foremen, because they would be held accountable for any production shortages. Another method involved the railroad tankcars used to transport oil products. The contents of a tankcar would be drained off through a hole drilled in the bottom. The loss would not be discovered until a string of tankcars supposedly loaded with cooking oil reached the distribution point. When the supervisor there discovered the loss and called the factory to ask why one car was empty, the manager would pretend to be surprised, since they were all listed as full on the shipping manifest. A delegation from the factory would go to the depot to verify that the tankcar was empty. A joint inspection would lead to the discovery of the hole in the bottom. What then, but to declare that a saboteur, an enemy of the Soviet Union, had drilled the hole. An investigation would ensue, and the security police would begin looking for the saboteur. Who was going to blow the whistle when so many ranking officials were in on it? The small thief made a small profit; the big thieves, police, and ranking Party officials made big profits.

Similar scams were in operation in the textile mills, the silk factory, and in other industrial plants. Surprisingly, despite the many guards, the same stealing went on in the factory in the prison on Pioneer Street.

With such large quantities of merchandise being lost, it was inevitable that the NKVD would investigate. Occasionally culprits were caught, managers as well as workers, and they paid dearly, sometimes with their lives. Nonetheless the stealing continued. Habit, desperation, greed all contributed; stealing was a way of life in the Soviet Union.

Every day, my father and brother went to the town center to trade, until one afternoon, in the middle of September 1941, they came home ill. The entire family fell ill with malaria. When it hit me, I shook terribly. Despite several layers of blankets I was cold, and shaking so hard I thought I would hit the ceiling. Procuring quinine pills was close to impossible. The troops had priority.

A neighbor, seeing our plight, told us about Dr. Wasserman, a Polish Jewish doctor who, like us, had been released from a labor camp. Luckily he was sympathetic and able to obtain some medicine for us.

Shortly after our recovery, we heard that the Polish army was recruiting and training in nearby Margelan. My brother Shmulek wanted to enlist. My father said he too would enlist if they accepted him. Father was fifty two years old at this time. To our dismay, the Polish army refused to accept Jews. Other Polish Jews told us how they had been rejected. One man, who never even reached the point of having a medical examination, was told he did not meet the physical requirements.

The Poles had lost their country, they had allowed Hitler to disperse and destroy talents and culture that had enriched their country, but they clung to their virulent anti-semitism.

General Anders's army did accept token Jewish enlistments, of which one was Menachem Begin. A leader of the

Betar Zionist organization in prewar Poland, Begin had been sent to a camp in Siberia but enlisted in General Anders's army, and went with it to Persia. From there he went to Palestine to become the leader of the Irgun, an underground organization working to establish a Jewish state.

My father and brother had black market dealings with a Jewish family from the Polish city of Wilno. It was in their house, near Pioneer Street, that we met Begin. My father, Shmulek, and I had gone to their mud house with a bread deal. There we saw a soldier in a Polish uniform. We were introduced to their friend Menachem Begin, also from Wilno. I had never heard of him before; now, shaking hands and briefly talking to him, I felt his greatness and destiny. Begin and I shared an interest in history and military affairs. I look back on that meeting as a special privilege in my life. I met Menachem Begin again in 1982 in Jerusalem. I had gone to Israel with a delegation from the Zionist Organization of America, and we visited Prime Minister Menachem Begin in his Jerusalem office.

The school term began, but Hella and I were not registered. Our first thoughts, upon arriving in Fergana, had been to find a place to live, familiarize ourselves with the city, and provide for ourselves. By the time we got our lives in order, it was too late to enroll in the Fergana school.

Around the end of September or early October 1941, the Communist authorities ordered all Polish citizens in the Soviet Union registered, which we thought of as nothing more than a census. Nothing in the questions asked by the registration agents aroused fear or distrust. The implications of this census did not surface for a while. Meantime, we were preoccupied with my mother's poor health. The last to contract malaria, she was hit hardest. Weak and listless, she would become exhausted by the household chores. Hella took over most of the cooking and cleaning. We began to call her Little Mama. She was able to cope with all of the family's needs except for washing linens and clothing. We had no water in or near the house, having to carry it from the irrigation ditch. To carry enough to launder our things was staggering, in every sense of the word.

We found a Russian woman on the outskirts of the town who would do the washing for us. That was her way of earning money. I was designated to take the laundry, bed linens, and clothing to her. I would tie up the heavy bundle, toss it on my back, and walk to the woman's house.

Once, while I was doing so, I was suddenly stopped by a militiaman. He grabbed my bundle and looked inside.

"Thief," he yelled out. "You stole this linen from the hospital."

"No!" I protested. "We're from Poland and it's ours. My mother is very sick, and I'm taking it to a lady to have it washed."

"You liar! No one in Fergana has so much bedding and laundry," the militiaman yelled.

In that respect, he was probably right. The Soviet people could claim very few household amenities. We had been carrying the bedding since our departure from Lwów. We had little else.

He took me to the militia station and accused me of stealing socialist property from the hospital, a very serious crime. The penalty could be many years in a gulag.

I cried and pleaded. I was able to explain in Russian, "I am a Polish citizen! This is all we have left from Poland!"

"Let me see your passport for proof!" The officer sneered, holding out his hand.

"I am only fourteen years old. I am listed on my father's documents." In the Soviet Union, those over sixteen were issued internal passports. Children under that age were listed on their parents' passports.

He began shouting. "You're lying! You're older than fourteen."

He had a militiaman accompany me to our house to verify the story. Because of my delay, my parents were already alarmed. Now I walked into our mud house with a militiaman and the bundle of unwashed laundry. Fortunately, my father was home, and he showed his identity document with my name listed on it. Polish citizens holding an *udostovereniye* were held in some respect. My parents verified that the bedding and other laundry was ours, brought from Poland.

The militiaman was satisfied with the explanation and left.

Shaken, I vowed never to go anywhere near a militiaman or an NKVD officer. Others had warned us, but it took this experience to bring the lesson home. From now on, we avoided them like the plague. Whenever I saw a militiaman on one side of the street, I ran to the other side. Given their name, you might think that the Workers and Peasants Militia was there for the good of the people, but Soviet policemen did not protect the people, they were an arm of the government, scrutinizing everyone's activities. The other, more important force, the NKVD, was divided into several directorates. The directorates were further divided into internal and external departments. The external were involved in espionage in foreign countries. During the war, Stalin set up a directorate called Smersh, an acronym for *Smert Shpionom,* which meant "Death to Spies."

We refugees were carefully watched; we were statistics on official records, restricted in the work we could do. We expected little sympathy and little assistance. What was becoming more difficult was the shortage of food.

As the war continued, more and more people fled from the advancing German armies and looked for a haven in Fergana. The need for housing and food became more severe. Having a ration card for bread did not assure us of getting our allotment. We spent many hours in line in the hope of getting our bread and other rationed items. The wait was always long, with people pushing and shoving and being generally irritable. By the time we reached the doors of the store, we might find the bread or oil or sugar gone. If it was there, you could buy either bread or *lepiosh-ka* as long as the weight was the same.

There were times when we left empty-handed. The signs of hunger were everywhere evident in the drawn cheeks, hollow eyes, shuffling weakened bodies. Desperate for any kind of food as long as it filled the stomach, people began to eat *zmicha,* patties made from by-products of pressed cotton seeds generally allocated for cow feed. We still were more fortunate. Father and Shmulek had sources for bread or vegetables that supplemented our rations.

As Polish citizens we had ration cards that were not predicated on work. Soviet citizens had to work, otherwise they did not get a ration card. Article 12 of the Stalinist Constitution specifically stated: "He who does not work, neither shall he eat."

The sorry fact was that working offered small compensation, hardly enough to cover needs. Consequently, many resorted to stealing or the black market. Most of the Polish people were involved in black market activities, one way or another. They traded in American dollars and sold soap, cooking oil, and cotton textiles stolen from the factories.

Desperate to earn a living, the Uzbeks on our street were subletting parts of their mud houses. Two new tenants moved into our street. One was a Polish Jewish family named Hoiberg, a mother, father, and their daughter

Rela, who was my sister Hella's age. The other family was
Russian Jewish, a father, mother, and young son. The
father had sustained a severe injury to his leg in the war.
Because he was a veteran, he was given a job in a store.

The family made a point of talking about the war. The
father asked me when England was going to invade
Western Europe and take the pressure off the Russian
front. I was careful with my responses to their questions.
Strangers to us, they could very well have been government informers. We did not trust the Russians, and they
did not trust each other. Spy nets were cast among the
poorest as well as among the prominent politicians. I was
not about to get into discussions with Russians about the
war, especially since it was going badly for them.

By the end of October 1941, the news from the front
was frightening. The Germans had just about completely
encircled the city of Leningrad. They had invaded the
Crimean peninsula and were within sight of the strategic
port of Sevastopol. The capital of the Ukraine, Kiev, was
now in German hands. The lives of many soldiers had been
lost in its defense. Large stores of equipment had fallen into
German hands.

News was coming through that the second-most-
important city in the Ukraine, Kharkov, had been captured.
Kharkov had once been the site of a huge tractor factory.
With the intensity of a general on the headquarters staff, I
followed every move on my large map of Russia. I had an
uncomfortable feeling that were my uncle Lemel here to
see me tracing war movements, he would hiss in my ear,
"Marshal Wenig! Still stuck on strategy?" Couldn't he
understand that these events were shaping my destiny, the
destiny of a young man who longed for an end to running
across the street when a militiaman approached? That
what I would like to do was attend school, find some pur-

pose in life. That I had to keep my mind occupied and not tremble in fear of this organized oppressive anti-human government.

Everyone was frightened. Panic-stricken newscasters on the radio appealed to soldiers to stand fast and defend Moscow. One broadcaster, a woman, tearfully announced, *"Vrag rvyotsa do Moskvy"* ("The enemy is tearing toward Moscow") and urged civilians, members of the Young Communist League, every patriot and soldier, to defend Moscow with their last ounce of strength. In the Moscow *Pravda*, Ilya Ehrenburg wrote stirring columns on the same theme. The Jewish columnist had a galvanizing effect on the Russian people; he gave them courage and his opinions were revered. The popularity of his column is shown by the following anecdote.

There were no cigarettes or tobacco to be had. Consequently, many were smoking a concoction of green grass and wood chips called *machorka*. A person would tear off a sheet of newspaper, make a funnel from the sheet, than would pour the *machorka* from a pouch into the wide upper opening of the funnel, fold it closed, light the wide upper part, and smoke it by inhaling at the narrow end of the funnel. This became so common a practice that one day an officer in the army, addressing his front-line unit, told them they could use any part of the Moscow *Pravda* to roll their *machorka* except the part in which Ilya Ehrenburg's column appeared.

I wish I could have felt the same reverence. I thought his writing was brilliant, but I couldn't reconcile a Jew writing with such fervor on behalf of a politically inept and corrupt government.

But perhaps the country needed someone with his rhetoric to prop up patriotism. The situation on the Moscow front became so precarious that Stalin summoned

General Zhukov from the northern Leningrad front and put him in command of the defense of Moscow. A million Muscovites were mobilized to dig deep trenches, build antitank obstacles, and string barbed wire. Many volunteers from the Komsomol—the Young Communist League—were ready to make any sacrifice necessary to defend the capital.

In Fergana and in the Uzbek countryside, more and more people were mobilized by the army. They began to draft older men. Draft boards were recalling soldiers recuperating from wounds. The people were imbued with the need to rally around their country for fear of the tyranny of a conqueror. Fear was the common cause solidifying their effort. The Russians may have despised their rulers, but they fiercely loved Mother Russia and expected everyone to defend it.

Occasionally, we would hear about a draft-dodger. The Russians were repelled by such reports but treated them with a touch of humor. One ironic story of a shirker had a message for the unpatriotic.

A Russian who did not want to be drafted shot off the index finger of his right hand. When he came before the draft board, he held up his hand.

"Look, comrades, I'm just not of any use to you because I do not have my right index finger. I simply could not pull the trigger of a gun."

To which one of the officers responded, "No problem. We really need people like you to run in front of our attacking troops and shout inspiring slogans. Practice yelling 'Hurrah!'" And the man was drafted.

The commitment to country was admirable. Perhaps the resolve to defend it came from the history of those who had tried to conquer Russia in the past. They were able to advance just so far before the formidable winter snows fell.

Every Russian knew that winter was a cruel deterrent to invasion. By the middle of October, heavy snows were reported in the Moscow region. By the middle of October, supplies from England were beginning to move through the Persian corridor.

And with all the adversity, with armies in fierce battle on several fronts, the leaders still went on planning an international Communist takeover. There was an institute that trained revolutionary leaders for other countries, the School for Eastern Studies, "Institute Vostoko Vedenia." That school and a Moscow medical university in the path of the advancing German armies had to be evacuated. The students and teachers were dispersed to remote areas, and we began to see Oriental students: Chinese, Korean, Indochinese. They were exceptionally well dressed, wearing finely tailored suits and overcoats and carrying briefcases. Although dispersed, they had their own quarters and avoided the rest of the populace. Their exclusiveness made us suspicious.

From the wife of a Russian Jewish man who worked together with my father in the black market, I learned that these students from China, Korea, and Indochina were being trained as future Communist leaders of their countries. She warned me not to approach them in the street or elsewhere. I took such warnings seriously, particularly because any inadvertent remark could be misconstrued and might endanger my father and Shmulek.

One of their business connections was puzzling. Alex, a young Polish Jew a few years older than Shmulek, was married to a very beautiful Korean girl he had met in Fergana. Not only was he a wheeler-dealer in the black market but he had good connections with the militia and the NKVD. In other words, if you got in trouble, he acted as intermediary with officialdom, charging a fee which he split with the authorities. The question was, who was this stunning Korean girl and what was she doing in Fergana? Had she arranged his introduction to the police? I never found out. The black market operators offered no clues or comments, an indication of the secrecy that enveloped every aspect of life. But in my fantasies, I spun international spy tales with a Korean seductress.

In Fergana, where the autumn temperatures hovered around fifty degrees, we did not have snow. Instead, we had heavy rains. When it rained, the mud hut with its mud roof was no protection, the rain dripping through the roof and turning our earthen floor to mud. It became a mud hut, mud roof, mud floor—a muddy mess. We covered our meager food supplies and what little clothing we had with a bed sheet, hoping to protect our possessions.

Father spoke to our landlord about the rain coming into our room from the roof. "Come see," he shrugged in reply; "the rain is coming into my room too." To him, this was as normal as the moon rising in the evening. There was no leak in the cow's room. The roofing was thicker over that room and more protective. A cow has more value than a human being. Could you get milk and dung from the humans in the other rooms?

Outside, the unpaved streets turned into a quagmire. Walking, putting down one mud-laden foot after the other, was like stirring and dredging up the muck in a marshland. It took forever to walk one block. And when it turned a little colder, but still not cold enough to harden the mud, it seemed that a crisis arose every day of our lives. Every crisis diminished our will to survive. Only father and Shmulek, who bore all the burdens, showed a ferocious resolve to plod through the difficulties. Mother, Hella, and I took solace in their strength. They found ways to relieve our distress. They brought rubber shoes for us, presumably obtained by barter in the black market.

Late in November, with the colder weather, our travail with the mud came to an end. The ground hardened, as did the roof, and the water seepage ceased. If the rainwater could have been used, I think we would have collected it in every pot and bowl, but the rain had come through a muddy roof, mud-laden, and was not fit for use. Now a clean-up began, not the least of which was cleaning ourselves.

Our method of bathing was to bring in a pail of water, place it in the middle of the mud room, and sponge ourselves down as best we could. Trying to maintain some delicacy toward each other, we only exposed the upper parts of our bodies. What we hid from each other were the hairy clumps around the genitals, which became nests for lice that bred there and, as well, infested the hair on our heads and armpits. They crawled into the seams of our clothing, black species and blond species. Were there parasitic varieties for bodies of different colors? If so, they were indiscriminate with us. The Polish Jewish people in Fergana referred to the lice as *mendeveshki*, a word they spat out with disgust, a word I had never heard in Poland. But then, I never knew of lice in Poland. Their crawling, biting presence in my hair itched, embarrassed me, shamed me. It was no consolation to know that everybody was infested. I spent the best part of each day using kerosene to scrape the lice from my body.

Lice infestation became epidemic not only in Fergana but throughout Uzbekistan. When typhus broke out, the health officials took steps to eliminate the pests. A public bathhouse installed a disinfection unit to kill the insects in our clothing. That November 1941 marked my first trip to the *banya*, or public bathhouse. The fee covered a Turkish steambath, a shower, and a *sano bezrabotka*, a sanitary cleansing of my clothing. It did not include my shoes.

Inside the bathhouse, which had separate sections for men and women, I was directed to a locker. No sooner was I undressed when two middle-aged women attendants came in to pick up my clothing for the *sano bezrabotka*. I wanted to scurry like one of the lice from the light of their eyes. I had never stood nude before a woman. I knew my face was reddening. Like Adam with the first flush of truth, I covered my genitals with my hands.

A buxom, fleshy woman reached over and pulled my hand away. She laughed heartily. "*Molodoi chelovyek, ty zhe durak, chto ty delaesh?*" ("Young man, are you stupid, what are you doing?"). I heard the male bathers around me joining in the laughter. Why hadn't someone prepared me for the fact that there were women attendants in the Russian bathhouses? Perhaps I, too, would have bared my body and casually walked among the other naked men. Perhaps, but I don't think it would have been with the same nonchalance. I, who had hidden from the eyes of my mother and sister, despairing when I had to use the human litter box in the yard, hardly had visions of myself as a princely figure, nor assurance of masculinity. Perhaps nude men developed an ease with one other after frequenting the bathhouse. Perhaps their egos inflated with admiring female glances. But I was not initiated. A mud hut in lice-ridden Fergana was hardly a good training ground.

Timidly, I gave my clothing to the woman for disinfection and gingerly stepped into the steamroom, where the steam hit me with cyclonic force. My first thought was that the steam emanating from the hot stones would kill my *mendeveshki*, but my next thought, less than a second later, was to run from the heat. It was just too hot for me. I settled for the showers. As I was about to enter the stall, I noticed some men lying on the floor with their eyes to the low cracks in the door, laughing uproariously.

"Come, boychik," one man called over to me, "Take a peek."

As I lay on the floor, I saw there was an adjacent room with a white enamel bathtub. On the floor was a middle-aged man pumping away on top of a young girl.

"Not one of us, boychik," the man slapped my shoulder. "Such accommodations," he laughed heartily over the use of the word and then went on to explain, "They are for the *vlasti*, the ones in power, the party elite, the secret police, not for the pro-le-tar-i-at." He stretched out the word to emphasize the class distinction.

I peeked and saw the two naked rutting bodies squirm, bounce, pant on the hard floor, then rose and turned my flushed face from the comrade. Through a crack in a door, I peeked at the mysteries of sex exposed, a hesitant peek, an indecisive quickening of interest. As I went to the shower stall, I wondered whether the comrade frequently tutored young boys in the bathhouse. I took a hot shower, scrubbed my eyes as I washed my hair, and prayed that my body was rid of the *mendeveshki*. Standing stark naked before the attendant, still embarrassed, I handed her the ticket for my disinfected clothing. Absorbed as I was in the recollection of that brief experience in the bathhouse, another thought superseded. I was no longer scratching.

In November, the city government tried to put some cheer into the lives of its people for the twenty-fourth anniversary celebration of the Great October Revolution. White bread appeared in the bread stores. In the gastronome, marmalade and jam appeared on the shelves. Milk was available for children only. There was some cooking oil, and for the first time, a brighter-colored soap rather than the usual very dark version. The oil and the soap came out of the same factory. Foods like milk, butter, cheese, and vegetables might be found in the farmers' market, but the price was prohibitive. Few people could afford such luxuries.

The story of poor nutrition could be read on a multitude of faces: gaunt hollow cheeks, dark-rimmed lusterless eyes, dry skin. If food was a primary concern, second to it was safety. Not only were the newscasts from the front frightening, but the sight of the wounded soldiers brought to Fergana from the battlefield was sickening. Some had lost legs or arms, many had lost both legs. Their cries, more like the sound of animals clamped in traps, and curses heedlessly hurled against the Soviet leaders, were alarming. They openly condemned their leaders for signing the treaty with Hitler in 1939. We were concerned that their criticisms could bring more blows and pain to them, and in some perverted way direct vengeance against the townspeople.

In our minds, the wounded soldiers were real patriots. They had fought valiantly for their motherland and were maimed for life. They spoke out in front boldly, saying they had been sent into battle with outmoded weapons, poorly trained, led by incompetent officers. They openly blamed Stalin's execution of the very capable generals during the purges of 1930. They told us of whole battalions encircled by the Germans and forced to surrender.

The government had been telling the people that the armed forces had abandoned certain areas in order to move to more defensible positions. What they were telling us was contrary to the official reports. In one instance, while I was taking a walk in the Park Kultury i Ordykha (Park of Culture and Rest) I saw a large crowd gathered around some severely wounded soldiers who were imprudently condemning the government for losing the war. Suddenly, militiamen arrived and started to yell at them.

"You're talking against the Soviet Union, you traitors!"

The wounded needed little to ignite their anger. These insults added fuel to their fury. A fight broke out, I saw a one-legged young soldier throw both his crutches at the militiamen. He yelled and cursed until foam ringed his mouth. He began to rave, wildly swinging his fists, daring them to add more injury to what their clumsy leaders had already done to him. I saw distraught, unhinged warriors wailing against their fates. I knew that the confrontation boded ill for the disabled Russian patriots. Militiamen were not trained to be compassionate. I ran from the scene, fearful they might arrest me for listening and observing all this. A few days later, the local paper criticized the wounded demonstrators for speaking out against the country and called them hooligans. A sorry tribute to their sacrifices.

The park scene in Fergana was like the twitch of a fly's wing on Stalin's nose. The great leader was intent upon turning the public eye to the fanfare in Moscow. The movie house showed newsreels of the military parade in Moscow's Red Square. On top of Lenin's mausoleum, the Russian leaders saluted the strutting soldiers and hailed the display of weapons.

In Fergana, large portraits of the members of the Politburo and the army commanders hung along Lenin Street. The importance and standing of officials could be gauged by how close to, or far from, Stalin's portrait their pictures hung. Malenkov, Beria, Bulganin, Molotov, and Zhdanov were very close. Farther away were Mikoyan, Kaganovich, Shvernik, and Khrushchev. Kaganovich was the only Jewish member of the Politburo.

A disgraceful event that took place after the establishment of the State of Israel will be an eternal blemish on Kaganovich's name. When Pfeffer, Mikhoels, Kvitko, and more than twenty other Jewish writers and artists asked permission to visit the newly established state, Stalin had all of them executed as enemies of the Soviet Union. This cruel act was done with Kaganovich's approval.

There was not as much fanfare over the November 7 observance in Fergana as in Moscow. The Young Pioneers, wearing their red scarves, marched down Lenin Street to the blaring martial music over the loudspeakers. I have an unguarded weakness for military songs. The vigorous rhythms stir something inside me, perhaps a longing to belong to a country, to be a patriot, to have a nation to cheer for, to be a person among the throngs that line the streets, waving a national flag and singing a spirited anthem. I try to fathom why, so many years later, I still remember the lyrics and melody of the song the red pioneers sang as they marched through the street.

> *Artileristy, Stalin dal prikaz.*
> Artillerymen, Stalin gave the order.
> Artillerymen, your fatherland is calling you.
> From the thousands of your batteries,
> For the glory of your mothers.
> Forward! Forward!

Is it that such songs help us forget our miseries? Take us outside of ourselves to visualize a better life? Hypnotize and inspire men to offer their lives for the promise of a better life? The trumpet, the drum, the human voice have magical, magnetic powers. Music is a language that mystically probes our deepest longings and makes an indelible imprint on our minds.

Events laden with meaning and passion also leave an imprint. The war years, when we were stranded in a foreign country, are unforgettable. Everything that happened impinged on our safety, our survival. Every word issued by the Party leaders was of consummate importance. Was there a word of hope in the speeches they made in Moscow during the October Revolution ceremonies?

Several days after the celebration, the Moscow papers arrived and we read of the speech Stalin had given to an audience of Party officials and army officers in the Mayakovskaya subway station. Why there? Usually important celebrations were held in the Bolshoi Theater, but not this time, because the beautiful building had been damaged by German bombs. There, on the underground platform, Stalin had spoken to the Russian people, quoting Hitler's vile references to the Slavs as subhuman.

"The Germans are intent upon conquering the land of Russia, intent upon enslaving and annihilating the people of the Soviet Union."

From atop the Lenin mausoleum, after accepting the salute from his soldiers, Stalin addressed his troops. He spoke of the glorious heroes of the past who had defended their country and whose victories had made it great.

Alexander Nevsky, who defeated the Teutonic Knights in the year 1240; Dmitry Donskoy, who defeated the Tatars in 1380; Aleksandr Suvorov, who won a great victory against the Turks in 1789; Mikhail Kutuzov, who was victorious against Napoleon in 1812.

On that morning of November 7, when the battalions that had paraded before him left for the front lines, he appealed to their patriotism.

Impassioned speeches replete with patriotic fervor, a contrast to another item in the newspaper, informing the public that the diplomatic corps had been moved from Moscow to the city of Kuybyshev. From the information in the paper, we deduced that the report of the withdrawal had been withheld for quite some time.

The streams of refugees from the capital were vivid proof of the chaos in Moscow. The refugees added quite a bit to what we read in the papers or heard on the radio. German units had occupied villages no more than twenty miles from Moscow. Widespread German brutality had panicked the civilian populace. Initially, the Ukrainians had embraced the Germans as liberators from Communist tyranny, but when the Nazis began to tyrannize and plunder the people, and conducted public hangings, partisan bands formed and fought the invader with whatever weapons they could get their hands on. There was little hope that the Red Army would be able to save Moscow.

The refugees arriving in Fergana brought stories of Communist decrees that threatened our meager sustenance. Rumors abounded. We treated the rumors with skepticism and dubbed them the O.B.S. Agency—O.B.S. standing for *odnaya baba skazala* ("an old woman said"). By the end of November, we were hearing rumors supposedly emanating from the highest authorities. While we pooh-poohed these as wild tales concocted by spiteful people, one was very frightening: The Polish populace of Fergana were to be rounded up and transferred to the Kazakh Republic.

Without notice, before noon on the first or perhaps the second of December, a horse-drawn cart driven by an Uzbek driver pulled up in front of our home. Two NKVD officers, easily identified by the blue braid on their hats, stepped down and shouted orders.

"Get your stuff together. We are sending you away from here. You'll be driven to the train station where you'll be told your destination."

Despairingly, mother and Hella clutched each other, calling out for pity. Father, always the strong, determined protector of his family, stepped forward.

"What's it all about?"

"Orders."

The officers were not rough, just formal, no comparison to the way we were treated in June 1940 when we were deported from Lwów to the slave labor camp. Perhaps their knowledge of the existence of a Polish army in the Soviet Union made the difference. Nevertheless, we started to pack our few household articles and scant wardrobe into some shabby suitcases and boxes.

Our Uzbek landlord seemed grieved over what was happening to us, but did not say anything. Obviously he was afraid. We did not know at the time that he had cause to be afraid. Fear was a by-product of authoritarian government. It was like a communicable disease that contaminated everyone. The first sign was loss of speech.

We felt the clamp of fear on our tongues as we complied with the instructions to board the wagon that was to take us off for our third Babylonian exile. We neither spoke to one another nor looked into one another's eyes. Each of us had an overflow of grief. To see it in mother's eyes, or Hella's eyes, or in the eyes of the Hoiberg family, our neighbors, added to our helplessness and guilt. We could do nothing to assuage the sadness.

As the wagon creaked along, the horse's body heaving with every hoofbeat, we joined a convoy of wagons carrying displaced Polish Jews. We saw no Christians. Most of the Poles had joined the army. Their loved ones were lodged close to the training camps. We Jews were not wanted as volunteers.

At the siding, NKVD personnel and railroad officials politely informed the assembled Jews that they were being sent to a camp in Kazakhstan. They told us to board the long line of waiting cattle cars. They provided food and told us to be patient. They must have known there would be a delay. Several days went by during which nothing happened and no one told us anything. There was nothing to think about except the ineptness of a government at war that would assign trained soldiers to herd harmless Polish citizens when the front lines were faltering and the Germans were twenty miles from the capital. One would have thought they needed all their resources to hold back the impending collapse, yet they were using valuable man-power and transport facilities to move us around. What threat did we present? How paranoid could this political system be?

Occasionally, the guards shared news about the war. On December 5, 1941, they announced that General Sikorski and Stalin, meeting together in Moscow, had issued a joint communique about the common struggle of the Polish and Soviet peoples against Hitler's Germany. We were to be set free. We could disembark from the cattle cars. Awaiting us were the same horse-drawn carts that had brought us to the train and now took us back to our mud houses. Another instance of wasted effort. The Uzbek collective farmers assembled to carry us could have used their horses and time more productively for the war effort. Did their God shake in disbelief?

Were there warring gods somewhere in space playing poker, placing bets, raising the stakes with every ante? How much cruelty did there have to be, how much havoc, to win? Was the folly on earth the fallout of their game? Was the Almighty King watching the human folly on earth? How long would it be before Almighty God stayed the hand of mankind from the slaughter in our day as he had done with Abraham so long ago? How I wanted to believe that God was in His heaven and would set the world aright.

While I waited for God, the clod-driven horse took us back home, where our landlord welcomed us and asked to talk with father, Shmulek, and me. Not mother or Hella. Moslems exclude women from serious matters. It was then that we heard how the NKVD had brought him up on trumped-up charges. They had handed him a prepared confession to sign. The confession, he told us, implicated him in counter-Revolutionary activities. When he refused to sign, they beat him, yet he still refused to sign. Recognizing that their obstinate victim would not bend, they decided to send him home.

He may have wanted to voice hatred and disgust for the Communists, but he kept his silence. What he considered necessary was basic insight and sense. In his simple way, he made a valuable point. "If you have your bones, you'll get your flesh back."

The simple homily in peasant language meant that if you were asked to confess to something and did not comply, expect them to beat you and torment you. But don't sign anything, for if you stand your ground, they'll let you go. They may beat you and destroy your flesh, but remember: If you have your bones, you'll get your flesh back.

We were now back in our former situation: hungry, since we had no food. Fortunately, we had not discarded our bread coupons. Unfortunately, our stock of rubles was dwindling day by day. I volunteered to stand on line at the bread store. I also went to the farmers' market in hopes of finding other items. What I found was that the food shortage was even more acute, the prices at the market higher. I managed to buy some *lepioshkas*, milk, potatoes, and dried fruit.

Mother prepared hot potato soup, our first warm food since the day we were ousted from the mud house. After we finished our dinner with tea and dried apricots, father and Shmulek discussed our financial situation. Father began by saying,

"We have some dollars and gold coins, but they have to be held for emergencies only. We have enough rubles for the time being, but we'll soon run short."

Weighing the facts, Shmulek said, "Even if we get jobs, what you can earn in Fergana in a month won't buy one day's food."

"True," my father agreed. "The people working in the factories all supplement their pay by stealing on the job."

That was the picture. The black market revolved around dealing in American dollars and gold coins, buying stolen property from the thieves and reselling it to a retailer, who in turn sold it on the black market at the *tolkuchka*. All this was dangerous, but the choice was starve or steal. Starving was a slow death, stealing also led to an unhappy end. Caught, you ended up in a slave labor camp in Siberia. Starve or steal. And if you chose the path of honesty? Officials, for their own political purposes, would uproot you, seal you into a cattle car, and ship you to a camp in Siberia. Starve, steal, stick it out! Some choice!

The plan was for Hella and me to enroll in a Russian school. In addition, I was to help out by doing all kinds of daily chores at home and acting as a runner for father and Shmulek. Although illegal trading was more dangerous than ever, father and Shmulek decided to take their chances in the black market on Lenin Street, which our people were now calling Wall Street. They certainly were not trading in stocks and bonds, or puts and calls. They were trading in ration cards.

After resting from the cramped, unnerving days in the cattle car, father, Shmulek, and I went to Lenin Street to find out how the war had been going. There, from the loudspeakers, we heard the stunning announcement that Japan had attacked the United States fleet at Pearl Harbor. With the initial shock and the pity for lost lives came the realization that America was now in the world conflict. Since Japan, as one of the Axis powers, was linked with Nazi Germany and Fascist Italy, the United States would be, in essence, allied with England, France, and Russia.

Father and Shmulek went on to pursue their business contacts. I went to the library to catch up on the Moscow newspapers. The librarian gave me a large stack of old issues of *Pravda* and *Izvestia*. New names appeared. Harry Hopkins and Averell Harriman from the United States were in Moscow, with Lord Beaverbrook from Great Britain, to discuss plans for rendering aid in terms of military equipment as well as raw materials. The Soviet Union had been clamoring for the English to open up a second front that would divert German forces from the eastern front. This strategy was now a serious possibility.

More recent editions of the papers showed heavy snow around Moscow. It was one of the most severe winters in Russian history, with temperatures going down to forty below. That was good news. I remembered the freezing weather during our imprisonment in the Mari Republic, a winter I had never expected to survive. History recorded the defeat of many invaders whose armies could not endure the harsh Russian winter. The weather was the Soviets' natural weapon. Perhaps that accounted for the fact that the Wehrmacht was at last being stopped by fierce Russian resistance.

I still remember reading about a unit of Russian soldiers under the command of General Panfilov on the Mozhaisk road. They threw themselves under the German tanks, blowing themselves up with hand grenades to destroy the Germans.

There was another encouraging news item: The Soviets were producing a new tank, the T-34, equipped with a 76-millimeter gun, that was superior to the German tanks. They were also deploying another new weapon, the Katyusha, of which the details were kept secret. Later, we saw these weapons on newsreels in the movies.

Reversal of the War

On December 21, 1941, the Red Army began a counter-offensive on the Moscow front that lasted into the early spring of 1942. The Russians were able to throw back the Wehrmacht as much as fifty kilometers. And for the first time, we saw pictures of enemy prisoners-of-war—half-frozen German soldiers surrendering in droves.

I was absorbed in the progress of the offensive. My father and Shmulek were absorbed in the realities of earning money to support the family. They were familiar figures on Lenin Street but had to be very careful. The security forces were checking everyone, pulling people off the street to examine their bundles, even the smallest that might contain the daily bread. They were looking for the goods that were disappearing from factories, warehouses, stores, and offices. Moreover, they knew very well that the missing goods were being sold in the farmers' market, because these were the same security officers who took bribes to ignore the thefts.

In disrepute among the people for their shameless pursuit of bribes, known to condone and assist workers lifting goods from the factories, the security police had to make a show of doing their job by cracking down on illegal traders and on dishonest workers in the factories. The answer to the problem was more NKVD recruits, more emphasis on public awards to Stakhanovites.

Toward the end of January 1942, father was picked up by a militiaman and taken in for interrogation. He had to appear before a *sledovatel* (interrogator) named

Tabachnikov, a vicious young man well known as a womanizer. Tabachnikov regularly had prisoners awakened in the middle of the night and fired questions at them under glaring lights while they were drowsy and befuddled. The questioning would go on for hours. His men would beat prisoners severely, especially around their genitals, and used tortures of all kinds, such as pulling out fingernails or knocking teeth out, to make them confess. Sometimes they even wrote the confession out for the prisoner to sign. Tabachnikov's brutality was so well known that many prisoners confessed just to avoid the torture.

My father was held for several days and nights. And he remembered our Uzbek landlord's advice: If you have your bones, you can put flesh on them later. Never confess!

For hours, Comrade Tabachnikov, the tough inquisitor, persistently questioned my father.

"How do you support your family?"

"We receive packages from my brother in the United States."

Tabachnikov did not beat him. I shall always believe that had he done so, father would have raised his fists too. He was a tough, strong soldier. Tabachnikov got no confession. Another interrogator was assigned. Father confessed to nothing. They found no illegal money on him, and had seen none being passed in the street. This was because the transactions always took place in our mud room, from which my mother rarely emerged. The paper dollars and gold coins were sewed into special pockets in her corset.

Back home, we were frantic. We spent sleepless nights worrying about father. We had no way of finding out what was happening. Shmulek looked for a fixer who might get father out. Shmulek had no contacts, but he thought that Alex, who was married to the beautiful Korean girl, might be able to do something. As it turned out, Alex was not able to help. Shmulek then approached Adek Weinstein, another of the Polish Jews who had been with us in the slave labor camp. Adek had the right contacts and was able to get father out.

When father came home, his brows were more strongly set in a straight line, his eyes deep and dark as caves no man would want to enter, his lips so tightly clamped that a breath could hardly sneak by, and a new quiver along his cheeks. That quiver, more than anything else, showed how frightening the interrogation had been. When he finally felt able to speak, he told us about the excruciating screams he had heard at night, some from women who were being beaten heartlessly.

I guess he must have stored those memories in the caves around his eyes, because, having lived through it and talked about it, he went back into black market deals, saying he had no choice.

The winter of 1942 was cold but not as unbearable as in the Mari camp. We faced the problem of heating our mud house with nothing but cow dung. When my father explained to our landlord about mother's failing health and sensitivity, he told us we could try a wood fire but we would have to cut our own logs. He showed us some trees beyond his fence. In all probability, the trees we were cutting down belonged to the adjoining small collective farm, but we had to take the chance. Fortunately, there were no complaints. We also purchased some *zmicha,* the light-brown paste that was a cottonseed oil by-product. When hardened in a press, the paste could be used as fuel.

Food was a bigger problem. The Soviet Union had lost a lot of territory to the Germans, especially the fertile land of the Ukraine. The government claimed all the produce from the collective farms and sent it to the army. That left very little, and at exorbitant prices for the civilians. We faced the winter without much hope.

Our only recourse was to write to Uncle Irving in New York for help. We could not openly tell him how badly we were faring. If we said anything unfavorable to the Soviet Union, the letter would never be passed by the censor. So we wrote that we were fine but had decided to move. There was no need for him to write back; we simply wanted him to know our new address. We hoped, of course, that he would be able to read between the lines and detect our impoverished state.

Uncle Irving got the carefully worded message and understood. Several weeks later, we were notified by the mailman that we had two parcels at the post office. Shmulek and I went there and presented the card from the mailman in order to claim the packages. The clerk went to a bin and returned to say that he could not give them to us because our name was not the same as the one on the packages; in fact it was spelled differently.

Our two years in the Soviet Union had prepared us for just such an eventuality. We knew that the clerk was simply waiting for a bribe. Shmulek folded the card around some rubles and handed it to him, upon which two large parcels appeared. The rubles had worked their magic.

To our delight there was a generous supply of food and clothing in the parcels. Canned meat, fish, Crisco, coffee, hot chocolate, soup cubes, jam, chocolate, tea. Just looking at this collection of extraordinary groceries appeased our hunger. There was also a ten-pack carton of colorfully wrapped cigarettes. Can you imagine ten packages of cigarettes in a country where people were smoking straw rolled in newspaper? There were stockings, shirts, and a pair of patent leather high-heeled lady's shoes. A decadent capitalistic country producing high-heeled shoes when the world needed food. An absurd item to send to a family living in a mud room? Not at all. Uncle Irving shrewdly knew the exchange value of a product that would ultimately buy favors. I was already spinning stories in my head of a high-ranking officer seeking the favors of a vain woman, offering her the glamorous shiny high-heeled shoes in exchange for state secrets. The fate of a country teetering on high heels.

It was as if a genie had crossed the sea in the package, appearing with a huge fortune when we rubbed our hands over the shiny shoes. Every can was a ruby, an emerald, a pearl that could be redeemed for necessities, or used to buy attention or consideration, or goodwill or privilege, or to gain access to whatever stubborn bureaucrat the future might put in our path. We talked into the night about the practical uses for the gifts. My parents decided that for the time being, not a single can was to be opened. They would all be stored for an emergency, for a pay-off to a commissar one day.

Except for the clothes. The socks and shirts from Uncle Irving came at the right time. Fergana was indescribably harsh that winter. From December 1941 through March 1942, it was bitterly cold. We had no snow, but on many days cold rain poured down, seeping through our clothes, chilling us to the bone.

Food became more and more scarce. The only food allocated us was the daily ration of coarse bread, four hundred grams (less than a pound). The whole ration could be consumed in just a few bites. If food came to the farmers' market, it was prohibitive in price. It wasn't difficult to fathom why the prices were so high. The Uzbek farmers stole the produce from the farms, then had to bribe the authorities to look away, and at every juncture someone had to be paid off.

The economic conditions affected everyone. Ethics went to war and were fatally wounded. Doctors stole medicine from the hospital and sold it to their patients. With the money received from the patients, they were able to buy food at the farmers' market.

Then news filtered through that ships from England and the United States, making their way to Russia via the northern route to Murmansk and the southern route through Iran, were bringing vast amounts of weapons, raw materials, clothing, and food. A trusted Polish person in Fergana, the *mozh zaufany*, appointed by the Polish embassy in Moscow, received a shipment and distributed it to us.

Father, Shmulek, and I received new leather shoes. The feel of them, the look of them, the comfort of them was just undescribable. Toes that did not have to curl against rain seeping through cracked shoes. Mother and Hella also received some clothing. There were shirts, there were blankets, and there was food: powdered milk, white soap, some canned food, tea, and coffee. Such gestures restore one's wizened view of humanity. I shall never forget that the Joint Distribution Committee, an American-Jewish relief organization, prevailed upon the Sikorski Polish government in London to forward the relief items to us. They fulfilled the biblical command to be charitable to others.

Relief that this was, our daily conditions were still abominable. The rain kept coming through the roof. Going out to the toilet in freezing temperatures, making your way to the hole in the ground, settling yourself on the wooden board which partially covered the hole, was profoundly embarrassing. It took its toll. Many of us took sick with colds. When typhus erupted and raged through Fergana, it was difficult to get into the hospital and difficult to obtain medicines.

Only once there was a moment of distraction. Our landlord invited us to share pilaf with his family. When a family like his had food to share, there could only be one explanation: he had stolen some mutton from his collective farm.
The meat was not kosher, but we ate it anyway. When
there is no meat hanging on your bones, your skin detects
and lunges at the smell of animal flesh. Every cell develops
taste buds that cannot resist the aroma of meat. We felt sure
that God would forgive our transgressions, particularly
when He offered no other way for us to alleviate our
hunger.

Despite our being guests at their table, the landlord's
wife, who observed the tradition of covering her face with
a long black veil, hardly spoke to us. She averted her eyes
from the men in our family and ignored mother and Hella
as well.

The Uzbeks were conditioned to the land, to the weather, to whatever conqueror ruled over them. They seemed
impervious to threats and ignored edicts. They clung to
their traditions and adhered to the code of their Moslem
society. They had their *tchai hana*, their tea houses, where
they met and socialized. The Uzbek men poured their tea
from china teapots into china cups. The women were never
included in their social functions. In the teahouse, which
had no chairs, the men sat on a platform with their legs
folded under them, chatted, drank endless cups of tea, and
listened to Uzbek music which was beamed to them from
Uzbek radio stations.

The Communist authorities tried to teach them that
women should be treated equally, but they would not
change their tradition or the treatment of women. The
younger Uzbek women tried to bring about a change.
Tamara Chanum, the popular and famous Uzbek female
chanteuse of the time, appealed to the men for acceptance

and equality, but was unsuccessful. The men listened to her songs and applauded her talent, but considered them Allah's gift for their pleasure. Their eyes glazed and their heads nodded as they inhaled the smoke from a nargileh, the local version of the Near Eastern waterpipe, which cools the tobacco smoke by passing it through a reservoir of water. Familiar melodies and lyrics reaffirmed their cultural habits. They countenanced no breach of tradition. Their teahouses were recreational, they were sacrosanct.

Neither Russians nor Polish exiles were welcome in the Uzbek teahouses. As Moslems, they considered both Christians and Jews to be infidels. The Uzbeks on our street did not talk to or look at us. Their attitude toward other religions was but one more example, for me, of the prejudice and malice that prevailed on our planet.

Next to our house lived a family that had been exiled from Russia many years before. The best I could figure out was that they were kulaks, well-to-do farmers who had opposed the Soviet collectivization of the land or had perpetrated anti-socialist crimes. They told me they were Russian Orthodox Christians. Because they too were persecuted, they understood our plight. They told me that they were not hated as Russians, but as Christians, since the Uzbeks considered them infidels.

Knowing that others suffered religious stigma or deprivations was of little solace when we looked into unfriendly faces or when our stomachs rumbled for food. The winter months brought more shortages and more obstacles to obtaining food. At no time did we touch Uncle Irving's provisions. We lived like the others, lining up in front of the *lepioshka* bakery or the government bread store, sometimes in the middle of the night to be there when the gates opened in the morning and before supplies ran out. Many in the line were very tired from their day's work but knew of no other way to assure their rations of bread. They were irritable, pushing and shoving their way into the line. Some sat down on the ground, securing their spot, and fell asleep.

One night, not far from where I was standing, an old man sat down, fell asleep, and began snoring, his chin resting on his chest. His intricatedly embroidered *shapka* began to slip down his forehead. A young boy eyed the bright *shapka*. He took a few steps toward the man, assured himself the man was soundly asleep, removed the cap, and tried it on his own head. Alas, it was too big. He put it back on the man's head, took a hesitant step or two, turned back, tried it on again, moved it to one side of his head, then to the other, held it down with the palm of his hand, lifted it, put it back. His capers were amusing. It was as if with each try he was pushing a current of air into his head, as with a balloon, to blow his head larger. Finally, the boy walked away with the *shapka* on his head. The old man snored and slept on, oblivious to the loss. The onlookers had a moment of amusement. No one stopped the boy from engaging in this act of theft. They remained in their places on line and hoped the shipment to the bread store was not stolen in transit.

All kinds of stories circulated: the flour expected by a bakery was stolen; one store paid off the bakery to get its daily quota earlier; a warehouse or a flour mill preferred one bakery over another; delivery men skipped one store for another that passed them a bribe.

There were long lines for every product. We learned to walk around with knitted cotton bags crumbled in our pockets because we might happen on an unexpected delivery anywhere along the row of stores. All of a sudden, while walking, you would see a person running. Your immediate instinct told you that he had seen a delivery cart carrying bread, so you would take off after him. Others seeing you pulling the cotton yarn bag out of your pocket would run too. In a split second, people were running from all directions with the same thought in mind, coming to a halt before a bread store. It would be like the childhood song of Old McDonald who had a farm and everyone ran after the farmer's wife who was chasing a goose. And like that song, it often turned out to be a wild-goose chase, because the bread cart that stirred up the activity very often was empty and returning to the bakery, or the bread delivery was going to a different store. Once, after running with a crowd, we found that people were lining up only to discover that up front, at the head of the line, there wasn't a bread store at all.

Bread became an obsession. There were days when we did not get any bread ration. Many resorted to eating *zmicha*, which was normally used as animal food. We could not face the thought of eating it. My mother mournfully remarked, "It does not seem possible that President Roosevelt could sit there in the United States, knowing how much we are suffering, and do nothing about it."

Poor mother was losing her ability to see the world practically. The real world was coveting and stealing to stay alive.

That reality was whittling away at my own ethics. On one of those days when we barely had anything to eat, and only a small bread ration was left and there was no outlook of obtaining any for the next day, father urged us to go to bed early, hoping to stave off hunger with sleep. Father wrapped the small remaining piece of bread in a newspaper and placed it under his pillow.

Hella and I could not sleep. If we lay down on the straw-filled burlap sacks, we would hear a chorus of stomachs rumbling and grinding on emptiness, so we stayed up reading by the light of the kerosene lamp. But when you are that hungry, words on a page become a blur. When you know that the only food in the room is under your father's pillow, that scrap of bread looms larger and larger in your head, more fragrant and tantalizing than you can bear. Hella told me she was going through the same torture. We conspired to get the bread from under father's pillow and eat it. Hella would raise the edge of the pillow and I would slip my hand under to pull it out. The movement close to his head, the crackling of paper close to his ear, woke my father. He turned into a raging animal, physically beating Hella and me.

"How could you do such a thing?" he screamed. "How could you think only of yourself?" Mother cried uncontrollably, for our pain and for our shame.

Ever since then, I have anguished over the sad fact that this incident teaches, that hunger can become so acute that it eradicates all one has learned of ethics and decency. I anguish over my shame that I would have sated my hunger at the price of making the others face greater hunger. I anguish over the selfishness my father and mother recognized in me. I anguish over the fury my act provoked in my father, who must have suffered more deeply than I from his grim awareness that we were in such straits that a small piece of bread had to be hidden from hungry children because it might be needed the next day. I had succumbed to the behavior of an animal. I had forgotten love, respect, and consideration for the people most important to me. That was the lowest time of my life.

That his children were starving and desperate enough to pilfer the bread from under his pillow had its impact upon my father. The man who had within him a strongly constructed sense of pride that defied the humiliation of Nazi and Communist subjugation, the man who grieved over land, stores, and home stolen, who, after his community was scattered and driven to barren, icy, hostile regions, was trying to hold his family together, now witnessed the moral breakdown of his own family. He knew he had to do something to ameliorate our hunger.

Remorse and responsibility for our act may have contributed to the change. I saw a solemn determination in his eyes, more than the usual hustling toward the marketplace. His innate sense of where and with whom to make deals was as acute as ever. He had an intuitive compass that picked out the right apparatchik, the one he could deal with. It took a while, but he made a connection with the manager of a bread store, and this resulted in more bread for us.

Marcus, the manager, was a Jewish war veteran from Minsk, a city in Byelorussia. Seriously wounded in combat with the Nazis, he had been rewarded with an appointment as manager of the bread store. Father and he entered into a business deal wherein he would supply father with several loaves of bread daily, to be sold on the black market, for which they would divide the profits.

The store manager had his own axe to grind, for he was still bitter against an army command that sent foot soldiers into battle against tanks. When his beautiful wife died of typhoid, he could not overcome his grief. Screw the government! He would make his crippled life easier by playing their game, skimming off a bit of profit for himself.

For us, the logistics of this arrangement presented several problems. First, how does someone, particularly an emigre, get several loaves of bread out of a store without arousing suspicion? After all, even with a ration card, you would not receive a whole loaf. We decided that Shmulek and I would pick up the loaves during the night, when it would be difficult for anyone to see what was going on. We delivered the bread to a designated retailer who was the other partner in the scheme.

The bread we delivered to him was still warm from the ovens. Warm bread weighs more than cold bread. The shopkeeper would weigh the warm bread on the scale for a ration card holder, meting out the regulation amount. A few grams could be taken off each loaf as a consequence, and he was able to set aside a sizable stock that he could resell to black marketeers—at a substantial profit, of course.

The bakery itself was also skimming off a profit by altering the ingredients that went into in the bread. Since flour was in short supply, the baker was expected to add fillers to the dough. By increasing the proportion of fillers, the baker stretched the number of loaves he could produce. He obliged the government by filling his quota, and the extra loaves were sold to the bread store manager at a profit.

The ration card system offered the bread store manager another opportunity. The monthly ration card had dated stubs that were each good for one daily ration of bread. There were thirty or thirty-one stubs, depending on the month. When a customer presented the card, the store manager cut off the appropriate stub. At the end of the day, he pasted the stubs on account sheets provided by the ration card commission. Every few days, he delivered these sheets to the commission, three trusted members of the Communist Party in Fergana. The chairman of the commission was also the secretary of the Komsomol.

The three-member commission, after examining the pasted coupons, was required to burn them. Required, but by tacit agreement, not executed. Why burn the sheets when they could be sold to people like my father and Shmulek, who would resell them to a store manager? The store manager would present the sheets to the baker for a supply of bread equivalent to the ration coupons, and would thus have a larger stock to sell. Then back to square one. Trim off a piece, black-market the shaved pieces, collude with the authorities, bribe, steal, survive. There were several bread stores in the area, all with the same operation, but father dealt only with the war veteran, Marcus.

The chain of operators and profiteers went down the line.

The most trusted members of the Communist Party were corrupt. The entire population of the Soviet Union witnessed and perpetrated thievery. The NKVD, the Workers' and Peasants' Militia, factory managers, workers, men and women, everyone. A comic picture could have been drawn of the typical Soviet "new man" (or woman) as a split figure with one hand outstretched to take, the other shoveling out. Taking in and meting out. The system made a farce of the clause of the Stalinist Constitution that declared: "He who does not work, shall not eat."

What also helped was that Shmulek got to know the chairman of the commission. He was a familiar figure on Lenin Street. A handsome man who attracted attention. I often saw him with the most beautiful Uzbek girl in Fergana. He was well aware that heads turned when he was out walking with her. She was tall, her nut-brown skin like honey poured smoothly across her forehead, cheeks, and tiny nose. Her brown eyes were ringed with black lashes, the color of the long black braided hair that shimmered along her tall body. She had the grace and elegance of a princess, unlike the gait of a Communist milkmaid. She made me recall Mania, my touch on her young body, the smell of woodland in her dark hair, and I wondered if there would be a time when I would again walk with my arm around a girl, lift her face to meet my eyes and yield to my desire to kiss her.

Whenever I saw the Uzbek girl walking with the Communist chairman, I remembered the schoolroom where Mania and I had shared embraces and transitory seclusion from the mounting crisis for Jews in Poland. I looked at the Uzbek girl and concluded that she had to accept the embraces of the chairman because her world too was threatened. Many times I would see her father, a factory manager, on his way to work. Once, long ago, he had owned the factory and had been a capitalist entrepreneur. After the October Revolution, he had agreed to turn the factory over to the Communists. Since they needed his expertise, they had spared his life and allowed him to manage the small factory.

The lovely princess and the chairman did not live happily ever after. The chairman, still a young man, was hit by a truck as he crossed the street. I don't know whether she grieved over his death. I did not see her at the state funeral where he was eulogized as a true disciple of Comrades Lenin and Stalin, and an honest member of the Communist Party. Shmulek lost a good business connection. But the good and honorable members of the commission picked up the scent of rubles. Father and Shmulek continued to ply their trade in bread and ration stamps.

Much of the profit went to pay off the good honest members of the Communist Party. Father and Shmulek considered that the cost of doing business. Enough remained to pay the high prices of potatoes, cabbage, onions, milk, and occasionally some butter, yogurt, and eggs. We considered ourselves affluent. True, we still lived in one room of a mud house, and our toilet still consisted of a board over a hole in the garden. There was nothing better in the area. Even the local representative of the Polish government lived in a similar mud house.

Life became easier, but not safe. Black marketeering was a serious crime, often punished with the death penalty. We lived in continual danger. If any of us was late coming back to the mud flat, mother would faint from fear that we had been arrested by the NKVD.

We tried to spare her fright by telling her to expect us at a later hour than we actually anticipated returning. I myself was not involved in any of the business deals and tried not to worry her by staying too late at the Agitprop office, where I went occasionally to attend lectures on the military situation.

The lecturers were tried-and-true members of the Communist Party, wounded veterans no longer fit for battle. Their accounts of the progress of the war were combined with propaganda for the Communist cause. I knew what they were doing, but lingered anyway, eager to hear the war news and study the maps.

I was especially interested in the many changes being made to motivate the troops and enhance their patriotism. A regime that had shot the tsar was now decorating former tsarist generals in order to show its citizenry that everyone was united in the war to defend Russia. A warm wind to fan patriotism and arouse the army to greater sacrifice blew from the government propaganda.

The medals, bestowed ceremoniously, were the Order of Suvorov and the Order of Kutuzov, named for famous Russian generals of the eighteenth and nineteenth centuries.

The second change was the reintroduction of shoulderboards on the army's dress uniforms. Shoulderboards had been abolished during the October Revolution as an exploitative capitalist device intended to emphasize the difference in status between ordinary soldiers and officers. Reintroduced, they became a colorful addition to the drab uniforms of the Red Army.

The third change was in the national anthem. Starting with the October Revolution observance in 1944, the

"Internationale," the song of the Revolution, was replaced by a less revolutionary, more patriotic anthem heralding a new world order, the "Hymn of the Soviet Union." The common man was the Soviet man. The new anthem, more melodic and lyrical, did not call for world revolution but for solidarity. The Soviet leaders thought this would make a favorable impression on President Roosevelt and Prime Minister Churchill, their new allies.

At the Agitpoint office, I learned that key Party functionaries were exempted from military service. This in itself said something about Soviet politics, but before long rumors were circulating about a number of cases in which unimportant people had bribed highly placed officials in order to obtain an exemption document, known as a *bron*. Another example of the unsuccessful attempt to create a classless society.

I frequented the Agitpoint as often as I could, eager to hear the war news. In the summer of 1942, after the Germans were pushed back from Moscow, weakened by the Soviet counterattack in the winter and spring fighting, Hitler rebuilt his shattered divisions and chose a different strategy. His thrust, more to the south, was meant to cut off the Soviet army and gain control of the Baku oil fields in the Caucasus. His armies advanced deep into the Caucasus and, from there, advanced on the Volga River toward the city of Stalingrad.

Heavy fighting ensued throughout the summer. The Red Army was again on the defensive, trying to hold back the powerful and newly equipped German armies. Hitler's forces pushed forward to the Volga.

As the autumn of 1942 approached, rumors began to spread that the Polish army, known as the Anders army, would be leaving the Soviet Union to go to Iran, and from there it was to join up with the British. Talk was already circulating about a plan to bring the Polish army from Iran to North Africa, to participate in the battle against the German and Italian forces there, the famous Afrika Korps commanded by Field Marshal Rommel.

That must have been a joint decision with England, but it clearly differed from the original plan for the Polish army to fight side by side with the Red Army on the eastern front. In my young mind, it looked like a betrayal. Most of the Polish volunteers had only too recently been released from Soviet slave labor camps, and the Russians apparently feared that they might be bitter and unreliable as a result.

There was another, more political consideration that came to mind. Should Hitler be defeated by the combined Russian and Polish forces, the Poles would be partners in the spoils. If a Polish army helped to liberate Poland, this might interfere with Soviet plans to control this neighboring country as part of the postwar Communist world order. The Soviets certainly knew that the Poles disliked the Communist system and would not voluntarily accept it.

When news spread that the Anders army would be fighting outside the Soviet Union, in another theater of the war, Jews who were Polish citizens saw this as an opportunity to leave the Soviet domain. Shmulek was one of the many Polish Jews who once again attempted to join the Polish army. But again he was rejected. Jews were not wanted.

Appeals were summarily rejected or ignored. Jewish volunteers were turned down even in the rare instances where there were social connections between Jews and Polish officers. In Fergana, the Simon July family had befriended a Polish *porucznik* (lieutenant) who used to visit their home, obviously enjoying the company of their son Leon and daughter Sala. When they asked him to facilitate Leon's enlistment, he responded:

"The flowers will go, and the garbage will remain here."

His meaning was: The Christian Poles were flowers, the Jews were garbage.

The comment was reprehensible. Many of the Polish Jews in Fergana were professional people: doctors, lawyers, engineers, architects, teachers, and businessmen. The lieutenant showed little sense of breeding. He wouldn't have known one flower from another. He wouldn't have been able to hold an intelligent conversation with those he referred to as garbage. Prejudiced, warped minds! Because of its deeply ingrained antisemitism, Poland was deprived of virile, scientific, creative, competent volunteers when it could have used all the help it could get. And so, the Polish "flowers" bore arms for the Allies, and the garbage, such as my family, was left to rot in the Soviet Union.

While we brooded about being locked into an unalterable situation, we struggled to survive. So did this vast, unfriendly country. The winter of 1942 was harsh. In our mud house, we could find no solace or comfort. Cold winds and rain battered the insubstantial frame. Hella and I tried not to talk about our parents' hardships and the danger. We blew on our cold hands and concentrated on our schoolwork. In Russia's so-called Ten Year School System, I was registered in a high school class, she on the an elementary level.

Some of my classmates were Russians, probably the children of refugees who had escaped from the advancing German troops. The majority were Uzbeks, who kept to themselves and conversed with one another in the Uzbek language. Each ethnic circle seemed to have a fence around it. I was curious about the schism between Russians and Uzbeks. When I finally broke through the Russian aloofness, I asked about the hostility.

The first burst of dislike was directly at us, the "Polacks." As for the Uzbeks, who were Moslems, anyone who was not a follower of Allah was an infidel. Bluntly, if the Moslems had the power, they would slaughter all of us because we were not Moslems. These inbred hatreds were restrained because there was strict discipline in the school.

We were given instruction in algebra, geography, history, Russian literature, and gymnastics. In the literature course, we had weekly assignments to memorize Russian poems. My having learned the language helped. For most of the Polish students, it was difficult. We had an excellent male teacher for algebra. The textbook, written by Kiselev, was logically arranged. Algebra was not that dependent upon knowledge of Russian, which helped the Polish students to cope.

History was taught in two parts: one covered the ancient and evolving civilizations, the other was known as "The Short Course History of the Communist Party, the Bolsheviks." The course on general history had a Leninist slant. With every advancing civilization, the emphasis was upon the revolts that had taken place during those times. Roman history was defined by the Spartacus rebellion: its causes, an analysis of why it failed, the inevitability of its failure because there was no Leninist revolutionary party then. If there had been such a party, the revolution would have succeeded. Throughout the ages, every society failed because government was predicated on favored classes. Kingdoms collapsed because there was internal unrest. Empires expired because the people were exploited. Parliaments had no future. Communism was going to change history for all time.

As for the obligatory second course, we traced the origins of Bolshevism: the conditions that bred discontent, the leaders who took action, the events that led to the October Revolution and the subsequent success of communism.

The former course was a world view; the second, a national view. Both courses were considered very important. The
Russian and Polish students took these courses seriously
and did fairly well. The Uzbeks were not as diligent. To do
well required many hours each and every day of homework assignments and memorization of poems.

Fizkultura (gymnastics) included military exercises,
such as climbing barricades, jumping, and marching to
military songs. There was a song for every aspect of the
curriculum. With all the difficulties of the past three years,
I had not lost my innate response to military songs. I
learned the lyrics and sang gustily with the rest of the class.

Although I had heaps of homework, and had to schedule time to wait on line for our daily bread rations, I continued to be fascinated by military matters. I went to the
farmers' market to make food purchases whenever they
were available and then to the library to read up on the
news from the various war fronts. I followed every move
of the brutal battles at Stalingrad where the Russians put
up a valiant resistance, fighting from street to street and
from building to building. We were overjoyed when we
heard that the German Sixth Army at Stalingrad, under the
command of General Paulus, was surrounded. One Soviet
army from the south met with an army from the north at
the city of Kalach, on the Don River, a pincer move that
trapped a huge German army there.

I felt a shiver of excitement when Rommel was defeated at El-Alamein by General Montgomery in November
1942. I hoped this marked the beginning of a turn of events.
I was even more excited by the Allied invasion of French
North Africa under the command of General Eisenhower.
This surely signified the beginning of the end of Hitler. But
the war was far from over, and our struggles were far from
finished.

The Soviet Union had lost most of its food-producing areas during the first year of the war and was now relying upon food supplies from the Central Asian republics, including the Uzbek Republic. The government confiscated food supplies in and around the villages of Fergana. Little was left for the civilian population in the area, creating acute shortages and ever increasing prices.

I continued to pick up the loaves of bread from the store manager for my father's business operation. We became more and more dependent upon that source.

Insufficient food was one problem for the Soviets, the casualties that decreased their armed forces were another. The Red Army began drafting older men to serve in the fighting forces and in essential wartime projects. They drafted our landlord, who was about fifty years old and the father of three children. His wife, his children, and the neighbors bewailed the heartlessness. The best they could hope for was his being sent to a construction project largely manned by civilians.

The construction project, the Farhad Stroy, was a large dam and hydroelectric power station on one of the major rivers of the Uzbek Republic. Posters urged patriots to enlist. Tens of thousands of civilians were drafted for the project. People were rounded up in the streets. Old people were taken off the collective farms in spite of their being essential to the production of food, which was in such short supply. An aura of urgency hovered over the project. Looking back, was this a Soviet response to rumors of atomic energy research in Germany? Their frantic scurrying for equal power? Or, more reasonably, preparing power to produce the weapons for an extended war. In fact the Soviets were beginning to stem the tide of the German onslaught against their country.

The War Is Coming to an End

In the spring of 1943, the Red Army defeated the Germans at Stalingrad and commenced a drive into the Ukraine in the area of Kursk. One small victory, however, did not mean the end of war.

Many battle tales would unfold about the atrocities committed. There was a shocking report that burst upon our horizon and had a devastating effect upon the Polish community in the Soviet Union. A hideous war crime in a forest area near Smolensk, in a place called Katyn.

Back in September 1939, when the Polish army was defeated by the massive German blitzkrieg, its remnants escaped to the eastern part of Poland. There, unexpectedly, they met units of the Red Army that had just entered eastern Poland. The Polish officers thought the Red Army had come to join forces with them in the war against Germany. What they did not know was that in August 1939 Hitler and Stalin had agreed to divide Poland. The Red Army was moving into Poland to take over the part of the country allocated to the Soviet Union. It disarmed the Polish warriors, carting off thousands of them to prisons inside Soviet territory.

Two years later, the Germans invaded the Soviet Union. In due course they occupied the area around the city of Smolensk, including the Katyn forest. The Germans claimed that Russian peasants had led them to mass graves in the area of Katyn where thousands of Polish officers and soldiers had been executed by the Soviet security forces. They said they had begun digging and found the graves. The incident provided Germany with powerful propaganda, exposing the brutality of the Soviet Communist system. The Germans exploited this information, a good ploy to turn attention from their own callous conduct toward Jews and other non-Aryans. They invited the International Red Cross and the Polish government in London to investigate the heinous massacre.

The Polish government-in-exile, upon learning the facts, submitted an inquiry to the Soviet government expressing the wish to send a delegation to visit the site. The Soviet government issued a total denial of the German charges and accused the Germans of trying to divert attention from their own guilt in mass executions. The Soviet government also accused the Polish government of complicity with Germany in fostering the lie. The accusations and invectives from both sides resulted in the breaking off of diplomatic relations between the Soviet government and the London-based Polish government.

In Fergana, where the population was now predominantly Jewish, the German version was more credible. The Jewish refugees reasoned that with Germans advancing on Moscow, the Soviets could have evacuated the officers, imprisoned since 1939, to serve in General Anders's Polish army. Furthermore, the Soviet government had never mentioned being unable to evacuate the Polish officers and had never apprised the London-based Polish government of the need to do so. Nor had it ever reported that the Polish officers had fallen into the hands of the Germans. Had the rules of international warfare been observed, there would have been no blame.

In addition, so it was reasoned, if the Germans had captured the Polish officers imprisoned by the Russians, they probably would have drafted them into the Wehrmacht or sent them to their own slave labor camps. Germany had prison camps, but not in a frigid subhuman wasteland. We based our opinions on our own experiences in Siberian slavery. We never doubted that the Soviet government had executed the Polish officers.

When I discussed the reports with a Russian, one I trusted, he said, "If we killed them, that was no reason for the Polish government in London to raise the issue at a time when the Red Army is losing thousands of its own men every day in the war against Hitler."

He was echoing the Soviet propaganda that accused the Polish officials of duplicity, of playing into the hands of Hitler's propaganda machine and undermining the alliance against Germany.

As a consequence of the accusations and counteraccusations, the Soviets broke off diplomatic relations with the Polish government. The local Polish consulate was closed, and we no longer had a representative to watch our interests. The Jewish refugees in Fergana felt orphaned.

Not too long afterward, we felt the repercussions of the severed ties. The Fergana radio station reported that Polish citizens in Fergana were clamoring for Soviet citizenship. To assure an orderly process, Polish citizens were asked to line up in front of the office of the local NKVD to request Soviet citizenship, the order said. A shudder went through the Polish Jewish community in Fergana. Obviously, the Communist government intended to force us to become Soviet citizens. They were testing our commitment to the country that offered sanctuary to us. They could not know our hearts, the veins of which stretched back to our ancestral homeland, waiting for the day when we could return to Poland.

My family, like the rest of the Polish community in Fergana, would rather have seen themselves dead than accept Soviet citizenship. We considered Soviet citizenship a verdict of life imprisonment. I would have put a bullet through my head rather than accept Soviet citizenship.

Most of us went into hiding. Our house was located behind a vegetable and corn field. The corn stalks were very high. Father and Shmulek built a hideout in the corn field. Wood branches, tall enough to cover our height, were lashed together with rope. Small pieces of wood were pressed into the soft ground. The lashed twigs were fastened with rope to the wood in the ground. We could easily see through the twigs. It was a flimsy contraption, but the corn stalks provided added secrecy. We called it our little sukkah because of its resemblance to the temporary shelter built for the Jewish holiday of Sukkoth. Somehow it worked.

My sister Hella stood watch in the street and alerted us when officers of the NKVD appeared on our street. The moment Hella saw them at the end of the street, she let us know and the four of us jumped into the hiding place. At night, father and Shmulek and I slept there in a standing position. The NKVD looked for us at least twice during the next three weeks.

We lived like that, hiding in fear, until we heard a local radio announcement that the NKVD could no longer contend with the overwhelming demand and would accept no further requests for citizenship. The Soviet cancellation of this project sent a clear message that it had not succeeded. Tentatively, we let our guard down, but only partially, for we simply did not trust the authorities.

They tried other schemes to woo Polish settlers into their Communist ranks. A few weeks later, we heard a radio announcement to the effect that Polish patriots in the Soviet Union had formed an organization called Zwiazek

Patriotów Polskich (Union of Polish Patriots). Wanda Wasilewska, a Polish woman novelist, was its leader. She was married to a Ukrainian or Russian, which is why I associated her name with the Communist Party. His name was Korneichuk, also a poet or novelist. Wasilewska was the author of a novel, *Tecza*, meaning "Rainbow," which had been translated into Russian and later became a movie. Other names in the Union of Polish Patriots were people I had never heard of before. One of them, a Colonel Zygmunt Berling, was said to be organizing a Polish volunteer army in the Soviet Union to fight side by side with the Red Army on the eastern front.

At this juncture of the war, Hitler's armies were being turned back on all fronts. On the eastern front near Stalingrad, General Paulus's Sixth Army had been captured and its soldiers herded into Soviet prison camps. The German losses, including those killed, injured, or captured, amounted to over three hundred thousand men. The Germans had also been pushed out of North Africa. The Allies were in Sicily, making plans to invade Italy. It looked as if Hitler and his Axis partners, Italy and Japan, would be defeated. If the Soviets were victorious, they would have a greater impetus to spread Communist doctrines. This was the right time for the Soviet Union to prepare a Communist-oriented government for Poland. Thus, the appeal to Polish patriots.

From the beginning, we understood the Union to be a Soviet scheme. It was a Communist committee and not a government agency, thus it had no legal power to draft Polish citizens into the army. They could take volunteers. My brother Shmulek had tried very hard to enlist in the Polish army organized by General Anders, but had been rejected because he was Jewish. He was willing to sign up, but not in a Polish Communist army.

Generally, the Poles in Fergana were skeptical about the Union of Polish Patriots. They were convinced that many of the troops in the new volunteer Polish army were actually Polish-speaking Russians and Ukrainians. There was little response to the call.

To provide itself with an aura of legitimacy, the Union of Polish Patriots opened schools in areas where there was a Polish population. They opened one in Fergana. All the Polish students in the Russian school were transferred to the Polish school, Hella and I among them. The textbooks were printed in Polish, and the teachers were Poles. Like the teachers in the Russian schools, they tried to lure us to Communism. Again, we were amazed at the revolutionary schemes to convert us. The diversion of money and manpower to this end, at a time when the country was coping with a major war and its resources were taxed to the hilt, was amazing.

Of course, we Polish students were happy to be in a Polish school. At least here, we thought, we'd be learning and speaking in our own language. And it was good to read our own Polish literature, especially the great poet Adam Mickiewicz. Our teacher was a woman named Marysia, a Polish Jewess, who revealed no allegiance and expressed no belief in the Communist system. We regained a sense of connectedness when we heard our Polish history again, in our native Polish language. For social studies, we had two male teachers. Another teacher, a young lady named Tabachnik, taught algebra. Attending this school was like a homecoming. It was pleasurable to meet and speak to Polish students. Hella felt the same way. I met and liked Sala July and Marysia Stillman, Hella's classmates, because they, too, took their studies very seriously. We had a great deal of homework, but we had a sense of doing something important, at long last.

Despite my heavy homework schedule, I continued helping my father with his business activities. He and Shmulek continued the transactions with the bread store manager and the ration cards. Shmulek had ingratiated himself with the secretary of the Komsomol, the highest-ranking officer of the local Communist youth organization. A trusted and highly respected leader, this man, an Uzbek, was chairman of the ration card control committee. He and two other trusted Party members were charged with burning the used bread coupons every few days. Trusted, respected, yet watched by higher officials. These higher officials may have been collecting bribes themselves, but someone on an even higher rung was investigating the disappearance of foodstuffs. When the pressure was on, arrests had to be made to prove officials were doing their job.

One evening in the fall of 1943, Shmulek was late in coming home. We had all gone to sleep when suddenly we heard hammering outside. Two militiamen were breaking down the gate to our landlord's garden. A moment later they broke down the door to our apartment and barged in, demanding to know Shmulek's whereabouts. Jerked from his bed, half-asleep but half-expecting this disruption at any time, father's judgment was clear. "Shmulek is out with friends this evening."

With fists as brutal as sledgehammers, they struck him on the head, chest, arms, accusing accused him of lying. But father stuck to his story.

"If there were any reason for us to worry about him, would we have been sleeping?"

"We've seen your son with a batch of bread ration coupons and chased him."

It was enough for father to know that Shmulek had escaped. When they demanded that he tell them where

Shmulek might be hiding, not a syllable of disclosure would pass his lips. Father insisted that he did not know where Shmulek was and denied that Shmulek had any bread ration coupons. They beat father more horribly, but he yielded no information. The militiamen screamed and cursed and showered him with blows, but father could not be forced to incriminate Shmulek. The militiamen left with threats to the family. The militia were the regular police. Had they been NKVD officers, the more cruel political police, they would not have left us alive.

Through all this, my mother and Hella stood horrified, their mouths agape, their cries trapped in throats petrified by fear. My heart, too, was full of emotion; my eyes, too, filled with terror; and my mind marveled at my father's stoicism. And a strange human thought wrenched itself from the grip of terror. Father had endured the beating and insults because he was taking the blame for Shmulek's crime, accepting the penalty that might appease the Communist lust for brutal punishment. I whispered words of thanks that father had managed to withstand the blows. I whispered thanks that Shmulek had escaped, and I whispered a hope that the God of these men would be satisfied with the vengeance.

Shmulek had escaped, we figured, but where to? Had the NKVD gotten hold of the coupons? If so, they would have evidence to implicate him in the illegal operation. We would be unable to rest until we had located Shmulek, but we dared not venture into the night to look for him lest we be followed. Shmulek did not return to the house that evening, but we had an idea where he might be. Next day we went to the house of father's business associate, Mark Wrobel, and found Shmulek there. We felt the sweet sweep of relief.

Shmulek told us that he had picked up the bread ration coupons from the Komsomol secretary and put the packet under his shirt.

"It was an unusually bulky package. The secretary needed rubles, a lot of them, and so he gave me more coupons than ever before. Well, the militiamen spotted me on the street, my shirt bulging from the concealed package. They ordered me to stop, but I ran as fast as I could into the bakery, the Socialist Artel."

One of the workers in the bakery was Simon July, the father of Leon and Sala July, our school friends. Like us, he and his family were Jewish citizens of Poland. They would not betray us. Nor did we want to jeopardize their safety. A knowing look, a mute exchange, conveyed Shmulek's trouble to Simon July. Shmulek flung the package of bread ration coupons behind the flour bags piled high against the back wall and ran toward the Wrobel apartment to hide. The two militiamen and a detective, hot on Shmulek's trail, ran into the bakery, but Simon July revealed nothing about Shmulek or the package thrown behind the flour bags. Father remained with Shmulek, and I ran to tell mother and Hella that he was safe, at least for the time being.

The problem now was how to squelch the case against Shmulek. It was obvious that the militia officers could not identify the man they had chased. They had probably come to our apartment because my father and Shmulek, so often seen loitering on Lenin Street, dubbed Wall Street because it was the scene of so many transactions, were already under suspicion. Or maybe a competitor had informed on them. Whatever the cause, the question now was how to find a fixer, someone who could be paid to take care of the problem.

For safety's sake, my father and Shmulek never discussed such matters with mother, Hella, or me. They were keenly aware that we were more vulnerable if interrogated. I do not know exactly how it was done, who was bribed, or who did the bribing, but it got done. For sure, some high official was contacted, which came as no surprise because in the Soviet Union everyone could be bribed. It was just a question of arranging things diplomatically. Many rubles and even dollars changed hands, but Shmulek was a free man again and came back home to resume his life and business.

Sometimes incidents of this kind took on elements of a game. Stakes, pursuit, hiding places, ransom, players dressed up in uniforms or rags depending on their role. So much imagination, surreptitious activity, struggle, and fortitude went into it. Of course! Life was the prize. That's why father and Shmulek went back into it. For expatriates, wheeling and dealing was the only way to survive.

Trouble shadowed our movements. Several weeks after Shmulek's run-in with the militia, my parents entrusted me with a sizable sum in rubles to purchase food at the farmers' market. I had enough money to buy a quantity of potatoes, cabbage, onions, dried fruit, or whatever the collective farmers brought in to the market that day from their small private plots. What they sold was supposed to be the share of production allowed for their own use. Everyone knew, though, that the farmers hid, stole, and sold produce from the collective farms. Food was so scarce that prices soared.

I was toting two large cotton-knit shopping bags which I soon filled. As I made my way through the crowded bazaar, I heard a roaring command, *"Obysk!"* (Search!).

The two gates to the enclosed area slammed shut and the bazaar swarmed with militiamen. Anyone carrying a shopping bag with produce was ordered to the side. I was pulled over by a militiaman who examined my two full bags.

"Where did you get the money to buy so much?" he shouted.

Of course, I was carrying suspiciously large quantities in my two bags. One bag had ten kilograms of potatoes, equivalent to twenty-two pounds, for which I had paid fifty rubles per kilogram, a total of five hundred rubles. What might seem like an inordinate quantity had to be measured against a family of five whose main diet consisted of potatoes. Our family could eat ten kilograms of potatoes in three days. But measured against the average monthly salary in Fergana at the time, about a hundred and fifty rubles before governmental deductions, one of my bags was equivalent to four months of a worker's salary. In the other bag were items for which I had paid another 400 rubles. Together that amounted to about six months of a worker's salary before deductions. Those of us who had full shopping bags were marched off at gunpoint to the militia headquarters.

Paling with terror, feeling the breath of death on the back of my neck, I followed the others. The militiamen were marching us off to what I felt was sure death. Russians, Ukrainians, Uzbeks—a brigade of guilty people, and I, probably the only Polish citizen, was carrying more produce than anyone else.

I was one of the first called in before a militia officer, and when he saw the contents of my two bags, he accused me of being a German spy, the logic being that only a spy would be able to buy so much.

"I am writing out a confession for you to sign," the militiaman said gravely. "You are a German spy."

Spying was a capital offense. He was condemning me to the firing squad. My heart was full of terror, my lips trembled with emotion, crying out,

"I'm Jewish! How can you accuse me of spying for Hitler?"

This meant not a thing to the officer.

"You're a German spy!" he repeated. "I'm writing out a confession for you to sign."

My blood was leaping over pebbles of fear. My head was spinning, my body cringing with dread.

Did the interrogators know what hunger was, I wondered. Did they know what it was to scrounge for a piece of bread hidden under a pillow? What would they do in our circumstances?

These were the buddies of the first Russians I had encountered when we had crossed the river San into the part of Poland occupied by the Soviets. These were the buddies of the Russians who had ordered everything on the menu in the local restaurant to fill their bellies. Here I was trying to do the same. But for my act, I was going to be forced to sign a confession of spying.

I knew enough to be aware that forced confessions were a favorite Russian tactic. During the purge trials, ranking officials had condemned themselves to death rather than endure horrendous torture. A confession cleared them of guilt in what would otherwise be an atrocity. I had heard about an interrogator who told a suspect he would make him confess not only that he was guilty of the stipulated crime but that he was the king of England.

Fearing that I might be tortured if I did not give in, I remembered the advice of our Uzbek landlord, who had warned that one must never confess to anything. His words stuck in my mind: "No matter how much they beat you or torture you, you must never confess. If you have your bones, you'll someday get back your flesh."

I thought of my father and how the words "Do not confess" had protected his dignity. Those words had pulsated through his veins with every blow from the militiamen. The words now rang in my head as I was sent out to the yard and told to wait.

As I leaned against the grillwork of the gates, trying hard to be brave, I was spotted by Alex, my father's business associate. Alex was a fixer with contacts among the security police. When he asked what I was doing there, I told him the story.

Within half an hour, I was called in before the militia commander, Comrade Captain Wislow. He was a tall, stocky Russian with blue eyes, probably in his fifties. He gave me my two shopping bags and told me to go home.

Alex was waiting outside. I grabbed him and kissed him, and asked how he had done it. He explained that he have given Captain Wislow two flints for a cigarette lighter. Cigarette lighters and flints were something almost unheard of in Fergana during the war. The Russians didn't even have matches to spare, because matches were rationed.

It was like finding myself in an absurd surrealistic arcade where everything is out of proportion, and when you reach for a ladder to climb to safety, a cigarette lighter comes into view, floating and flaming, and a Polish hand grinds at you. I could not believe what had just happened. I had been accused of being a German spy, which would have meant the death penalty, and then, for two flints for a cigarette lighter, I was let off scot-free with two shopping bags of produce for which I had paid about nine hundred rubles. It was mind-boggling.

It was not euphoric, however, for I was drained of energy. My eyes stared unseeing, my face was fixed in shock, my legs trembled, and my feet stumbled as I held on to Alex. We were quite a distance from home, and Alex, knowing that I was in no physical or mental condition to get there by myself, helped me get there.

When I walked into our one-room apartment, I found my mother in a faint because of my being so long overdue. In those days, in the Soviet Union, in the city of Fergana, when you did not come back within the time expected, you were presumed apprehended by the security forces and whisked away to work on the Farhad Stroy dam project.

I told my parents what had happened. I wanted to tell them that having given me a role in making the risky bakery deliveries, they had primed me for life in the Soviet Union, where man has one goal, to protect his life. My parents were an example for me in spite of my doubts as to my own bravery or stoicism. I was not sure whether I had handled myself properly. I knew I owed my life to Alex and was sure that my father would repay him. I felt that the debt I owed Alex would come to haunt me in the future. At this moment, however, I fell onto the straw mattress, hungry but with no desire to eat, trying only to forget the day's events. I lay immobile just as I had in the cattle car upon our arrival in the Soviet Union, indifferent to the outward clatter, seeking refuge in the deep unknown. I was alone in the dark place which no one else could enter to hurt me, reaching an inner depth deeper and wider and higher than the mud house in which there was nothing but a trailing semblance of a self. I had to find a way to immunize myself against the pain and cruelty of life, a way to react to the terror I had to face. With the murmuring reassurances of familiar voices around me, I sank into a deep sleep.

The following day the family had a serious discussion about changing our activities. In view of my experience in the market, we were to make small purchases only.

"It is true that it will require more trips, but I can't stand the suspense anymore," mother argued. "I worry too much when each of you goes out. When you are late in coming back, I imagine you in the hands of the police and it is too much to bear."

She pleaded with father and Shmulek to curtail their business activities. They were becoming too conspicuous, and it was dangerous. But father and Shmulek answered that there simply was no alternative.

"It's that or starvation."

Father made his plans known. "I have to accumulate enough money to get us out of the Soviet Union as quickly as possible. The war will soon be over. We have some dollars and some things from America that we can sell, but we still need a great many more rubles to pay off the NKVD and get the proper exit documents."

Another reason he needed to raise money was to be able to get a better apartment, because the mud hut had become too depressing for mother.

My father's optimism about the war coming to an end was justified. On both the western and eastern fronts, there were heartening developments.

After the great defeat at Stalingrad, the Germans tried one more summer offensive against the Soviet Union. During the month of July 1943, they attacked from two directions to cut off the so-called Kursk Salient, south of Moscow. They planned to capture the salient and then drive on toward Moscow. The German high command threw massive forces into this offensive. The Wehrmacht was equipped with two brand-new heavy tanks, the Tiger and the Ferdinand. But the Soviet command was apparently forewarned of the German offensive and built up its forces inside the salient for a counteroffensive. At this juncture, the Red Army was very well equipped, not only with war materials from Russian factories, but with huge shipments from England and the United States: tanks, trucks, jeeps, airplanes, even shoes and soft goods. I was awed by the sight of an American jeep driven by NKVD personnel in Fergana. I also saw an American-made Studebaker truck. I had long hoped that the Allies would do something to stop Hitler. Finally they had begun.

Every day the radio announced huge battles taking place in the area of Kursk Salient and described the powerful forces deployed there. In a seesaw of emotions, we felt apprehension as well as confidence that the Red Army would beat back the German thrust. Before long we learned that the German forces had, in fact, been stopped, and better yet, that they had been beaten back at two strategic points. In the north, the Red Army had retaken the city of Orel. In the south, it had overrun the city of Belgorod. It was a great victory for Russia.

During the victory celebration, I realized that the head of state, Premier Joseph Stalin, was also the commander-in-chief of the Red Army. Stalin issued a statement that was read on the air by Yuri Levitan, Moscow radio's most important announcer. In a loud, booming voice, he named and commended the generals and units that had participated in a certain action, ending with the words, "*Vechna slava geroyam pavshim borbye za svobodu nashey strany. Smert nymyeckim zakhavatchikom*" ("Eternal glory to the heroes who fell in the struggle for freedom of our country. Death to the German invaders"). After Yuri Levitan concluded, there was a thunderous salvo of artillery, saluting the victories at Orel and Belgorod. Such acknowledgments followed each victory until the end of the war.

The news from the western front was also very good. The Allies had driven the German and Italian forces from North Africa, then had gone on to take Sicily, and finally had invaded Italy itself. Facing defeat, Italy's leaders overthrew Benito Mussolini, the country's Fascist dictator, and surrendered.

The Red Army continued its offensive and liberated the city of Kharkov. The Kharkov Army Group was now renamed the First Ukrainian Front. (The southern army groups were renamed the First, Second, Third, and Fourth

Ukrainian Fronts. The northern groups were renamed the First, Second, and Third Byelorussian Fronts.) The front armies continued their westward advance, crossing the Dnieper River and liberating the capital of the Ukraine, Kiev. Euphoria swept the country. Despite hardships and suffering and hunger, we began to feel that better times were ahead.

Then, a strange new development took place that affected the Polish community. During the 1943 fall offensive, the Red Army captured the city of Smolensk and the nearby Katyn Forest, where the Germans, as mentioned earlier, had discovered mass graves containing the bodies of ten thousand slain Polish officers. Soviet investigators claimed that the Katyn massacre had been perpetrated by the Nazis.

The Polish refugees in the Soviet Union, however, were convinced that the Soviets had murdered the officers. We dared not say so openly, for as instructed in the Polish school, we had to support the Soviet claim. Privately, among ourselves, we felt certain that the Soviets were lying. We swallowed the lies, and tasted the bitter bile of cowardice.

The end of November brought exciting news about the Teheran Conference between Roosevelt, Churchill, and Stalin. The Soviet newspapers did not discuss the agenda of the conference, but we were optimistic. The Russians were impressed by Churchill, who gave Stalin a sword made of gold as a gift from the king of England to the citizens of Stalingrad for their heroic defense of the city. We hoped that President Roosevelt would influence Stalin to behave more humanely. We also hoped that the future of Poland would be discussed, particularly the legitimacy of the Polish London government, which we favored over the Union of Polish Patriots, the Communist front organization. Although the meeting of the three world leaders was a sign that the Allied nations shared a common war goal and were acting cooperatively, the speakers at the lectures I attended continued to accuse Britain and America of deliberately delaying the opening of a second front in northern France.

Despite the good news, our living and food conditions did not improve. Hunger, like a black cloud, hung over Fergana. Most of the food grown locally was sent to the front and to the newly liberated territories. According to the papers, the Germans were conducting a scorched-earth campaign wherever they were forced to give up land. As they retreated, they burned towns and villages to the ground, ripped up the railroad tracks, and drove all the livestock westward.

War atrocities abounded and were splashed across the headlines. We saw innumerable pictures of mass hangings of civilians by the Germans in the territories they had occupied. The response was heightened patriotism among the Soviet people. The army fought more valiantly. Soldiers and civilians praised Stalin for the successes of the Red Army. They now called him a genius and the inspiration for victory. He took on the aura of a god, and students wrote odes to the "Great Stalin." We in the Polish schools were also required to shower praises upon the great, wise, and all-knowing leader.

Attributing the turnabout to Stalin's genius led to more forceful Communist propaganda. Only Communism could so inspire soldiers to be dedicated warriors. Everyone could learn from their courage and sacrifice. On and on, the propaganda campaign lauded the virtues of Communism and the Soviet system. Impressionable young minds were easy prey to the perpetual barrage of propaganda. Those of us who recognized the ploy but were hostage to the government joined in the praises, particularly the Russian students in our school. The propaganda was pervasive, constant. The outside world had no way of knowing how intensely Communism was purveyed.

One day, an officer at the Agitpoint was lecturing on Red Army operations.

"The Germans," he said, "sowed mines everywhere, so the Red Army brought in *shtrafnye bataliony* [long-term political prisoners]." With swaggering arrogance, the officer described how battalions of condemned political prisoners were forced to march through the minefields by soldiers with machine-guns. Any prisoner who hesitated was shot. The prisoners had no choice, it was death ahead or death behind. They had to blow up the mines. Those who survived had the honor of being free citizens again in the great Soviet Union.

Once again I experienced the stranglehold of terror in my throat. There seemed no end to the evil that man was able to contrive and gleefully describe. Could patriots really condone such cruel treatment of their own countrymen? Couldn't they see how evil the system was? What was even more galling and humiliating, we students had to applaud this fiendish apparatchik. Such experiences made me acutely aware of the need to be on guard, not to say a thing that might give the impression of criticism, not to allow a muscle in my face to move, not to show revulsion.

I was put to the test many times by Russian students at the school I attended. Once I was asked a loaded question about the three world leaders: Roosevelt, Stalin, and Churchill. They tauntingly asked me to place them in the order of greatness. I pretended to ponder the question and then responded.

"President Roosevelt is number two, Churchill is number three."

"And whom do you place in the number one slot?"

"How dare you ask such a question?" I showed surprise. "You know that the world's wisest and greatest leader is our beloved Comrade Stalin."

Had I answered differently, I would have been in trouble. I saw they were satisfied with my answer, especially my designating Roosevelt as the second-greatest leader. The Soviets liked Roosevelt better than Churchill, whom they regarded as a reactionary.

Why did I falsify my response? Because I had already learned that a man's responsibility was to his own survival. Principles would not have a fine funeral or lie in state. Principles would meet a quick death or imprisonment in a labor camp. It was comply or die. Knowing that, I had to come up with the politically correct answers. Knowing that, I had to avoid the daily minefields.

Such was my response to the daily threats. The Russian students expressed their own reactions to bitterness and frustration with foul language. I could not exchange vulgarities with them. I was always embarrassed when I heard students use coarse language, for I was brought up in a home that regarded cursing and vulgarity as uncultured. Good, faithful Jews never stooped to such behavior.

Later that day, after the test about the world leaders, I walked into the school building with the others, and we happened to enter a dark, windowless room. One of the Russian students snorted, *"Tyomno kak v pyzde,"* which in English means, "It's as dark as the inside of a vagina." I squirmed uncomfortably. In the darkness, my flushed face could not be seen, but I was embarrassed by a vulgarity that showed utter disrespect for the sanctity of a woman's body. A cultural disrespect. The Russian girls had their own store of insults.

Nonetheless, their open sexuality prompted me to ask these Russian fellow students how they avoided getting a girl pregnant, since there were no contraceptives available in Fergana. They were quick to inform me, "Urinate immediately after the orgasm inside the girl. The urine will flush out the sperms."

I, who associated intercourse with love, almost threw up. The closeness of a girl's body, its mysterious hollows configured to join with a boy's, the promise of ecstasy in that joining was sullied, denigrated, sloughed off with the sloughing off of the body's waste fluids. The romance of lovemaking was smudged with smutty connotations. Disgust for these crude comrades coiled in my scrotum like a snake. Yet if I had countered with a snide remark about their vulgarity, I would not only have been sinking to their level, I would have invited their hostility. I pretended to enjoy what they told me, and this led them to share more sexual secrets.

But, they advised, if you did get a girl pregnant, the baby could be placed in the *detski dom* (baby home), a government institution for unwanted children and orphans. For illegitimate children, it was a permanent home, where they were fed, clothed, and indoctrinated in Communist ideology. I was later to learn that many Communist leaders and security officers had come out of these homes.

As we entered the year 1944, the Red Army made spectacular advances. We began to believe that the defeat of Hitler's battalions was close. We needed to believe that. We needed to believe that we would once again be able to think, act, conduct ourselves like human beings leading a clean, ordered life. The mud room we habituated, sleeping and huddling like animals in a stall with one muddy wall between us and the cow, did not distinguish us as human beings. Scrounging for food and warmth reduced life to the animal level. Affection and respect for one another kept us from ultimate despair. But the seams that held self-respect together were fraying. The one who showed the most weariness was my mother, and this distressed my father enormously. His fondness for her, his concern, his risk-taking to protect and provide for her, countered the coarseness in my Russian schoolmates, giving me some balance.

Father knew that it was almost impossible to get a decent apartment, but he was determined to find better housing for us. Added to the crudeness and discomforts of the structure we were in was the distance from the center of town, where he and Shmulek carried on their trading. Now that Hella and I were enrolled in school, moreover, we had to walk quite a distance to get there.

Fergana was brimming with refugees. Even if an apartment were available, the homeowner had to comply with complicated regulations before he could rent it. The homeowner had to get permission from the local leader, who then had to report on the applicant to the NKVD. The process was slowed because the local leader had to administer a large area. In many instances, the local leader was a member of the NKVD, but most such leaders, even if good Party members, also liked money.

Our local leader was a woman whose husband was in the army. She maintained herself in ways we could only conjecture about; one did not ask questions in the Soviet Union, one drew his own conclusions. Father, in his inimitable way, filled her pockets. She in return found us a place on Pervomaiskaja (May First) Street, a thoroughfare that began at Lenin Street and ran south for quite a distance, covering a good part of Fergana. The houses were large by Soviet standards and more substantially constructed than the mud houses. Most of the houses were owned by Russians.

The house we were to move to was owned by three Russian sisters. It was divided into two. One part was occupied by the oldest sister, her two children, and her mother. She told us that her husband was in the army. The other two sisters lived in the other part of the house, which consisted of two large rooms and a kitchen, all with wooden floors. There was a large garden behind the house and, greatest of joys, an enclosed outhouse. Not to mention that the house also had electricity. The two younger sisters were unmarried and willing to sublet one of their rooms with permission to use their kitchen, if they could get approval from the local leader. Father assured them that he had permission.

Just imagine! We would not have to sleep on a mud floor. We would have a completely enclosed outhouse. We would have kitchen facilities. And best of all, rainwater would no longer pour into our apartment. An additional bonus, our next-door neighbor wasn't a cow. Our next-door neighbors were going to be two young, good-looking girls. This was like the Taj-Mahal to us.

We bid our good Uzbek landlord farewell, the landlord who, like his Russian compatriots, had learned to take advantage of his assigned job in the big cotton mill nearby. He was more rotund than when we first met him, daily getting more round and paunchy, not from eating, which he probably was doing well at, but from stealing and wrapping yards and yards of cotton material around his body which he hid under his long Uzbek coat. He had begun to look like a woman in her ninth month of pregnancy. He was sorry to see us go, not only because secret deals were sacred between him and my father, but because he understood that First Yang-Chek Street was not May First Street.

We knew little about our new landladies. We did not ask them about their personal lives. You did not ask such questions in the Soviet Union. What these Russian ladies were doing in Fergana could only be surmised. Why had they been exiled to Fergana? Because they were politically unreliable? This category would include relatives of people who had been capitalists or tsarist officials before the Revolution, as well as indiscreet citizens who spoke against the Communist government. The sisters had been living in Fergana for more than twenty years. They silently nodded when we told them we were Polish citizens. They got the picture.

Adjusting to the new environment was easy. On the very first day there, Hella and I did our homework by the light of an electric bulb. We did not have to smell the odor of the burning cow dung which our Uzbek landlord used for cooking and baking in the garden area close to our room. I no longer had to run to Lenin Street to listen to the news coming from the loudspeakers there. We now had our own radio, provided by our landladies. Our school was closer to our apartment, and the streets we walked to get there were tree-lined and tidy.

Our spirits were up, as was the mood of Fergana's populace in general. We were now into the spring of 1944, and the news from the front was still good. It looked as if the war was coming to an end. The weather was warm again, and the wide branches of the trees lining May First Street were sprouting leaves. Couples strolled the streets.

Perhaps because it was spring, perhaps because I was drawn to the reawakening of the earth myself, I yearned to walk freely and breathe the fresh air. One evening I took a leisurely stroll along Lenin Street. As I turned into May First Street, I saw couples lodged against the tree trunks, unabashedly embracing, women braced against the tree, feminine legs entwining with the man's, openly copulating. Like cricket sounds, "ooohs" and "aaahs" resonated audibly in the air, a human melody of pleasure. So abandoned were they to their sensuality, they paid no heed to passersby, many young and curious like myself, who chuckled as sounds and contortions shifted under the trees.

I must confess that I liked taking those walks in the evening. May First Street offered me my first witness to human intercourse, upright, out in the open. Beds and bedrooms and privacy were not common commodities. Young lovers in the Soviet Union had no such luxuries for their fundamental joys.

The day we had prayed for, waited for, arrived. June 6, 1944. The Allies invaded the northern coast of France. The second front had been opened. Jubilation in the Polish community and in the Russian neighborhoods. Throughout Fergana, celebrations and demonstrations. Two words, shouted over and over, louder and louder, reverberated through the streets: *"Nasheye sojuzniki!* Our allies!" There was no need to append the two words. They were totally comprehensive. They conveyed a union, a contract, to destroy Hitler's forces. Germany's imminent defeat became especially apparent in the middle of July 1944, when pictures appeared in the newspapers of fifty-seven thousand German prisoners being paraded through Moscow. In front of the marching prisoners were twenty German generals. Ah! The sweet surge of reversal! Now let the Nazis chew on their wilted pride and deposed glory. Make them pay for their heinous, ruinous ambitions. Let them march and be witness to the hatred and vengeance sowed on Russian soil in Polish hearts.

The Polish community in Fergana was particularly proud of Konstantin Rokossovsky, commander of the Soviet offensive, who smashed the German forces on the Stalingrad front and then on the Byelorussian front. Marshal Rokossovsky, born in Russia, was the son of Polish parents. The prisoners in the parade had been captured during his offensive in Byelorussia.

After liberating the Soviet territories conquered by the Germans, the Red Army advanced into Poland, entering the city of Lublin toward the end of July. There a Polish

Committee of National Liberation was formed, chaired by
Edward Osóbka-Morawski, and including Boleslaw Bierut
and Wladislaw Gomulka, the secretary of the Polish
Communist Party.

The Sovinform Bureau, the official Soviet information
agency, issued a communique naming the fifteen members
of the Lublin Committee. Three of them were known to be
Communists. We had never heard of the chairman and
were convinced he was either a Communist or a
Communist sympathizer. As for the other committeemen,
we had no knowledge of any of them. We had no doubts
about their being tools of the Soviet government. The communique lauded them as Polish patriots and said they were
more praiseworthy than the Polish government in London,
headed by Stanislaw Mikolajczyk. The die was cast. Poland
would become a satellite of the Soviet Union.

In August 1944, the Soviet advance in Poland came to a
halt. Radio reports and the newspapers informed us that
the Red Army was pausing to consolidate its gains and
resupply its forces for the final push into Germany.
Apparently the heavy fighting in Poland had depleted
munitions and food, because for the rest of the summer
and into the fall the Soviet government mobilized its school
population to work on the collective farms to help bring in
the harvest.

The farmers on the collective farms were notoriously
unproductive, as they had good reason to be. They were
treated like slaves and not compensated adequately for
their work. Consequently, city workers and students—all
of them supposedly patriotic volunteers—were sent to
help on the farms without pay.

The principal of our Polish school announced that we
would honor the victorious Red Army by volunteering to
do farm work. We were to be sent to a cotton-growing col-

lective to pick cotton for two weeks. We could not object. Moreover, we had to show enthusiasm and confirm our duty and loyalty to the great Soviet Union by volunteering.

And so, the entire student body of the Polish school was driven in carts to an unfamiliar Uzbek village. My sister Hella, who was twelve years old, was among the volunteers. We spent two full weeks picking cotton, more conscientiously than the collective farmers, who could be seen idling and talking in the fields. After two weeks of labor, fed insufficiently, our school administrators told us that we had fulfilled our socialist duty. When we returned to classes, we were praised for fulfilling the norms, praised for our good work and our contribution to the country.

On the wider, political scene, we learned, late in September or early October 1944, of an uprising by the underground Polish Home Army, the Armia Krajowa, in the city of Warsaw, led by General Tadeusz Bór-Komorowski.

We heard the Soviet version of the uprising. It was an action by reactionary forces, not connected to the Red Army. It was poorly planned, failed, and resulted in the loss of many innocent civilian lives. Knowing how the government distorted news to suit its policies, we found the report hard to believe. We interpreted the uprising differently. For one thing, if this uprising had been going on for several weeks, why had it not been reported to us before? The whole thing seemed contrived. More likely, the Soviet Union had deliberately incited the revolt and then arranged for the destruction of the Home Army. The Russians intended to reduce Poland to a client state. A victorious Polish army would be a demanding encumbrance, a political hindrance to a Communist autocracy.

A year later, our analysis was confirmed. A special Soviet radio station had called on the Polish people in

Warsaw to revolt against the Germans. The Red Army was actually on the scene, right across the Vistula River from Warsaw, and did absolutely nothing to help them. Prime Minister Churchill pleaded with Stalin to come o the assistance of the Poles in Warsaw. Stalin refused to do so, on the grounds that the Red Army was too exhausted from previous military operations.

The Red Army finally entered Warsaw in January 1945, but by that time the city was almost totally destroyed. After the fall of Warsaw, the Red Army kept up its offensive in East Prussia and continued its thrust toward the Oder River.

Wounded soldiers, coming home from the front, brought back tales of atrocities committed in captured and occupied territories by German soldiers and S.S. troops. Jewish soldiers told of an earlier uprising in the Warsaw Ghetto. Although the ghetto uprising had taken place in 1943, the Soviet news media had never reported it.

The returning wounded Jewish soldiers described the ferocity of the uprising. The Jewish ghetto in Warsaw had been totally destroyed, and any surviving Jews were annihilated. In 1939 the Jewish population of Warsaw had been more than 400,000. Now there were none.

The Jews in the ghetto had received no help from the city's Polish citizens during the uprising. The Polish populace went on with their lives as if nothing was happening.

The news was shattering to the Polish and Russian Jews in Fergana. The returning Jewish soldiers were inconsolable. Why was the Soviet government indifferent to Jewish suffering? Why had it withheld news of the uprising? Why hadn't it told us about the atrocities committed by the Germans and the mass annihilation of Jews in the Ukraine? The Jewish soldiers also told us that some Ukrainians had helped the German soldiers to hunt down and kill Jews. If the Russians had tried to help the Jews, wouldn't this have strengthened our allegiance to them? Wouldn't we have given our complete support to the war effort? Wouldn't we have urged worldwide attention?

The answer is: distrust. The Soviet system was ridden with paranoia. Paranoia breeds control and intolerance. The symptoms seeped through to the populace at large. No one dared criticize the government in front of anyone else. No one dared call attention to himself. No one raised a political voice. If you did, you would be reported to the security authorities. We were all guilty. The government silenced criticism, and suppressed decent human responses—human responses that might reflect ill upon Communist ideals.

Nonetheless, the news brought by the wounded Jewish soldiers returning from the front led to grumbling among the refugee Jews in Fergana. Murmured complaints about the government were heard.

I learned at this time that in the 1930s there had been an active Zionist movement in the Soviet Union. The government had reacted by creating a Jewish Autonomous Oblast in Birobidzhan, a Far Eastern region near China, to which Jews could migrate.

Not many Jews were tempted to settle there. Now, the horrendous stories told by the returning soldiers were bringing about a reawakening of Zionism among the Russian Jews in Fergana. Some began to speak confidentially about the evils of the Communist system. There were still not many of them, but they wanted to leave the Soviet Union if they could and settle in Palestine, fulfilling the Zionist dream. They talked about this goal privately, but as yet none did anything tangible toward achieving it.

Freedom But Not Liberty

The leaders of the three Allied countries met in Yalta, in the Crimea, on February 4–7, 1945, but the Soviet press did not mention the conference until it was over, nor did it give readers many details. The Yalta Conference came as a surprise to us, especially since President Roosevelt and Prime Minister Churchill had to travel such a great distance to accommodate Stalin. The two Western statesmen must have realized from his past actions that the suspicious, distrustful Stalin was reluctant to leave his well-guarded headquarters because of fears about assassination.

While we knew little about the details, several aspects of the agreement seemed clear. The most surprising was the inclusion of France in the four-power occupation of Germany. That the Soviet Union would enter the war against Japan after Germany's defeat, receiving territories in the east in return, seemed a quid pro quo for Allied help. That it had agreed to participate in the conference to organize a United Nations seemed like a step in the right direction. But it was the fourth point that concerned and affected us: the guarantee of a representative government in Poland. What this implied and how it would impinge on our lives was an open question.

We knew about the Provisional Government of National Unity established in 1944 in Lublin, which, in essence, was a Soviet-created puppet state, Communist-dominated. The Western powers had evidently agreed to cede to the Soviets most of the eastern Polish territories initially occupied in 1939 under the agreement with Hitler.

We favored the Polish government in London, headed by Prime Minister Mikolajczyk. To us, it seemed essential that the new government of Poland include members of the London government. We wanted to see the path cleared for us to leave Stalin and as quickly as possible. Were a coalition government to be formed, our chances of getting out of the Soviet Union would be much better.

We were also very much afraid that the Allies had given Stalin too much at Yalta. The Red Army, by this time, was in Rumania, Bulgaria, Hungary, Czechoslovakia, and Poland. What made the Allies think Stalin would release his hold on those countries once he had brought them under the Communist flag, thereby advancing the Communist world order?

I had too many recollections of lectures on the Communist vision of the future. One of the lecturers at the Agitpoint had spoken with intense glee about Bulgaria. To quote him verbatim he said: "*Byl korol tyepyer kolchozy*" ("Once there was a king there, but now there are collective farms"). The Soviet Union had established a Czechoslovak Legion commanded by General Svoboda. Most of its members were Communists or sympathizers.

At the Institute of Eastern Studies in Fergana, the Soviet government trained Communist revolutionaries for leadership roles in the Communist governments it intended to install in the many "liberated" countries now under its influence. Were President Roosevelt and Prime Minister Churchill naive, or were they unaware of these preparations when they discussed the future of Europe after the defeat of Hitler?

As is often the case when the public is bewildered and cynical, humor erupted. We Polish Jews in Fergana expressed our fears in the jokes we told. One story coming out of the Yalta Conference told about an argument between the two Western leaders and Stalin about Poland's borders and future government. Stalin invited Roosevelt and Churchill to join him for a ride through the Yalta countryside. The three got into a car and set out along a narrow road. Suddenly, they came upon a cow in the middle of the road. They were at an impasse. They could not go around her because the way was blocked by trees. Stalin suggested that Roosevelt speak to the cow and urge her to get off the road. Roosevelt addressed the cow:

"I am the president of the richest, strongest country in the world. Get off the road and permit the car to go on."

When the cow did not stir, he warned: "If you don't get out of the way, I'll have you locked up in Alcatraz prison."

The cow shook her head and said: "I'm not moving."

Then Stalin suggested that Churchill speak to the cow. And so he did:

"I am the prime minister of the British Empire, which controls one fourth of the world. If you don't get out of the way, I'll have you thrown into a prison in Africa or Asia."

The cow shook her head. She was not moving.

Roosevelt and Churchill then asked Stalin to try. He did so:

"I am Joseph Stalin, the first secretary of the Communist Party of the Soviet Union, the premier of the Soviet Union, the commanding marshal of the Red Army, and if you don't get out of the way, I will send you to a *kolchoz* [collective farm]."

When the cow heard this, she began trembling and bolted for the border.

The war news from all fronts continued to be good. The Red Army and the Allies were pushing into Germany. That part was good. Life in Fergana was not, for we were constantly hungry, and uncertain of our fates. We lived in fear of the unrelenting NKVD scrutiny. Emphasizing our powerlessness was the persistent voice of propaganda in school, on the radio, and in the newspapers. We were told to believe we were in the land of opportunity, a microcosm of the Communist world. In this land of opportunity, we had unwillingly lived on the frozen edge of civilization, lived in substandard housing with insubstantial nourishment, our nerves taut and tangled from constant threats.

The propaganda would have us believe this was Utopia. For the past five years, I had been in Eden, biting the apple of truth, chewing on knowledge that at its core was man's cruelty to man, spitting out the seeds of intolerance, humility, depravity, and left with an aftertaste of bitterness. And there still were more outrages left to bite from the apple.

Calamitous and devastating were the reports from returning Jewish wounded soldiers about places called Auschwitz and Treblinka, where the Nazis had built gas chambers and crematoria and murdered vast numbers of Jews—millions of Jews—burning their bodies afterwards. This could not be true. It was stretching Nazi cruelty to unbelievable limits, too inhuman, too infamous, too incredible.

If it were true, why hadn't the Soviet government told us? Why had they kept it a secret? Wouldn't it have been to their advantage to decry the genocide? Wouldn't every Jew in Russia have risen to praise the Russians for sending their armies in to punish the Germans? Or were the Soviets collaborators in this mad scheme to annihilate every Jew on the continent? Hadn't antisemitic Ukrainians, Lithuanians, Latvians, and Estonians helped the Nazis to perpetrate these ghastly deeds? Was there any truth to the stories of Ukrainian concentration camp guards prodding defenseless Jews into gas chambers? Did this information have to be hushed up lest the leaders of the West see Russia's shameful complicity and break off the alliance?

I did not want to believe any of this, but how could I fail to believe when the same sort of thing was going on in Fergana? The Soviet government deported trainloads of Tatars from the Crimea and Ingush people from the northern Caucasus to Fergana. They were Moslems who, so we were told, had cooperated with the Germans, embraced the German occupier, even volunteered to serve in the German army. Now they were classified as enemies of the Soviet Union, and the entire Ingush, Chechens, and Tartar populace of the Crimea had been exiled to the Central Asian republics of the Soviet Union. A camp in Fergana was the destination for many of these enemies and traitors.

I saw entire families, fathers, mothers, and children of all ages, with the haggard, bewildered, frightened eyes that had become too familiar to me. Even if I had known their language and could have spoken with them, it would have been too dangerous. We were not permitted to get near them. Some of them were transported to other places. One rumor had it that they were being sent to slave labor camps, to work on that big hydroelectric dam at Farhad-Stroy. This was an era when human life was expendable for political gain.

While this was having its impact, the retaking of Soviet territory meant that many Russian refugees could return to the homes they had left to escape the Germans. However, Russian Jewish refugees were not given the same privilege. The official explanation was that it was not safe for them to return while fighting was still going on against anti-Soviet partisan forces, especially in the Ukraine, where there was a guerilla war raging against the Soviet state. One of these groups, former Nazi collaborators now fighting against the Communists, was led by a Ukrainian named Bandera. These partisans, imbued with Nazi ideology, made Jews their special target. They were reputed to have killed the famous Russian general Vatutin, commander of the

Southern Front that had encircled Paulus's Sixth Army at Stalingrad.

Despite these tales, we hoped that we would soon be permitted to return to our homes, now that Poland was completely liberated from the Wehrmacht. The Polish Government of National Unity, we trusted, would arrange for our leavetaking from Fergana.

At the end of April 1945, information filtered through that there was an underground organization in Poland opposed to the puppet Lublin government. We heard that the underground was conducting guerilla operations against the Lublin Communist clique, and that it simply was not safe, especially for Jews, to return to small cities in Poland. Among other things, this was because the homes and businesses formerly owned by Jews had been confiscated by local Polish nationals who were now arming themselves to take action against any returning Jews who tried to reclaim their property. They were ready to kill in order to hold on to their loot.

Our family took this news seriously and decided that we would put off returning to Dynów even if we got permission. The next few weeks found us thinking, weighing the possible options, profoundly hoping to be able to leave the land of the Soviets. Every day brought news of great victories over Hitler's armies. We followed the movements of Generals Patton, Bradley, and Montgomery.

Then, on May 2, 1945, came the news that the Red Army had captured the Nazi capital, Berlin. General Patton's tanks entered Czechoslovakia, and finally, on May 8, 1945, the Germans signed a surrender agreement. In Fergana, as I am sure all over the Soviet Union, unrestrained shouts of joy rang through the streets. I wept even as I felt the straps of bondage slip from my body, feeling that I might soon reclaim my life, my future, a destiny I could choose for myself. Still, there was the overlay of sadness and mourning over the deaths of millions of righteous Jews.

In Fergana, that eighth day of May, there was a jubilee. The Russians took to the streets to sing and dance and shout hosannahs for their victory. The Uzbeks were more subdued. The Jews feigned joy.

Fergana had its own brewery. During the war years, most of the beer had been sent to the soldiers at the front and very little had been allocated for civilian consumption. On this day it was plentiful. With the war at an end, the local authorities decided to release enough beer for a celebration. There was continuous drinking of vodka and beer. At every corner, in any clear spot in the middle of the sidewalk, the locals sat drinking, sixteen-liter pails of beer propped between their legs. Two men with such a pail of beer would quickly guzzle it down, one liter-sized mug at a time. Empty pails of beer were quickly refilled. They drank themselves into a stupor, sprawling on the ground when their legs could no longer support them.

Nor was it only beer that was flowing. Although vodka was still rationed, it seemed to be more available. Those lucky enough to get a bottle would down the entire contents in one continuous gulp. During the war, those who could not get vodka drank cologne, getting drunk on its alcohol content. Since there had been an ample supply of cologne in Fergana throughout the war, you could often smell its scent on men in the streets. In the merriment of victory, anything with alcohol was consumed. Fergana was totally caught up in a wild, frenzied orgy of drink. They drank until they dropped. In Russia, drinking is not a cordial social exchange, Russians drink until they are drunk.

The victory celebration lasted for several days. Then Fergana was abuzz with scenes of refugees leaving for their liberated homes in the Ukraine and elsewhere. But the Poles were not included. The Polish puppet government did not contact us. It divulged not the slightest hint about its intentions toward us. We felt totally abandoned. We were weak, despondent, numbed, but we had survived. We still had the will to live, but not in Fergana.

At the end of May, the family sat down to discuss its future course of action. What was obvious was that no one, not even a Russian, could go from one place to another without proper documents and permits. Father and Shmulek began inquiring about documents for us to leave. The question was whether to go to the Ukraine or back to Poland.

The first break came when the Russian wife of a high school principal offered Shmulek a high school diploma for a large sum of rubles. She probably could have arranged for him to get a degree from a university for the right price, but that was not what we were interested in. My brother had graduated from elementary school in Poland but had not attended school since our departure from Dynów. Now our goal was to escape from the Soviet Union. Her offer did not help in that respect.

Finally, in June, Father and Shmulek made the right contacts with some ranking NKVD officers. The deal was that we would receive two sets of documents and two sets of travel permits. One set of documents gave us Ukrainian names and designated a town in the western Ukraine as our destination. The western Ukraine was prewar Polish territory annexed by the Soviet Union on September 6, 1939. We would get travel documents and railroad tickets to travel there. The second set of travel documents would give us permission to join our relatives in Poland, as well as the right to purchase train tickets to travel to the Polish city of Cracow. Strangely, I can remember the names of

generals, commanders, teachers, and neighbors, but not the
Ukrainian and Polish names we were given on the two sets
of documents. There are protective cells in the brain
against unpleasant recollections.

This was a very dangerous undertaking. If we were discovered using false credentials, we could be executed as
spies. But we were willing to take the chance. Life in the
Soviet Union was little better than death.

This arrangements for the documents took most of our
American dollars, as well as the gold coins, a hoard of
rubles, and the patent leather high-heeled shoes Uncle
Irving had sent us from New York. It may well have been
the shoes, more than anything else, that fixed the deal.
Such shoes would woo and warm the heart of a *dyevushka*,
the girlfriend of an NKVD officer. And so, the most
respected and trusted men in Soviet society, the truest of
Communists, the officers assigned to protect the government from its enemies, were bought by my father with
some capitalist dollars and capitalist goods.

The two sets of documents opened the way for our exodus from the twentieth-century land of the Pharaohs. We
told no one, not even our closest friends. Our secret was
too precious to mention. Even the most loyal person might
innocently blab about what we were doing or might try to
do the same thing and be caught. We secretly packed our
few miserable belongings, the fear in our hearts suppress-
ing the joy on our lips.

At the end of the first week of June, a horse-drawn
wagon pulled over in front of our house. It was only then
that we told our landladies that we were leaving Fergana.
We were going to Bukhara, we said, to join my mother's
sister there.

And so, less than one month after the war ended in
Europe, after three and a half years in Fergana, we were on

the train from Fergana to Tashkent, the Uzbek capital. Traveling on the same train was one other Polish Jewish family: Marek Wrobl, his wife Liutka, and their infant son Danny. Marek Wrobel had been father's friend and business associate in Fergana. They had obtained the same documents and travel permits through the same source as we did. Throughout the journey, we had to be very careful to use our assumed names as listed in the new documents.

In Tashkent, chaos greeted us. Streams of refugees and military personnel were trying to get to their various destinations. We slept in the railroad station for three nights because we could not get on a train out of Tashkent. On the fourth day, we were able to board a train for Saratov, a city on the Volga River. It proved to be a slow-moving train that had to stop often to let other more important trains go through. During one of these very frequent stops, we noticed long trains carrying troops and tanks. When some Russians asked the soldiers where they were going, they responded, *"Sey chas Yapontsov yebat budyem"* ("Now we're going to fuck the Japanese").

After three days more, we arrived in Saratov, which proved to be a major rail center. Here the mass of humanity and the chaos were even greater than in Tashkent. From all directions, people shoved, pushed, clawed toward the ticket windows to have tickets approved for the next destination. People were literally jumping over each other, roughly pushing the older ones aside, unheedingly buffeting one another in the effort to secure a seat for themselves. It took two full days for us to get our tickets to proceed to the city of Voronezh.

We encountered the same waiting, jostling, pushing, shoving, and disregard at the station there. There simply was no courtesy. It was always the stronger and meaner who got to the front of the line. Shmulek, father, and I began to use our own strong arms to protect mother and Hella and to move forward. From Voronezh, we took the train to Kiev, the capital of the Ukraine. We never left any of the railroad stations. We slept on the floor in shifts, one of us always up and on guard to protect the few pieces of luggage we possessed. We were well aware of the stealing going on.

The trip to Kiev took more than two days, and at the Kiev station we again waited several days to get a train to Lwów, the city from which we had been deported on June 28, 1940 to the slave labor camp in the Mari Autonomous Republic. What slowed us down was the destruction left in their wake by the retreating Germans. From the windows we could see crews repairing the tracks, letting trains go by only intermittently.

In Lwów, we again spent several days getting tickets and documents permitting us to travel on to Cracow. Going through Poland, at some local stops, we were harassed by Poles who recognized us as Jewish. Attitudes had not changed. The travail of war had not made them sensitive to our displacement and suffering.

We arrived in Cracow on July 2, 1945, three weeks from the time we left Fergana, but at last, we believed, we had escaped from the Soviet Union. We'd had some close calls during our lengthy trip when the militiamen checked our documents. We'd had some trepidations when railroad cars were uncoupled and reconnected to another train, fearful that our route would be reversed and we would find ourselves stranded in another lonely outpost. There were several times when I felt my heart stop beating, as if the sharp stabs of fright had severed my arteries. It was an odyssey of helplessness. Being alive was not a matter of bravery. It had been like a game of chance, and each move had been determined by how many steps forward or back-

ward were meted out to us. We had been buffeted by per-
secuting, greedy, calculating players. I did not even think
of God in these movements. I thought He had forgotten us
or had lost His own war with evil. And in the way of all
games that are based on mazes, we had reached an exit. We
had made it!

At the Cracow railroad station, we were met by representatives of a local Jewish committee and were assigned
temporary housing in a residence it maintained. There we
met concentration camp survivors and other refugees who
had just come out of hiding. The Wrobel family was taken
to the same residence, and each family was given a room.
The building was like an army barracks. There were quite
a few people there. Although we were dead tired, we could
not sleep. We had too many uncertainties on our minds.
Our minds were brimming with questions. What was
Poland like now that the war was over? How would we
reassemble our lives? Would we be able to go back to our
home? Father's business? Would we find our relatives, our
friends? What lay ahead?

After a decent meal provided by the Jewish committee,
the first in five years, I roamed the halls and met a survivor
from Auschwitz who had a number tattooed on his arm.
He told us about the brutalities and bestialities that had
been perpetrated by the German nation on the Jewish population of Europe. Of the six million slaughtered, three million were Polish Jews. He told us what he had endured in
the Auschwitz and Mauthausen concentration camps. He
described the sadistic brutality of the camp guards, the gas
chambers, the ovens.

One of the first decisions we made that very first day
was to go to Auschwitz, which was not far from Cracow, to
see for ourselves. We went there the following day. That
day in July 1945 and the sights I saw are imprinted on my

brain. Thick ropes made out of human hair. Soap made from human fat. Crowns pulled from human teeth. Thousands upon thousands of leather shoes. This was a death factory where human beings had been gassed and cremated.

Who were the accursed monsters who had committed such unspeakable crimes? What kind of creature orders and commits such heinous acts? Human beings could not have done that to one another. They had to have been wild animals cloaked in human skins.

I looked long and despairingly at the bars of soap, at the long ropes. I wondered whether any of it could have been made out of my cousin Gonia's body. She had been such a beautiful girl. I thought about those gorgeous Grossman girls, Tonia and Hania. I thought of that beautiful young girl Mania, who had given me that first soul kiss when I was a little boy. Was it possible that the rope I was looking at had been made from the hair of those lovely girls? Was it really possible that these bars of soap had been made from the fat of those youthful beauties?

My eyes seemed drawn from my sockets, unforgiving, glazed to the exhibits. My legs felt drained of blood and buckled under me. I felt excruciating pain all over my body. I was not only anguished, I was experiencing an empathized extinction with the victims. I don't know how long I was in that trance. When I regained the sense of separateness, I said Kaddish, the Jewish prayer for the dead, except that I said it for all the people who had perished there, both Jews and Christians.

I returned to our residence, but the veil of travail followed me. I could not eat, I dropped down onto the cot and covered my eyes with my hands. My thoughts wandered off in many directions. I thought about us. If we had not fled, we too might have fed the flames. We had suffered frost, we had suffered deeply in the Soviet Union, but their sufferings had been so much greater. They were dead and I was still alive. How many other nations had contributed to that evil? Why had it not been stopped?

Mingling with these horrors was another nagging thought: What lay ahead for me? Where would I live? Being alive after all this, what was expected of me? What did I expect of myself? I gazed at the gray ceiling. There was no crack that revealed the future. I could not fall asleep. I found no answers to my questions.

The next morning I went to get a haircut. My hair was wild and bushy. The barbershop was owned by a Pole, and there were several other customers. After waiting quite a while, I was called by one of the barbers. While he cut my hair, I listened to the conversations around me. Mostly they were about the war, how terrible it had been, what tremendous destruction it had done. As the clippings from my hair fell to the floor, so did my heart when I heard one say,

"We must forever be grateful to Hitler. He got rid of the Jews."

They all nodded in agreement, yet I could say nothing. If I had said anything in defense of the Jews, or even had announced that I was a Jew, my throat would have been slit. I felt my throat closing as if that were actually happening. I could produce no words, make no outcry of protest; I just sat silently, absorbing the pervasive antisemitism.

From the barbershop, I went directly to the office of the Jewish committee to tell some of the people there about what had just happened. They told me I had made a mistake in going there, that it was quite dangerous for Jews in that part of town. Obviously, nothing had altered the hatred of the Poles toward the Jewish people. It was precisely because of this antisemitic atmosphere that Hitler had built his extermination camps in Poland, where the people not only permitted but welcomed them.

I learned that there were very few Jews left in Poland. Most of the survivors were in Cracow, but that was no consolation. Jews, we were told, had no future in Poland; we were advised to make every effort to go to Palestine and build a Jewish state there. I was told about several Zionist groups making preparations to do just that.

While I was making my own inquiries, father and Shmulek asked the committee whether it was advisable to go back to Dynów, our hometown. Father was sternly advised not to go there. All Jewish homes and properties had been taken over and expropriated by local Poles. It was dangerous, especially in small towns, for a Jew to try to reclaim his property. Jews making such attempts had been severely beaten and in some instances killed by those now in possession of their homes and property.

Father and Shmulek gave up the idea of returning to Dynów, but we had to find out about Mundek, our oldest brother. He had not been home the night we were deported from Lwów, and we had no idea what had happened to him or whether he was alive. When father and Shmulek made inquiries, they finally got the sad and expected news. Mundek had gone back to the area around Dynów. Shortly after the German invasion of the Soviet Union, he had asked a villager he knew, a man who had done business with father, to hide him.

This "friend" had invited Mundek in and served him a meal. While Mundek was eating, the villager sent one of his sons to notify the German police that there was a Jew in their house. The German police came immediately. My brother saw them approaching, darted out, and ran toward the river San. The police ran after him and began shooting when he jumped into the water. According to what we heard, the bullets hit their mark and he died in the river. His body was never found. Such was the nature of friends of the Jews in Poland.

The Jewish committee in Cracow told us that during the occupation, the German authorities in Poland had issued a proclamation promising to pay two kilograms of sugar to any Pole who turned in a Jew. Obviously, a bit of sugar was more valuable than a Jew's life to many Poles. Through this enticement, the remnants of Polish Jewry had been decimated.

On September 1, 1939, there had been about three and a half million Jews in Poland, constituting almost eleven percent of the total population. The Jewish population in Cracow in July 1945 stood at less than two thousand. They were mostly survivors from concentration camps, and a few like my family who had just returned from the Soviet Union. A mite on the surface of the antisemitic country, an unwelcome pest in the eyes of the Poles. We agreed that we must leave as soon as possible.

My family declared themselves ardent Zionists. We saw that the only solution was to build and establish a Jewish state in the ancient Jewish land called Palestine. The problem was how to get there. Poland was a satellite of the Soviet Union, situated behind the Iron Curtain. Its borders were sealed, and no one was able to leave. Great Britain, as the mandatory power in Palestine, had issued a White Paper restricting the number of Jews permitted to enter Palestine. Inevitably, a Zionist underground organization had come into existence. Its name was Berichah, a Hebrew word meaning "escape," and it was organized by agents of the Haganah, the Jewish self-defense force in Palestine. Quite a number of Polish Jews affiliated with Berichah.

The purpose of Berichah was to get the surviving Jews out from behind the Iron Curtain and into the displaced-persons camps in the American-occupied zones of Austria and Germany. From there, hopefully, they could be smuggled into Italy, on their way to Palestine.

I was eager to make contact with the organization and go through this process, but there were impediments. I would have been glad to leave the continent of Europe, which had been a landscape of pain and travail for my people. My mind whirled and raged with schemes to get going. My heart yearned for peace and a chance to reconstitute my life. The thought of getting to Palestine, to a haven where being a Jew was not a blight, was thrilling. The prospect of living among accepting, encouraging, practicing Jews again was like feeling the sun rise after an endless stormy night. Thoughts of a promising future were exciting, tantalizing, and yet distressing. Getting to Palestine was close to impossible. Every nation seemed to conspire against our traveling in a civilized and humane way. Why should people weakened and emaciated, who had suffered so much in concentration and slave labor camps, now have to go through the further agony and denigration of being smuggled in like contraband?

Leaving Europe soon became imperative. On August 11, 1945, while out for a walk in Cracow, I suddenly heard shouts and screams. Like a stampede, people were running through the street, shouting that the Jews had killed a Christian boy and used his blood to bake matzos for the Passover holidays. In one instant, I saw them severely beat a man. I had to assume he was Jewish. I turned from the mob and, although barely more than a skeleton myself, ran as fast as I could, the fastest I had ever run in my life. I managed to elude them and ran into the building where we were living. The door to the building was shut tight against the raging mob.

It took the police quite a while to respond to the uncontrolled throngs on the streets. Several hours later I looked out the window and saw Red Army troops with machine guns patrolling the streets, dispersing the mob. At the end of the day, we heard that many Jews had been severely beaten, bloodied, and injured. There were similar mob scenes throughout the day in many parts of the city. What amazed me was the stupidity, the irrational motive, for the demonstration. Passover, occurring around March or April, was not being observed in August. What had stirred up a riot at this time?

The bloodshed on the battlefields, the wounded, crippled veterans, the bombed-out cities, the scorched earth had made no impression on the cold-hearted antisemites. The Holocaust had not been complete enough for them. Ignorant reactionary elements of the Catholic clergy relentlessly stirred up hatred. They raised glorious gilded churches, carved saints, and saviors on the walls and pews, then let the hooligans whip up fiendish antagonism that replicated the ancient Roman riots. Where in all this were the teachings of Christ, in whose name the slaughter was committed?

I knew in my heart that I could not condemn all Poles for these dastardly acts. There were Polish people during World War II who saved Jews, at great risk to themselves. They will be remembered as righteous people. But the horror spread by the virulent antisemites who could not abide the fact that a small number of Jews were still alive will never be forgotten either.

If we were to survive, we had to get out of Poland as quickly as possible. We contacted the Zionist underground organization and pleaded with them to help us leave. A member of the Berichah organization visited us and explained the escape operation. We would be traveling in a small group with one or two leaders. The leader would have a forged document showing that we were Greek concentration camp survivors on our way home. The men were to wear Greek-style berets, to make them look like

Greeks. The women would wear headscarves. If stopped at the border and questioned, especially by Soviet guards, we were to respond by reciting a Hebrew prayer, which presumably would sound like Greek to them. He warned that this was an illegal operation and almost anything could happen. Each person was permitted no more than one knapsack, and we were not to have any documents revealing our true identity. All such documents must be destroyed. Our leader would have a list of our Greek names. We would be given one day's notice to assemble and go to the Cracow train station.

That was it, no questions to be asked. It was like a top-secret military operation. First, we disposed of all our miserable possessions, except for the few pieces of clothing that fit into a knapsack. I really did not know my Greek name. As for the Hebrew prayer, I decided that if questioned by a border guard, I would recite, *Mah tovu ohalekha Yaakov, mishkenotekha Yisrael* ("How goodly are your tents, O Jacob, Your dwelling places, O Israel").

Numbering somewhat fewer than fifty, wearing our Greek berets, we assembled at the Cracow railroad station toward the end of August 1945. Two operatives of the Berichah underground were assigned to escort us. They repeated the instructions we had received from the counselors. We boarded the train and soon were on our way to Prague, the capital of Czechoslovakia. We made two stops, one at the Polish border, and the other on the Czech side. Our leaders spoke to the guards at both points, and we were not interrogated. After crossing the Czech border we felt somewhat more confident, for we had passed the first obstacle on our journey.

At the Prague railroad station, agents of the Zionist underground met us. They drove us to a building where we were given a decent meal. They told us we would have to stay here for several days and must be constantly on guard, because the city was full of Russian soldiers. Although we were given permission to visit the city, the situation was not conducive to sightseeing. I ventured out for an occasional walk but never wandered far.

After several restless days in Prague, which took us into September, we left by train for Bratislava, the capital of Slovakia. This trip too went smoothly. We were met at the station by another Zionist agent, and were taken to a building owned by the organization. We were told to be vigilant: Bratislava was a border town, and just opposite lay Soviet-occupied Austria. Again, we were to wait for several days and were cautioned to remain inside.

Confined to a room, shut away from the sights of a city about whose history and past grandeur I had read, I craved the experience of walking the winding cobbled streets. The underpasses and overpasses that led to the secret entrances of old houses lured me. I yearned for freedom to visit the museums and universities that could satisfy my curiosity. I prayed that there would be an end to hiding, that I could close the picture album in my mind, forget the alleys and huts, the filthy train stations. I wanted to be rid of dodging oppressors and border guards, and fleeing from mobs.

Now we were at another way-station. What next, before we reached the holy soil? Would the horrors of the last seven years shackle me forever? What was I like as a person? In the crude scrambling to survive frost and famine, I had not thought much about myself. Neither was I preoccupied with the fate of nations during the war. As Jews, the fraying thread that bound us to mankind had threatened to snap at any moment. Our numbers had dwindled, extinction had threatened us. Now, granted life and the freedom to choose, how would I approach the future. I wanted to believe that life would be better.

I glanced down at my clothes. They were faded, rumpled, threadbare. My body felt thin, bony. There was a mirror in the room; facing it I wondered how long had it been since I had seen my reflection. An unfamiliar person, a hollow-eyed underfed face, skin barely covering the bones, stared back at me. What had the Uzbek landlord said? "If you have the bones, you will cover them again with flesh." I wanted to believe that too. I wanted to believe I would be able to convince the border guards that mine was a Greek face, but with the oversized beret, I looked more comical than classical. I couldn't believe that anyone would take me for a Greek.

Occupied with thoughts of myself, I was aware that the Greek beret was part of a carefully orchestrated scenario. At every step of the journey, we had reason to admire and be grateful for the care, supervision, and efficiency with which the Zionist organization had plotted our course and attended to our needs. The Berichah agents were taking personal risks for us, operating as they were behind the Iron Curtain, an apt metaphor for the totalitarian Soviet empire.

Finally, on the tenth of September, word came that we would be leaving Bratislava for Vienna, the capital of Austria. Vienna was divided into four zones of occupation: American, English, French, and Soviet. We were to be taken to the American zone, the most friendly one. This would be the most dangerous part of the journey. We would have to pass a Soviet border crossing point, and, as our rescuers told us, "One never knows what the Russkies may do." We were to leave the next morning.

Our joy was mixed with apprehension. We would be leaving the lands behind the Iron Curtain and entering a territory occupied by American soldiers. However, we would have to make a stop at the Soviet border. My family and I had every reason to fear the Soviet border guards.

On September 11, as promised, the delegated guides drove us to the Bratislava station. There we saw another group of fake Greeks. We kept quiet, not a word was exchanged among us or with them. We were all obsessed by the fear that someone would and blurt out a Polish or Russian word and reveal our identity, the end of the line to our journey.

The Vienna train pulled into the station. As we boarded it, our underground escorts assigned the members of our group to different cars. All five of us got on the same car so that we could stay together. Surging in our blood but suppressed in our facial expressions was the growing excitement: we were just one hair's breadth away from the free world. Please let it not be an illusion, I prayed. We were made uneasy by the sight of so many passengers in Soviet army and NKVD uniforms.

The train rolled on, its heavy steel wheels pounding and clacking against the rails. I felt my blood coursing through my body in its rhythm, and my anxiety propelled the engine faster. I glanced at the others, but we said not a word, hoping nothing would betray our true identity. I must have stopped breathing, thinking, or moving as we entered the Soviet zone of Austria. When the train stopped to pick up some passengers, I sat suspended in a vacuum until it regained momentum and we were on our way again.

About two hours into our journey my brother Shmulek decided to go into one of the other cars to see which of our people were there. We thought nothing of it; getting up and walking around the train was not unusual. We watched him exit our car as the train continued on its way to the monotonous clack-clack-clack against the rails.

Suddenly, we heard a loud thump and heart-twisting screams from the car Shmulek had entered. We had a premonition that something awful had happened, but the train did not stop. We were about twelve miles from Vienna. When Shmulek did not return, father and I went to look for him. We made our way into the next car. The passengers, our "Greek" compatriots, uttered sounds and made gestures with their hands, but refrained from speaking. In this dumbfounding way, we learned that Shmulek had either jumped or been pushed off the train.

My throat clamped, the muscles in my face went into spasms, I could issue no sounds. I looked at my father and saw his ashen face, and I thought that his heart had ceased beating. It took a split second for my mind to function again, and I had horrible images of the fate that had befallen Shmulek. Father and I could say nothing, neither could our people in the car, for there were Soviet military personnel all around us. As the train pulled into Vienna, we just stood there, paralyzed with ominous thoughts. Maybe someone had recognized Shmulek and made a move to betray or capture him, and Shmulek had jumped from the train, or was he pushed? We could only exchange looks, but that exchange conveyed mutual knowledge of tragedy. Then we went back to mother and Hella, to help them off the train.

Ironically, it was in the freedom of the Allied zone of Vienna—American or English, we weren't sure which—that my father had to tell my mother and Hella what had happened. Whatever their instincts might have been, they did not betray our origins with words, but their blood-curdling animal wails rose above the noisy, confused sounds of departing passengers. We were being propelled, forced to debark from the train. Nobody made room or time for grief. Father and I guided mother and Hella off the train. Our baggage was light, but our hearts were heavier than we could bear.

The underground escorts and the agents from the Vienna office tried to comfort us. They took us to a building in Vienna that I believe had once belonged to the Rothschild banking family. It was probably too late in the day to find out anything about Shmulek, they said, but they would do their best.

We were offered food but had no desire to eat. They provided beds but we could not close our eyes. The hours crawled through the long dark night. Finally, on the morning of September 12, we received the terrible news. Shmulek had sustained serious brain injuries. He had been taken to a hospital in the Russian-occupied zone, unconscious. The Berichah people arranged for us to be transported to the hospital to see him.

We were thus confronted with the most serious and dangerous dilemma of our odyssey. We had no identity documents and were posing as Greeks but did not speak the Greek language. We were going into a Soviet-occupied area contemplating what language to use at the hospital, where there would surely be Soviet soldiers and police.

Father and I conferred, and since I could speak a little German, I was to claim I was a Greek who had learned some German while in a concentration camp. If asked where we came from, I was to tell them that we were Athenians.

At the desk of the hospital receptionist, I asked, in my limited German, about Shmulek. I explained that he was my brother, and pointed to my father. She replied that Shmulek was in a coma and took us to his room. Shmulek was indeed in a coma, making strange, incomprehensible sounds. I spoke to the doctor, who told me there was nothing they could do for him medically; he would soon expire.

If there is an ironic spirit that hovers over human beings, a devilish creature banished from God's kingdom, who out of revenge plays with God's goodness, twisting it and watching the agony that paradox produces, this must have been its supreme victory. Shmulek had survived six years of eluding Nazis and Communists, had leaped over walls, swam across rivers, hidden in stalls. He had been chased through villages and countryside, been a slave laborer for fourteen months in the frozen outreaches of Siberia. He had lived like an animal in the Moslem republic of Uzbekistan and had been hounded by the NKVD for more than three years. Shmulek had been arrested on criminal charges, had faced the gallows, had wormed his way out of troubles to which there seemed no end, and then, on the journey to freedom, had been caught in a pogrom in Cracow. Having surmounted all this, disguised as a Greek in his final thrust to freedom, only ten minutes away from his goal, he was pursued, and either jumped or was pushed off a train, to end his life on a railroad track.

Irony, with your veiled intentions, you spared him through so many horrors. Then you stole his right to enjoy freedom and life just when it beckoned to him. Was there no end to your caprice or venom?

Shmulek died on the afternoon of September 12, 1945, but the heartache was not over. The hospital in which Shmulek lay was in the Soviet-occupied zone. They refused to release his body for burial. He had no documents or identification papers, he was a nameless person.

Father and I were helpless, we too had no identification documents to prove that he was son and brother. Even more frightening, if masquerade was uncovered, we might be considered spies. The Soviet Union was paranoid about foreigners, branding them spies. A foreigner, an *inostranyets*, was looked upon with suspicion. Since we would not be able to produce documentation, we would be accused of spying and sent to Siberia or even executed. Of course, it seems as if both sides were paranoid. A thin line divides normal fear from vindictive fear. While we still had sense enough to make that distinction, we left the hospital as quickly and quietly as we could.

What we shall ever be grateful for was that our pleas to Berichah to obtain Shmulek's body brought results. The Zionist organization had its own connections, methods, and influence. They persuaded the Soviet and Austrian authorities to release Shmulek's body. He was buried on September 25, 1945, thirteen days after he died, in a Jewish cemetery.

On this sad note, heartbroken and dispirited, we were sent to a temporary DP camp in the American-occupied zone of Austria. We spent several weeks there and then moved on to a permanent DP camp in Badgastein, also in the American zone.

The atmosphere was a sharp contrast to a Soviet or Nazi camp. Just about everyone became an ardent Zionist. Everyone decried the persecution, humiliation, annihilation endured in the concentration camps. All agreed, there must never be another Holocaust. The Jewish people found a new slogan: "Never Again!" This time, they declared, we will defend ourselves, no matter what it takes.

Jews saw that no one had come to their help, not even the United States, the world's most democratic and humane country, so loved and admired. The United States had refused to bomb the railroad tracks leading to the gas chambers and ovens of Auschwitz. As for England, its White Paper had prevented Europe's Jews from saving themselves by going to Palestine. Europe was now the cemetery of the Jewish people. We wanted to leave it, we wanted no part of it. And I, who at this point became a leader on the central committee of the camp's Jewish organization, swore with the others that we would create and build a Jewish state in the ancient land that other nations referred to as Palestine. During this interval, my father asked me to write a letter to Uncle Irving in New York City, to inform him of our whereabouts and of Shmulek's tragic death.

The camp was divided into two groups, young people and older people. History played a big role in the attitude of the younger ones. The Jews had suffered too much, especially on the European continent, during the Crusades, the Spanish Inquisition, the pogroms in Poland, Ukraine, and Russia, and the only solution was a Jewish homeland. They were determined to go to Palestine by any means and by any route, no matter how long it took to get there.

The older people may have shared this view, they were too tired, too drained, especially from the war, and they were not willing to undertake the danger of trying to break through the British blockade by illegally immigrating to Palestine on a dilapidated boat.

My sister Hella and I decided to go to Palestine. When we told our parents, father pleaded with us, practically going down on his knees.

"Please don't break up the family. My oldest son is lying on the bottom of the San River in Poland, where he was shot by the Germans. Now I have lost my second son, who has just been buried in Vienna. My heart tells me we should all go to America."

He did not have to add that we had lost so many other relatives in the Holocaust, that he was tired, weak, despondent, with only one brother left, Uncle Irving in New York.

"I want to see him before I die. I want what is left of my family to stay with me, to join him there."

It was not that Hella and I did not want to go to America. It was simply that we felt it our moral obligation, a duty we owed to the Jewish people, to help create and build a Jewish state in the ancient Jewish homeland. But seeing our father unabashedly crying was heartrending, especially for Hella, who adored him. The man who had endured hard labor with the strength of a bear and the wiliness of a fox, was crumbling before us. The sallow face, which had faced down so many enemies, was deeply etched with worry and pinched with hunger. He had lost his hair. His flowing mustache was limp and gray. We could not forsake him. He had been our mainstay, our mast, our rudder through the stormiest times. He had protected us, provided for us, sacrificed for us, exposed himself to the worst conditions and punishment to keep us alive. We could not forsake him.

Nor could we forsake mother. Her hollow eyes were brimming with tears that wordlessly pleaded with us to stay with her. Her shoulders drooped wearily. It was as if her frail body, encased in the corset that had hidden our family funds, had come this far and could go no further without our helping hands. Hella and I had come about-face. We were needed now to lead the way. We could not fail our parents now. We would go to America, if that were possible. We would not split the family.

I had lost two of our dearest, my two brothers, and had no way of knowing how many other relatives as well. Our family had emotional scars that were buried deep in the trenches and fortifications we had dug in the expanding hollows of hunger. We had lived with the perpetual clamor of fear, been carried in rumbling, stifling trains to unknown, debasing destinations, suffered subhuman climate and treatment and heartbreaking separations. But this conviction was seared on our consciences: We were bound to our fellow Jews, who treasure family relationships, who think of each other in crisis, and cling to the tenets of morality. The first obligation was to those who had taught me this and who had lived this way with unquestionable loyalty and love.

I immediately wrote another letter to Uncle Irving in New York, imploring him to help us get to the United States. Uncle Irving took steps at once to bring our family to America. On June 13, 1946, when the converted military transport vessel *Marine Flasher* passed the Statue of Liberty, tears were streaming down my cheeks. But they were tears of joy, of liberation, of renewal.

I arrived in New York harbor without any baggage. I had only the clothes on my body, a pair of pants and a shirt. I did not even possess a jacket. Hella, too, was skimpily dressed. Her hands were nervously smoothing her blouse, but her large brown eyes were straining to see the new land. At thirteen she still looked like a child. She reached out for father's hand. I drew my mother's quivering body close to me.

Uncle Irving, his wife, Aunt Ruthie, and my cousins Norman and Jerry met us at the dock. They embraced and kissed us. Father, who seldom cried, sobbed openly and unabashedly. Uncle Irving wept with him. "You're in America now. Forget the past."

Uncle Irving and Aunt Ruthie gave us a home. They gave us back our dignity. But without memory, life has no dignity.

Epilogue

The Soviet Union, the monolithic Communist state that I write about in this book, no longer exists. Its various constituent republics are now independent states. How should the United States relate to the new Russia? What should our attitude and policy be? To answer this question, it is necessary to know the history of Russia and its people.

The Russians have always been brutalized by their leaders, whether the autocratic tsars or the Communist commissars. They have never lived in a democracy, and they do not understand democracy. They have always admired and liked strong leaders. In the days of the tsars it was *Batyushka*, the "Little Father." Under the Communists it was the *Vozhd*, or "Leader." But whatever the period, Russians always responded to the lash of the nagaika. They were whipped by the tsars, and whipped even more brutally by the commissars.

Nonetheless, they liked being an imperial nation. The Russians are very nationalistic and patriotic, and will fight to the death for Mother Russia.

I cannot speak about Russian life under the tsars, but I lived there for five years in the time of Stalin. Communism is a brutal, inhumane system where there is no freedom, no love, no compassion or charity. The Communist leaders and their secret police were brutal and sadistic. Stalin was an insane, sadistic, perverted, inhuman monster.

The Communist government was unable to provide even the most basic material goods for its people. It had liquidated the middle class that could have done this, and

321

its leaders were engaged in mass theft of whatever was produced. Theft and bribery were essential elements of the culture.

Yes, today there is a new Russia, but the new country is run by former Communist apparatchiks, and the same "state security organs," the secret police, still keeps them in power. The average citizen is still deprived of the basic material needs for a decent life.

We must always be concerned about the possibility of Russia reverting to either a Communist or a nationalist-fascist government. Its leaders do not like us; they will always engage in mischief and try to hurt us. That is why we must maintain a strong military establishment.

At the same time, it would better for us if Russia were friendly rather than an enemy. We should help them to develop a free-market economy and teach them to become good businessmen. If we help them financially, we must make sure that the money goes to help the people; otherwise it will be stolen by crooked politicians and business oligarchs, and will end up in Swiss bank accounts.

I have a message for the people of Russia. This book was not written to insult or hurt you. To the contrary, it is meant to remind you of the brutality that you and I were exposed to, I for only five years, you for your entire history.

You suffered from Ivan the Terrible and from Stalin, yet you fought bravely against Hitler and endured huge casualties in World War II. Do not forget, though, that World War II might have been avoided if Stalin had not made a treaty with Hitler in August 1939. Stalin made it possible for Hitler to start the war. Millions of people paid the price of his political cynicism.

As an American I want to assure you that we wish you well, and that my country harbors no ill will toward you. I hope that you will work out your problems and live in dignity in a democratic state, and that we can all work together to build a harmonious, peaceful world.

Finally, I have a message for my coreligionists in Russia. I plead with them not to make the same mistakes that my parents and the Jews of their generation made in the 1930s. When the Nazi evil took root in Germany, they waited until it was to late before deciding to leave Poland. As you are well aware, most of them lost their lives in the Holocaust.

Jews have suffered much in Russia, from the Black Hundreds and the pogroms in tsarist times, from Stalin's repression under the Soviet Union. The situation in Russia today is in flux. Should a repressive Communist or nationalist-fascist regime gain power, it will look for a scapegoat. As in the past, it will be the Jews. Leave that land while you can. Never forget that Europe was the cemetery of the Jewish people. Get out, each and every one of you, before it is too late.